W9-BBB-641

CHILDREN'S WRITING

By the same Author

POETRY

Imaginings	Putnam 1961
Against the Cruel Frost	Putnam 1963
Object Relations	Methuen 1967

FICTION

Lights in the Sky Country	Putnam 1962
Flesh Wounds	Methuen 1966

LITERARY CRITICISM

Llareggub Revisited	Bowes and Bowes 1962
The Quest for Love	Methuen 1965

ON EDUCATION

English for Maturity	Cambridge 1961
English for the Rejected	Cambridge 1964
The Secret Places	Methuen 1964
The Exploring Word	Cambridge 1967

ANTHOLOGIES

Children's Games	Gordon Fraser 1957
Iron Honey Gold (four volumes)	Cambridge 1961
People and Diamonds (four volumes)	Cambridge 1962
Thieves and Angels	Cambridge 1963
Visions of Life (four volumes)	Cambridge 1964
I've Got to Use Words (four volumes)	Cambridge 1966
The Cambridge Hymnal (with Elizabeth Poston)	Cambridge 1967

CHILDREN'S WRITING

A SAMPLER FOR STUDENT TEACHERS

BY

DAVID HOLBROOK

Sometime Fellow of King's College Cambridge

CAMBRIDGE
AT THE UNIVERSITY PRESS
1967

Published by the Syndics of the Cambridge University Press
Bentley House, 200 Euston Road, London, N.W. 1
American Branch: 32 East 57th Street, New York, N.Y. 10022

Library of Congress Catalogue Card Number: 67–18315

Printed in Great Britain
at the University Printing House, Cambridge
(Brooke Crutchley, University Printer)

CONTENTS

FOR SUKEY

PREFACE

This is a students' handbook to accompany *The Exploring Word*. That book is about the education of teachers of English, and it recommends an approach to the subject which begins with our experience of children and their writing, and moves from there towards work in literature.

Some time during their first year at a college of education, or during their 'Education year' at a department of Education, students will have their first 'professional' experience of children, during their teaching practice. If they work by creative methods they will begin to collect examples of children's work. They will learn to study and evaluate children's writing, and they can bring samples back to college, for discussion. Even if they don't embark on creative writing in their teaching practices (or if they aren't allowed to!) they will have the problem of trying to match their pupils' interests with material selected from English literature: so, they need to know as much as possible about meaning and symbolism in children's imaginative life. Later, there will be the problem of beginning their professional lives as students in a confident and knowledgeable way—yet before the young teachers have had much experience of children.

In my own work with students and with teachers who come to 'refresher' courses, I know that they find the greatest satisfaction in discussing children's expression, by close analysis, in the same way as they discuss examples of literature proper. Of course, we discuss poems and passages from literature too: but there is a particular excitement about exploring children's expression. This is surely because it is so awe-inspiring to find how full of energy, how unique, and how positive each child can be in exploring his experience by words. To study their work confirms the impression expressed by Sir Herbert Read that each human soul is impelled to seek order and beauty within by what he calls 'ikons'. Indeed, we find that each has to be creative in order to maintain a human identity at all, by symbolic 'as if' work, from dreams to high art.

Yet the study and discussion of children's creative expression is if anything more exacting than normal literary criticism and so requires a special training. I have tried to point out in *The Exploring Word* how difficult it is to discuss, say, a poem by Thomas Hardy, recording and making articulate one's genuine response. I also show that if students are trained in examination methods of 'appreciation' they find it very difficult to be positive and really perceptive in their approach to children's writing.

So, by the time they reach a college of education, students are often by no means ready to exercise their capacity to respond to works of naïve composition from children, when they take their first teaching practice.

This book is primarily intended to help to prepare students to 'receive' children's writing, throughout their course. One obvious use for it is before the first teaching practice. But its use is unlikely to stop there. Even if a teacher brings back work from his first classes there is always the problem of puzzling out whether he had been given the 'right thing' or not. The whole point of creative work is that there are no 'right answers': so, the more teachers go on comparing notes and discussing children's writing, the better. Since the process depends upon 'whole experience' we need to build up a shared wisdom. And here this book is intended to help discussion cover the main points: most of the examples given here have been found to provoke relevant discussions, over the five years I have been using them with students and teachers.

There are further points to make about the presentation of the material here. There have in recent years been many books published on creative work in English. In some of them teacher-authors like Jack Beckett have reproduced some facsimiles. But the general practice has been, of course, to print children's poems and stories set up in type. Moreover, one selects for a book the most interesting pieces of work—perhaps a dozen are selected from a hundred. Those selected by an author bear the stamp of his endorsement of their quality.

Experienced teachers allow for this, in reading one's books. But the beginner faced with his first batch of children's work is school may be puzzled. He thumbs through the children's books, and is alarmed to find that he can hardly even read half of their efforts! Even those he can read don't seem to have anything remotely resembling the examples discussed in books on teaching English. So, he may feel floored from the start, and retreat, deciding that 'free expression' is not for him. There's no one, perhaps, to endorse his best examples, or even to discuss them. I am judging here from the number of samples I get from teachers who have embarked on creative work and who seek reassurance.

This selection is intended to give a more balanced view by including work which is not hand-picked. Some pieces are here because they have been well-tried in seminar work, and some are exceptional pieces, it is true. But some have been included because they are the kind one is likely to obtain from any secondary modern school class, any day. They have merits, which are indicated in the notes. But they represent the average level of work. Where I have been able to trace the original, and where reproduction is technically possible, the piece is reproduced facsimile. *This is what the stuff looks like when teachers thumb through pupils' exercise books after school.* Often, as with exercise 19, student teachers are reduced to an unhappy silence when first presented with the best a backward pupil can do. But then they find that there is an excitement even in deciphering the child's hand: and later they find a greater excitement in discussing the possible deeper meaning. When a piece like George Green's *Sick Sow* (p. 117) is then linked with literature, so that one sees an opportunity of reading George an excerpt from *Mr Tasker's Gods*, the painful scrawl takes on a new dimension, in terms of 'meeting in the word'. Some pieces here are facsimiles of examples discussed in my other books on teaching English. I hope readers won't groan at seeing them here yet again: students who do not know them can compare their own first-hand responses with the use I make of them in my books.

The exercises here, then, are intended, briefly:

(1) to accustom student teachers to children's handwriting, and the 'look' of an exercise-book page, after the pupil has done with it;

(2) to train student teachers to approach children's work in a positive frame of mind, and, undismayed by its appearance, to practise exercising their capacity to read the piece for its *content*; and to learn to apply to the meaning of the pupil's words their most sensitive responses, and the literary critical faculties they have learnt from their work with literature proper;

(3) to give students some foretaste of the experience of being receptive to children's creative 'giving' in the special context of the teacher-pupil relationship;

(4) to train students in being able to see opportunities for links with literature, as children's poetic needs become apparent from their own expression.

Of course, in work with this book, there will be a missing complex—that is the teacher's knowledge of the pupil's personality and his acquaintance with his home and social background. The whole school environment is missing, too, and so the full background of the environment for creative work is absent from these exercises, and this must be borne in mind.

But this unreality will be made up for to some degree by the experience of collaboration which seminar work on such examples should be. That is, the equal relationship between lecturers and students, puzzling over the nature of children's literacy, should itself be an experience of 'give and take' which the students can translate into classroom terms. And so this would seem to be the point at which I should thank all the student teachers from whom I have learnt so much in the discussion of children's writing.

I wish also to thank the teachers and student teachers from

whose pupils' work I quote: David Schonveld; Geoffrey Hawkes; Miss Averne Shirley; Peter Watson; Miss Susan Macklin; Jeff Nuttall; C. Elliott; Mr Patterson and Mr Brown of Braehead School; Kenyon Calthrop; Dr Biaggini; J. H. Walsh; P. A. B. Peacey; J. Cleary, Peter Hancock, K. P. Cassidy, R. F. O'Sullivan, and others.

I apologise to teachers from whose pupils' work I quote, but of whom I have lost track: I would be glad to hear from the teachers of the authors of *Snakes and Ladders*, *The Brook* and *A Tale of Woe*, and any others for which I make no acknowledgement.

I am grateful to the following for permission to quote from published work:

Mrs Helen Thomas and Faber and Faber Ltd for *Melancholy* and *Gallows* by Edward Thomas from *The Collected Poems of Edward Thomas.*

Mrs Violet Powys and Chatto and Windus Ltd for an extract from *Mr Tasker's Gods.*

The County Council of the West Riding of Yorkshire and Chatto and Windus Ltd for four poems and pasages from *The Excitement of Writing.*

Alan Ross Ltd for the poem *In a Foreign Hospital* from *The Collected Poems of Bernard Spencer.*

George Allen and Unwin Ltd and Mr Arthur Waley for a poem by Li Po from *The Poetry and Career of Li Po.*

Blackie and Sons Ltd and Mr Jack Becket for six poems from *The Keen Edge.*

The Bodley Head Ltd, Prentice-Hall, Inc., Englewood Cliffs, New Jersey, and Mr E. R. Braithwaite for an excerpt from *To Sir With Love* © 1959 by E. R. Braithwaite.

Faber and Faber Ltd; Harper and Row, Publishers and Mr Ted Hughes for *View of a Pig* (Copyright © 1960 by Mr Ted Hughes) and *Pike* (Copyright © 1959 by Mr Ted Hughes) from *Lupercal.*

The Bodley Head Ltd and Random House Inc. for an extract from *Ulysses* by James Joyce. Copyright 1914, 1918 and renewed 1942, 1946 by Mrs Nora Joseph Joyce.

Mr Peter Hancock for the children's play *The Way to Go Home.*

Mr J. Cleary for the passages by Patricia Lynch and Michael Morris.

Messrs Heinemann, the Viking Press, Inc., and the Estate of the late Mrs Frieda Lawrence for *Song of a Man who is not Loved* and *Work* (Copyright 1929 by Frieda Lawrence Ravagli), both from *The Complete Poems of D. H. Lawrence*, vol. 1, edited by Vivian de Sola Pinto and F. Warren Roberts;

and for an extract from *The Fox* (Copyright 1923 by Thomas Setzer, Inc.; 1951 by Frieda Lawrence) from *The Portable D. H. Lawrence*, edited by Diana Trilling; Messrs Laurence Pollinger, the Viking Press, Inc., and the Estate of the late Mrs Frieda Lawrence for *The Mountain Lion* (Copyright 1923, 1951 by Frieda Lawrence) from *The Complete Poems of D. H. Lawrence*, vol. 1, edited by Vivian de Sola Pinto and F. Warren Roberts. The poem *Bowling for a Pig* by David Holbrook, p. 120, remains the copyright of the author.

Introduction for the Student

If you have written poetry, or have responded to a poet's 'intolerable wrestle with words and with meanings', you will know how much effort can go into creative expression. Of course, some uses of the imagination are false and facile, and in literary criticism we have to try to distinguish between genuine creativity and imitations. Everything depends upon the degree to which the poet or artist is being 'true to himself': the only way to discover this is by closely examining his work and its meaning, and the nature of symbolism.

What being 'true to oneself' means is a complex problem, since the artist who falsifies experience to himself is in a way being sincere, even though we find his work 'false'. (As obvious examples, compare *The Secret Garden* and *Little Lord Fauntleroy*, by the same children's writer, Frances Burnett: or *The Old Curiosity Shop* and *Dombey and Son.*) One root of the problem would seem to be that creativity is a symbolic engagement with aspects of one's inner world: a theory of art I hope to explore in another work. That is, after a certain stage in the development of consciousness the child's ego becomes capable of exploring aspects of its inner world in symbolic terms. There is a stage before this is possible, when there is no capacity to distinguish between word and thing. At this stage the child will have primitive beliefs, of the kind that to give one's name to someone is to give oneself into their power. This kind of belief is still found among primitive tribes: the Abipones of Paraguay, for instance, eradicate from the whole language any word which is part of the name of anyone who has died. All words having affinity with the names of the dead are dropped from the vocabulary. 'In consequence their language is most difficult to learn, as it is full of blocks and neologisms replacing forbidden words' (Hannah Segal, *Notes on Symbol Formation*). This primitive lack of discrimination belongs to that stage of childhood when, in order to annihilate you, a child will put its fingers over its eyes—so that neither you, nor itself, is there any more.

Later, we learn the capacity to use words poetically, to explore our inner world, and its dynamics of hate and love: and to seek to develop a sense of the self—who am I? As we grow better able to work at these subjective processes we become better able to deal with the outside world. To be able to use symbolism at all means we have reached a stage at which we can recognise that there are three entities—the self, the symbol, and the thing symbolised—the not-me.

Thus, creativity is a matter of relationship with oneself, that enables one to come to better terms with the outer world. Since we learn the media of consciousness from others (words, ideograms in painting, melodic intervals and key relationships in music), creativity is communication: but a primary aspect of it is communication with one's inner world, with oneself.

I won't elaborate here on the kind of problems we have in our inner world (see however the Note on p. 228). But one can see the major themes of children's phantasy by reading any book of nursery rhymes. They are:

(1) We can have bad things inside us which can harm others (poison, curses, spells, consequences of wishing, etc.).

(2) There are bad things in the world, some of which intend harm to us (wolves, witches, etc.).

(These two seem related: as indeed they are, for Red-Riding-Hood's wolf is a projection of her own phantasy urges to 'eat up the mother', which she has known as a hungry baby, and fears—because they threaten to recoil upon her.)

(3) Good work, patience, unselfishness, creative acts, love, bring rewards (*Jack and the Beanstalk*).

(4) Hate and destructiveness tend to perish because of their own nature (*Hansel and Gretel*) and can be overcome.

(5) Yet the world is often a crazy and unpredictable place in which one's identity and environment may at any time evanesce, or be threatened by disruption (see *The Prince and the Pauper*, by Mark Twain; also *Cinderella* and *The Borrowers*).

To use psychological phrases, we come to terms with the destructiveness of our own hate by becoming gradually assured of the integration and continuity of our own identity. How this happens is by our mother's continuing love and care, and our own creative efforts—seeking order and beauty within, and discovering the reality of others. To this development everything contributes—good company, relationships, happy experiences, work done: and symbolic creativity.

It is this kind of inward truth which nursery rhymes symbolise; and most children's creative work symbolises in one way or another the quest for integration of the identity, towards realism in dealings with the outer world.

In approaching children's writing then, we need to seek beyond the problem of spelling, and the look of the writing, and get to the symbolic meaning. Once we have some sense of this, we judge it not in terms of its 'psychological value' *but as poetry*. That is, from our experience of poetry of all kinds, we can ask ourselves, 'In its symbolic exploration of inner and outer experience how sincere is this?'. By 'how sincere' here I think we mean *how much real work is being done on problems of life*: and the clue to this will be in the freshness, the energy, the rhythm and feel of the language.

When anyone is really working on his inner world, he becomes excited—for he is making important discoveries and gains, as between his ego and the witches, princesses, and threatening shadows within. He sees connections and relationships, and possibilities of structures, patterns, richness of content: and in these, joy and beauty. Expression will convey the bodily feelings of experience, and the 'inscape' of an inward effort. So, if we are responsive, we can usually feel this excitement in the words (as we can tell the most stirring bars in a piece of music: if we look at the score we are likely to find them marked *express*.). In *English for the Rejected* I marked all such passages in the children's writing quoted in italics: study those, and you will perhaps see what I mean.

Of course, judging quality of expression is a subjective

matter: there is nothing to go on but your own response to the words. But then we can compare B's response, and C's response, and so on—to the extent to which people can ever exchange their responses. In the end, we can get something of an agreed consensus of opinion about the quality of a piece of writing (by which *The Shadow Line* is more sincere than *Goldfinger*, as a crude example). So, the problem is not entirely subjective: there can be agreed values which really exist, although they have to be continually recreated. But the work can only be possessed in the heart: as Dereck Cooke says, Beethoven expressed this in a nutshell when he wrote on the MS of the *Missa Solemnis* 'Von Herzen—möge es wieder—zu Herzen gehn!'—'from the heart—may it go back—to the heart'. (See *The Language of Music*, p. 210.)

With children there are additional complications, since one is not merely trying to establish values (though one is, inevitably, going to convey to a class of children what it is one values highly, and what not, by selecting work to praise). A teacher is trying to encourage children to be more energetic in exploring the world by words: so, he will be mostly on the look-out for good things—for achievements to commend. He will see failures of sincerity as 'failures to come to grips' rather than as the unfortunate elements they could be in a published piece by an adult.

Even clichés have a different value in children's work. Take this poem, for example:

The Fate of the Discontented

When flower's buds all open, there petals bright and gay,
And mountain streams awake, and start their freshning trickle,
And Soft, thick grass is a bright, emerald green.

When birds all fly, and swoop, and sing,
When childeren play, and bathe.
O what a peaceful life this is, so happy and so gay.

But the pirate is not sattisfied,
He must go off to sea.
He doesn't go to admire the Gulls,

So gracefull in their flight,
Or feel the blast of the spray in the breeze, and watch the
crested waves.

For he goes off to drink, and shout
To fight, and rob, and kill
For he is the most ungratefull,
discontented, and dissatisfied;
For he is the worst of all murderers
But he will pay well for his crime,
For the fate of the discontented, will be
dreaded, and feared, throughout time.
(Malcolm, second-year 'B' stream, secondary modern school)

At first glance perhaps this poem seems to be full of clichés: 'petals bright and gay', 'emerald green', 'O what a peaceful life this is, so happy and so gay,' 'crested waves'. One could easily dismiss it with a sigh. It seems like the trite poem in Exercise 43 below ('Oh, how I love the radiant spring...').

But if we look closer, prepared to make proper allowances, as for a child, we can find a few words which are unusual enough to suggest something more than mere facility: 'freshning' for instance, 'soft, thick grass', and 'swoop'. We have a touch here of a relish that recalls folksong, a relish for natural things. That is, behind the triteness we can feel a boy's delight in 'playing and bathing' in the open air. From our acquaintance with fairy tale we shall put these down as symbols of 'goodness'.

Then we shall notice that some of the phrases which seem like cliché are actually used ironically: Huh!—

He doesn't go to admire the Gulls,
So gracefull...

And in the next lines we feel we have a little boy expressing his contempt for 'sissy' enjoyments, such as girls have, of flowery things. The emerging youth's identity needs to pretend he is a Big Sinner:

For he goes off to drink, and shout
To fight, and rob, and kill...

Drum-banging stuff! But then we notice a change in the rhythm:

> For he is the most ungratefull,
> discontented and dissatisfied...

However did this small boy come to use such long words? Whoever called a pirate *dissatisfied*? Gradually we come to recognise it as an echo. Malcolm's mother has said to him, 'You are the most ungrateful, discontented and dissatisfied little boy...' We can hear the rhythm of nagging adult speech.

So, even in the small experiment in feelings which the poem is, we find the boy exploring guilt:

> ...he will pay well for his crime,
> For the fate of the discontented, will be dreaded, and feared, throughout time.

The last phrase is really rather striking: more so, when we realise that the child is perhaps haunted by a feeling of remorse at having allowed himself to utter destructive 'attitudes' to the life in the 'freshning', 'swooping' thing of spring. That is, he has attacked life—and his clichés were only a disguise for this. So, he is guilty. The poem is not very deep: on the whole it is not a success—or is only a success as an experiment. But if we respond to it closely, we can see how we can discover in literature verses about the same kind of guilt:

> 'Is it he?' quoth one, 'Is this the man?
> By him who died on cross,
> With his cruel bow he laid full low
> The harmless Albatross.
>
> The Spirit who bideth by himself
> In the land of mist and snow,
> He loved the bird that loved the man
> That shot him with his bow.'
>
> The other was a softer voice,
> As soft as honey-dew:
> Quoth he, 'The man hath penance done,
> And penance more will do.'

Malcolm's poem is a form of penance—of exploring the badness in oneself—not the braggadocio badness, but the dreaded badness, of guilt and hate. Despite his cliché, he reaches this: of course poems such as 2C and 19 below do the same at a deeper level. If we can glimpse the depths in even an 'average' poem like this one, we can see how to link our work with literature—here, besides the *Ancient Mariner*, various other seafaring works suggest themselves from *Treasure Island* to *Moby Dick, The Secret Sharer, Typhoon, A High Wind in Jamaica, The Golden Vanity, Admiral Benbow, The Flying Cloud*; and, in a lighter vein, the poem by Ogden Nash about boyhood, *A Boy is a Boy.*

In order to seize our opportunities, then, we need to be acutely attentive to children's language. The problem is exacerbated by the difficulty of handwriting. Take this:

A ~~poem~~

·A little yellow Birds sat on my window sill, he hop. and poped about,
.he wisheld he cherped.
I trid to chach my little yellow brid, but he flew in to the golden yellow sun,
O how i wish that was my yellow brid.

This was written by Joan Stall, whose case-history is given in *English for the Rejected* (pp. 54 ff.). Our reactions tend to be depressed by the feeble spindly writing, and the poor spelling. What point is there (we feel) in looking for poetic meaning in lines scrawled in this spidery way, and when bird is spelt 'brid'; whistled, 'wisheld'; and catch, 'chach' or 'chash'? Can a child who can't spell 'tried' and who can't get her verbs right (as 'hopped' and 'popped') write *poetry*?

But if we are responsive to literature we shall respond to:

> ...but he flew into the golden yellow sun

and we shall be able to adjust our minds to this poetic hyperbole, as we do with Emily Dickinson:

> How still the bells in steeples stand,
> Till, swollen with the sky,
> They leap upon their silver feet
> In frantic melody!

or Blake:

> Ah, sunflower, weary of time,
> That countest the steps of the sun...

We shall then remember Yeats's *Byzantium*,

> And set upon a golden bough to sing

and the Hans Andersen story *The Emperor's Nightingale*.

By now we shall have arrived at the essence of Joan's poem, which is to identify herself with a golden bird, free, valuable and beautiful—a 'good' self she yearns to capture. If we look up at her—plain, short-sighted, ineffectual—we shall be much moved, to see how the golden bird forever escapes her. But (as the rest of her work shows) praise for this poem will be praise for the aspiration—and so impel her to explore (as she did) the aggression and badness in herself, which, because she was so afraid of it, she could not 'include' in her personality, and so organise her quest towards golden-birdness more successfully.

But look back at her poem: who would, at first glance, see it as a clue to such an inward quest?

This raises many problems: can one not be reading all this into a child's work? Isn't one making too much of it all—the symbolism, love and hate, and so forth? Can one really base such generalisations on a few idly scrawled words?

Well, they aren't idly scrawled: not in the right context. The least piece of writing, if the teacher has established the context for proper 'giving', will be a 'meant' gift. Of course, it depends on what the teacher's attitude is to human beings. If he cannot believe that every human being has an inward need to find himself, in a struggle with love and hate, and between the subjective and objective worlds, then he probably won't get given poetry. But how can anyone read poetry and not see that these problems are universal? Of course, you can deny the whole area with which art deals. A colleague was told by a scientist in his staffroom, 'Children from decent homes don't write poetry'. This man meant that it was possible to live without 'working on one's inner world'. But it isn't! Of course such a person probably can't be convinced, for he tries to live by pretending the subjective problem doesn't exist: he tries to live by submitting the inner world, as much as he can, to the objective. Such a scientist may have substituted his neat and 'complete' intellectual scheme for life and whole being—at the cost of leaving out much that is disturbing. Poetry reminds him of this troublesome threat—so, he becomes hostile. Such an individual, if he tried to teach English, would be a menace, since he would wear everybody out by activities which seek to deny that works of expression deal with a subjective world that is undeniably 'there'. So, he would actually crush expression by concentrating on grammar, linguistics, 'practical' exercises, and the rest. He daren't accept that in English work we can never *know* what is going on, or what the results are.

Take a poem like this by Simon: is it sincere or not?

A Tale of Woe.

1. My soul bears a bitterness,
A bitterness so great,
That if I am not careful,
It will turn to hate.

2 The bitterness that comes with sorrow,
That comes but never goes,
It may lose me many friends,
And win me many foes.

3\. I dread the night and what it brings,
The pain, the terror and the stress,
And then, behold, the fear, the fear,
The fear so strong you cannot guess.

4\. My tortured mind does scream for help,
But help will never come
For my soul is oh so bitter,
And my heart feels oh so numb.

5\. The morning brings a new day,
New time, new hopes, new date,
But the new day is no better,
Because I'm a man of hate.

I couldn't say: and I don't mind that I can't say. I don't mind (and nor should you) if all the poems in this book are declared bad and worthless by a committee of English teachers, and my notes on them pronounced rubbish. I don't think this is likely. In any case, something constructive went on, and where we have constructiveness we have a creative effort towards peace—that inner peace that the world needs.

Even if *A Tale of Woe* is an exercise in feelings, it has a value, as had Emily Brontë's *Cold in the Earth*, as the exploration of possible feelings. For, as the exploration of hate in a poem, it involves the exploration of possible ways of *overcoming* hate. Of course, there is callowness—'if I am not careful' is weak beside the histrionic 'bears a bitterness': but, again, the well-trained sensibility will note the remarkable phrases: 'the terror and the stress...the fear, the fear', and 'My tortured mind does scream for help...' What one should avoid is supposing that such a pupil is in a grim personal situation, however: it may be that he is merely experimenting in feeling—where children—especially adolescents—*don't* experiment, perhaps we should be worried? But beneath the experiment we should be able to accept, from our knowledge of the universal themes of literature, and from history, that all human beings have a problem of hate. So, we ought not to be alarmed or huffy, if a child speaks directly about such a disturbing matter, even in experiment.

Of course, if we knew Simon as a teacher knows a pupil, we would know how this particular poetic exploration fitted into his whole personality. This would not mean that we could relax our attention to the quality of his writing, but it does give our search for felicities of expression an added zest. Take the sequence below (pp. 29–35) of work by Raymond (4B) for instance: read it through first and make a note of any striking or unusual phrases.

Here is my list of phrases:

> I thought of only the ground in front of me
> Not the fear behind

(I have already noted, in *The Secret Places*, the resemblance of these to certain lines in *The Ancient Mariner*);

> I am an orphan I live in the hedge
> I live on scraps and bits of waste
> Let's...walk under those dark evil trees...

I note that, though he is a 'tough' boy of fourteen he writes (*a*) a lullaby, (*b*) a fairy story about a princess being embraced by a gipsy although she is betrothed to a prince, (*c*) a story for a play about a man who tricks a girl into his digs:

> —Shall we go and see what the butler saw
> —Yes that would be nice. What did he.
> —If you come with me I mite demestrate to you

(she is later found to be pregnant), (*d*) a song in which 'my love' is invited under the 'dark evil' trees, where the nightingale sings, that is 'such a bird it never goes wrong'.

Now Raymond is a 'sexy' boy, over whose work I had considerable difficulty (see *The Secret Places*, pp. 103 ff.). Later I found out he was illegitimate. Illegitimacy is treated lightly by our 'enlightened' journalism today: for a child, as we know in school, it can be an anguish. There is a deeply moving poem by a child in Jack Beckett's *The Keen Edge* which conveys this:

> Ho, God
> Help me to get
> Over things
> That worry
> Me so, Help me
> As I get older.
> I feel that I get
> Left out of things.
> Over children
> Have fathers
> But I have not
> They talk about
> The trips they take
> With their perents
> But I say
> I am happy
> But deep down inside me
> I feel hurt.
> And it hurts more
> And more all the time
> No God please help me...

Our Raymond felt such anguish too. And once I knew that his was the anguish of the illegitimate child, much in his work was explained. He fears that he is (or was) an unwanted baby: so, he even writes in adolescence the lullaby he feels was never sung to him. Because he has never known his father, he is in a sense an orphan who lives in the hedge—on 'scraps and bits of waste'—bits of love—when he can get them: from these he makes a 'super paste'. That is, he has a deep problem of not having had a father to identify with, to take aspects of the father into his own personality. So he has to make a 'super paste'—he has to invent what life did not supply, something he persuades himself is good enough to hold his world together. His is a 'super paste' in that he pretends to be more than normally sexy. In fact all he reveals is that he is compensating for a felt deficiency of manhood (because he hadn't a father on whom to build a self by identifying): his sexiness is a way of making up for his anxieties about being illegitimate.

His fairy story he announces as being about a 'long lost love' (but it isn't in fact). The illegitimate has a problem of finding the mother good (perhaps because he also blames her for the catastrophe of his birth): so he is likely to over-idealise her. Here she is symbolised by Yellowsinger the Princess. Raymond has probably been variously told his father is 'playing the harp' (i.e. dead) and heard people say he was 'a gypsy from the next village'. In the 'complications' (I suppose he means 'characters'!) is included a King who is 'a fat stubby man', and a Queen who is 'a wild person'; and the Prince who is 'a Jeously sort of person'.

In the unconscious symbolism of fairy tale and nursery rhyme the princess's invitation would have a symbolic sexual meaning: Hans' reply is significant—'Why pick a scruffy gipsy like me?'—i.e. Raymond is asking, Why did you give me a gipsy for a father?

As I have said, the illegitimate child has a problem of identification: this makes it very difficult for him to work on his Oedipal jealousy. So, while Hans is Raymond's father, of whom the Prince is jealous, he also becomes Hans, making the jealous Prince his father. Hans is a boy

I must go my Mother will be cross...

The Prince is to be married to the Princess—

Just don't forget it's me your marrying not that gypis

and to Hans he threatens 'I will kill you'.
The lack of straightforwardness of his Oedipal problem makes it difficult for Raymond to accept sex: so, he overdoes it, and pretends to be very daring. Seduction is his theme:

Now That is a proplem. HA I know we will go to my digs...

and the consequence is illegitimacy:

—You look fatter.
— didn't I tell you she is going to have a baby.

Under the trees is 'dark evil'; in a sense, Raymond is echoing what Edgar says to Edmund about Gloucester:

> The dark and vicious place where thee he got
> Cost him his eyes...

That is, in terms of inner feelings, Raymond feels that lust is sinister and damaging, since it has made it difficult for him to discover his identity: so he is obsessed with sex.

But in his simple scrawl, through the odd touches of poetry in his writing, we can hear his sadness. And if we hear it, he will know: we could hardly fail to respond to the guilt in his first poem, and its expression of insecurity.

Of course, not all children's work will invite such close exploration (though the innocent utterance of 'low-stream' children and disturbed children often will). Nor should the teacher always be digging beneath the surface: often one can simply stop short at what is offered, at the level of striking words. Here, for instance, at the end of the first lesson with me, a little girl in 1 A writes her first exceptional phrases:

It was a fine sunny morning in the end of May. Jimmy and Susan were off on a bike ride in Norfork which is a sea-side place.

The salt water Crashed down in great speed, with it's white foam crawl-ing up the beach. Near the sea there was a great Cave. Gream tiny plants Crawled up the rocky side. Tiny bits of rock came jutting out, like sharp daggers protecting the master.

Later she wrote the poem *Only Sad* (see p. 67 below and discussion in *The Secret Places*, p. 21) and *The Lilac Tree*

(p. 27, Ex. 5 C). How does one get from one to the other: how does one foster and improve writing? The answer here cannot be given for every teacher. There are answers of various kinds, given by Jack Beckett, by J. H. Walsh, by Marjorie Hourd, by various teachers in *The Excitement of Writing* and elsewhere, and in my own books. Each teacher knows how to reinforce the creative experience, in his own way. I am sure the methods must be positive ones: that is, praise where it is due, exclaiming to the class (as one would over the phrase 'like daggers protecting the master')—picking out exciting phrases, paragraphs and poems and reading them aloud to the class next day. 'Publishing' is another important way of emphasising constructive gains—reading aloud of selected work, tape-recording it, pinning it on the wall, correcting work and typing it out on stencils for the class magazine, and so forth (always with the proviso that you obtain the author's permission first).

But another important factor is the continual enrichment of the child's experience of literature. Sometimes I hear from enthusiastic young teachers who have gone crazy on creative work. They've kept the children at it for weeks: then pupils have suddenly 'gone off'. No wonder—they'd done nothing else! The poor little things were quite exhausted. The teacher had put nothing back. Creative work can't be all giving: and so children need to hear poems and stories read to them—and if it is possible, what the teacher reads should be related to current themes in their work, and current interests shown in it.

Of course, this 'matching' needs to be done sensitively, governed by an understanding of the deeper implications of a child's work, not its mere explicit meaning.

Thus, if we come across a poem like this:

Black Skeleton

The knife-like cloud called Black
Skeleton came too far down one day,
The birds soaring into Black Skeleton
Never seemed to come back.

> It seemed as if it would lightning and
> light all the world up.
>
> And then to my surprise, I saw a
> Flicker of light come from
> Black-Skeleton
> It was like a sinking ship
> In a raging sea.
>
> The wind was roaring, the cloud rumbled
> Along like the blast of a cannon.
>
> The whole world shuttered that moment,
> The leaden cloud was every colour in the rainbow.
>
> And Black Skeleton thinned white,
> The wind blew through him.
> And the wind tore Black Skeleton
> Apart.
>
> (by Paul, 2B, secondary modern school)

the point is not that the boy only wants to read more about thunderstorms—though there is a good one in *Huckleberry Finn* and others in a poem by John Clare and in Lawrence's poem *Storm in the Black Forest*. First we have to look at the most unusual and striking phrases: 'knife-like', 'Black Skeleton', 'too far down', 'Never seemed to come back', 'shuttered', 'leaden—every colour in the rainbow...', 'thinned white', 'the wind blew through him', 'tore...apart'. What do these suggest?

To a person skilled in responding to the symbolism of poetry (and nursery rhyme) this use of black and white here would seem symbolic of good and evil, and also of 'being there' and 'not being there'. How are 'being there' and 'not being there' related to good and evil? There are black devils in Hell, and angels are white: that is, black represents perdition and loss; whiteness, eternity (the Albatross was white, in the white moonlight, in the 'seafog white': the Ship of Death was black, and transparent, with black 'restless gossameres').

What else in the poem has to do with good being and bad not-being? Well, the cloud is skeletal, black and *knife-like*. It threatens because it 'comes too far down': the birds going into it 'never seem to come back'. When there is a flash of lightning the world *shutters*, and for a moment (of beauty) the *leaden* cloud is every *colour* of the rainbow (the rainbow is a symbol of continuity—assurance of the world's not ending).

In the end the black thins white: and the wind tears 'black not-being' apart: 'death thou shalt die'!

The poem, then, surely, is a poem about a thundercloud as a symbol of a badness (hate) which threatens to dissolve the identity (and the world), but which is overcome by the act of organisation which is the poem. The poem itself assures the writer that he will go on continuing to be.

What then can we supply for Paul from literature? Lawrence's *Song of a Man Who is Not Loved* is an obvious choice. It even has a similar phrase

I am too
Little to count in the wind that drifts me through...

Lawrence's poem, too, is the attempt to overcome a harrowing fear that in the absence of love his identity will be overcome by hate: he goes further, in accepting man's minuteness when confronted by the universe: so, he accepts his evanescence, and triumphs over the fear. (The poem is given in full with a Note on p. 228 at the end of this book).

There will be disagreement among my readers, I am sure: that is the point of the exercises here. Discuss this poem together with the adolescent poems on p. 25, p. 37 and pp. 64–5 which express the fear of the identity being disrupted from within, by badness and hate. Links between children's writing and literature, following such underlying themes, will be suggested by various exercises in this book, and in the notes.

Such a pursuit of deeply felt themes will, I am sure, help to prevent the kind of detached playing with language promoted by the 'English through Experience' kind of approach. In this children are shown some bubbles, or water, and invited to throw out words suggested by these. As Mr Rowe says in an essay in *English Versus Examinations* (p. 99):

All kinds of starting points in experience may be used to set children writing eagerly and enjoyably—and often freshly and creatively, too. For example, a piece of wave-worn drift-wood, some dried bladder-wrack, and a bag of sea-shells was taken into a third-year classroom...The children handled it and the bladderwrack and smelt them...They were asked to spend a few moments getting to *know* these shells. They closed their eyes...Words provided by them and by the teacher were put up on the board...

That is, words were collected from a group and thus detached from the inward dynamics of each child's metaphorical, symbolic relationship with himself. This is the basis of an 'aesthetic' preoccupation with words 'for their own sake' that can easily become insincere. The examples reveal this superficiality, by the lack of relationship between the words and any 'felt' rhythm:

> Small shells, large shells, sharp shells, smooth shells,
> Pearly shells and dark shells
> Some shells might have been there for centuries...

'Very like a whale'...'or like a porpoise'...it is as if the children were taken for a phantasy ride as Hamlet takes Polonius!

> The great sea came thundering in
> The shells came with it,
> Pearly-bright and dark...

The words come from 'outside'; as Mr. Rowe goes on to say, 'certain words had been *provided for them*' (my italics): so, on top of the 'provided' words is superimposed, with equal insincerity, a cliché posture, which also feels as if it were 'provided':

> Alive with a beauty that only nature can produce...
>
> ...A shell is surely a great thing, functional yet marvellous?

'A masterly stroke', coos Mr Rowe; but surely horribly pretentious for a boy?

This process of giving children 'words to play with' for 'enjoyment' seems to me as dull as the kind of practical exercises we are given in textbooks called *English for Pleasure*. The pleasure in English is working in the inner world—and securing deep satisfactions there. Mr Rowe says that this 'creative game with words' didn't go on in a vacuum: 'What they were given first was a stimulating sense-experience...'

But a mere 'stimulating sense-experience' is itself a vacuum, unless something emerges which relates it to inward complexities. The fallacy of 'English through Experience' work is to suppose that the child hasn't any 'experience' inside him: it all has to be supplied, whereas the truth is that he has all too little time to use his capacity for inward symbolism, to build bridges between subjective and objective, and to tackle the backlog of psychic problems he inherited from the darkest ages of infancy, before the capacity for symbolism was developed.

What Mr Rowe's approach amounts to is virtually what used to be called 'vocabulary work' in a new guise: looking at a picture the children each use the same words to describe it—a sure sign that the words are 'provided', rather than emerge with a rightness of substance, for each individual inward world:

(1) The water comes rushing down in a torrent of fury,
Racing downwards, gushing around stones and over branches...

(2) The water came surging over the rocky cliff,
Splashing, spluttering, raging downward...
Roaring on its way, gushing and sparkling...

(3) With the rushing sound of water...

Some vocabulary has certainly stuck, hasn't it? and who can doubt that these children are enjoying their creative game with words. As to what is happening to their sensibility, that will be as obvious to you as it is to me...

What is obvious to me is that the sameness of 'vocabulary' marks a failure of engagement with 'felt' meaning'. (This seems confirmed by some of the more ridiculous experiments—'chatting' for rushing water, and 'splaying' for a bank, which are merely wild inaccuracies.) It sounds too much like the uninvolved way children write when they are asked to 'write 20 similes'. It is not mere *vocabulary* we wish to develop—but perception and the capacity to explore and organise experience, from inward sources, symbolically.

This can be set off by outward stimuli: but the stimulus must be left to provoke a unique response from each child (since each child will bring to it a different capacity for perception, and a different need to symbolise). Mr Rowe's approach seeks to force children into the same pattern: hence the insincerity.

A student teacher simply followed my suggestion and took in a bag of apples. Some children merely wrote down free associations: but gradually the words became humanised: see Exercise I below.

Old Apples

The skins of old apples tend to be wrinkled, like an old woman's skin. There colour is often a dull red, which however hard you rub, will never shine, and there are lots of small brown patches, They are no longer juicy and soft and are best eaten soon.

Bad Apples

They are mostly brown and squash with maggots climbing in and out. They are covered with a white crust of mould and are best thrown away.

Some used the apple as a symbol of goodness and badness, wholeness and inner decay: they came to these processes of projective identification themselves:

An Apple

An apple on the window sill looks so queer, you'd be surprised how luch and juicy it is inside, but there it stands, green one side, red the other, it stands there, an ornament. It's been there some time but no-one has touched it, they've been told not to. One day, when it is old, it will get rotten and brown and will get thrown out with the rubbish.

These pieces are less showy than Mr Rowe's: but they are more genuine—and more essentially creative, because the children have been left to make use of the stimulus in their own way, for their own symbolic inward purposes—without having too much 'provided' and thus imposed.

From this point we can go straight into our first exercise: a comparison of these very passages with others obtained by the same student teacher, in a follow-up with the same children.

Please—for your own sake, as part of the whole approach, don't look up the notes until you've discussed the passages, or committed your own opinions to paper. There are no 'right answers': commitment and disagreement are part of the whole process of gaining benefit from one another's experience. Here it isn't the answers which count, but the process of developing 'openness' to symbolic experience, an important aspect of which is the need at times to be very, very wrong. Indeed until we are prepared to 'allow' ourselves to be wrong we can't even begin!

1 *Symbolism in Children's Writing*

EXERCISE 1

A student teacher gave her eleven-year-old pupils an apple each and asked them to associate freely with the word 'apple'. Here are some of the results. How satisfactory would you consider them if you were the teacher? What would you do next?

[A] *Old Apples*

The skins of old apples tend to be wrinkled, like an old woman's skin. There colour is often a dull red, which however hard you rub, will never shine, and there are lots of small brown patches. They are no longer juicy and soft and are best eaten soon.

Young Apples

The colour of young apples is a shiny fresh green or a rosy, polished red. Their skin is smooth and they are the best you can buy.

Bad Apples

They are mostly brown and squash with maggots climbing in and out. They are covered with a white crust of mould and are best thrown away. (Girl)

[B]

An apple on the window sill looks so queer, you'd be surprised how luch and juicy it is inside, but there it stands, green one side, red the other, it stands there, an ornament. It's been there some time but no-one has touched it, they've been told not to. One day, when it is old, it will go rotten and brown and will get thrown out with the rubbish. (Boy)

[C] In January when the snow and frost comes
The apple trees are dull and bear
With only scars to show that leaves and fruit once were there.
The apples kept throughout the winter
Start to soften and wrinkle,
And the air smells of maturing fruit.
In the spring the buds all open.
And the apple flowers all bloom and blossom
And bees go back and forth
Busy getting pollen from the blossoms

And from each flower comes forth an apple.
Small green and hard but still an apple.
All through the summer months
The apples grow and ripen
Wasps fly round among the trees
Stopping here and there and eating at the apples
The branches are weighed down
With their heavy load
And many a mouth tries an apple to see if it is time.
About September in the autumn
The apples will be picked all rosy and shinney
The people get out baskets ladders and bags.
And slowly but surely the trees are relieved of their fruit.
The people tell old stories of William Tell,
How Isace Newton discovered gravity and other tailes.
While they make cider and store and eat the apples. (Girl)

[D]

Apples, rosy, crisp, smooth, or you can have rotten apples, dotted apples, crisp apples, soft apples, fun. Fun from picking apples, throwing apples. Apples green, yellow, brown or red, orchards places of delight! Apples growing, apples falling, apple cores...Cox's Orange Pippins. Worcesters cookers; which are bitter; continental apples, smooth; red, soft, English apples greeny yellow, hard crinkly, many colours. Apples large, Apples small, apple cores upon the wall. Apples in large clumps, single apples. Thrushes, Blackbirds, pecking boring "apples evil?" Adam and eve. Artists painting. Apples rosy roundish, bitter apples. maggots crawling sickly looking, people chokeing, apple pieces stuck in the throat. Apples do good, loose toothe? bite an apple. Apple skins, chopped apple, babies eat them. Apple shrivelled up.

BARE APPLE TREES (Boy)

[E]

In early September when the small green apples are turning into juicy, sweet, crisp apples, we take our baskets and go and pick them from the orchard...we twist them gently...sometimes it seemed you could jump on them clinging with your hands the tree would swing and apples in their millions cascading down on you like an avalanche reaching the cliff...not many usually missed our eyes and lay rotting among long tufts of grass... the wasps often sung to us above the rotten apples...the farmhouse (where we went apple-picking) was quite large and it was a mystery to us as we had never been further than the kitchen...All over the orchard were tiny flowers many of them were really weeds, but not to us... (Girl)

EXERCISE 2

The same student teacher (as the one in Exercise 1) went on to explore fire as a theme. Perhaps she lit a small fire on her desk: or read an account of a fire. Discuss the following examples of her pupils' work.

[A] *The Bonfire*

The flames leapt high
Into the sky,
As far as one may see
Their dazzling lights betrayed one's sight
And sparkled on the lea

We threw on wood to make it burn
And hay and twigs and fern
And then when it was very hot... (Girl)

[B] Sir fire is a creepy thing,
a crawling thing a weeping thing
He dances as he tears along with a roaring gutter and a wild song
Where ever he steps his footsteps lie black,
In burnt up grass and smoky hay stack.
He is feared and known far and wide.
'Beware' says one 'do not lie where Sir fire lies,
Or else with screms and burning cries
You too will be where his footstep rides.'

Sire fire did first bread his breth,
when A cave man found him in stone and wood,
And made him burn as best he could.
In front of his cave house door.
To keep the wicked mamals away from him once more
True when he was found
while just a babe
His eyes were black and blue
and green,
His breth was hot and dry while burning.
and he was everywhere.

I'm sorry if this pome seems short but to me it's full (Girl)

[C]

Fire is not understanding; he is reckless and ruthless. He bites when you touch him, he is angry. Why? Who has upset him? Why does he roar when devouring one thing and purr when devouring another? He is a giver of heat but he doesn't want you to take it. The naked tongues of flame reach high into the sky as if searching for food.

He hates the wind and the rain, the wind makes him curl up and hide and the rain makes him spit in a fury of rain and smoke.

What makes him so reckless? Why does he find pleasure in destroying things? Why does he gnash his teeth in anger at metallic objects? He is so powerful, he stops at nothing!

What would we do without fire? He gives us our power, he cooks our food, he is our angry helper! (Tom, aged 13)

[D]

I fear not death alone
But fire
Fire burns ragingly
My nerves are uncontrollable
When I think of it. (A spastic boy)

EXERCISE 3

Compare the following passage with **C** in Exercise 2. Why do you think this comparison is invited? What similarities can you find?

Who can discover the face of his garment? or who can come to him with a double bridle?
Who can open the doors of his face? his teeth are terrible round about.
His scales are his pride, shut up together as with a close seal.
One is so near to another, that no air can come between them.
They are joined one to another, they stick together, that they cannot be sundered.
By his neesings a light doth shine, and his eyes are like the eyelids of the morning.
Out of his nostrils goeth smoke, as out of a seething pot or cauldron.
His breath kindleth coal, and a flame goeth out of his mouth.
In his neck remaineth strength, and sorrow it turned into joy before him.
The flakes of his flesh are joined together: they are firm in themselves; they cannot be moved.
His heart is as firm as a stone; yes, as hard as a piece of the nether millstone...
Upon earth there is not his like, who is made without fear.
He beholdeth all high things: he is king over all the children of pride.

(The description of Leviathan, Job xli)

EXERCISE 4

Discuss the use of fire as a symbol here:

The Fire

The man stared with unblinking eyes into the red-hot coals and in and out flickered and danced jets of yellow flame that licked hungrily around the coals and up the side of the dark, sooted fireplace. Twirls of gray smoke twisted and meandered until they were lost to the darkness of the chimney. The fire cracked and spat, now and then, and died away to a distant hum. The room fell silent again and everything was still.

From the fire came a transparent orange light which picked out the outline of the man's face and every line and wrinkle and contour on it. His face seemed to change from orange to yellow and back again, over and over again in an unending cycle of the changing lights.

The boy was watching the man from on the hearth rug where he had been playing with his model cars, ploughing them through the jungle which was the hearth rug. He had left his cars several minutes since and was watching the old man, studying the contours of his face as they changed and shadowed in the flickering of the fire. The man's chest heaved occasionally, and his eyes shut and then opened again. He licked his lips and made a clicking sound with his mouth. The boy had often heard the sound and had hated it; now he felt warmed and contented, he didn't know why.

Suddenly the man yawned noisily, breaking the silence startlingly. The boy jumped and stared at the rows of yellow, uneven pointed teeth and felt himself shudder.

Then there was silence again and there was only the crackle of the luminous coals. The old man looked tired and small. The light was yellow again and the air was hot and heavy. The boy felt he had woken from a dream. He picked up a car and pushed it across the carpet.

(Boy, 4th year, grammar school)

EXERCISE 5

In this exercise the object is to compare the following poems. But first of all discuss the symbolism in **A**: what is it about? Then compare it with **C**. Now discuss all four.

[A] *The Lilac Tree*

The lilac tree stood over the gate
Its young leafs moved in the breeze
The little green flowers not probly out

Exercise 5

Heafely laden it sways this way and that
Soon my little lilac tree we'll be out
Each day it gets whiter and whiter brighter and brighter
Very soon it's like a crown
A crown worn by an angle
And angle in white the best to be seen.
(Florence, aged 12, secondary modern school)

[B]

In a Mirtle Shade

Why should I be bound to thee,
O my lovely mirtle tree?
Love free love cannot be bound
To any tree that grows on ground.

O how sick and weary I
Underneath my mirtle lie,
Like to dung upon the ground
Underneath my mirtle bound.

Oft my mirtle sigh'd in vain
To behold my heavy chain;
Oft my father saw us sigh,
And laugh'd at our simplicity.

So I smote him and his gore
Stained the roots my mirtle bore.
But the time of youth is fled,
And grey hairs are on my head. (William Blake)

[C]

The Lilac Tree

How pretty is the lilac tree
How full of pride she seems to me;
Her purple flowers for to show
She only does it cause she knows,
How beautiful she is
How beautiful she is

Her leaves all dressed in the prettest green
The best of leaves I've ever seen
She only does it cause she knows
How more and more her splender grows
How beautiful she is
How beautiful she is
And more and more her splender is
How beautiful she is

But one day, up a gale comes
The wind it howls, and the sky hums
They steal the pretty little flowers
And now my dears theres only the boughs
How ugly she is now
How ugly she is now
And now my dears theres only the boughs
How ugly she is now.
(Susan, aged 12, secondary modern school)

[D]

I fear'd the fury of my wind
Would blight all blossoms fair and true;
And my sun it shin'd and shin'd
And my wind it never blew.
But a blossom fair or true
Was not found on any tree;
For all blossoms grew and grew
Fruitless, false, tho' fair to see. (William Blake)

EXERCISE 6

Discuss this piece of writing, by a grammar-school boy.

The lighthouse-keeper

He was watching the rain out of the window; his face was lean and intense,—looking out over the grey air. And he was solely independent of the world. His only contact with life was the ships—the black, barren shapes of metal which drifted close to his tower. His long, piercing beams of light shot over the black waters.

Then his eyes sharpened as the beam lit upon something tiny in the dark. Something shot towards the open glass and fluttered madly about his room, He shut the window on an impulse. It was a bird, a black thing with tiny, darting eyes and ugly claws.

He knew he should set it free. He could not keep it in his room; it was not right. He and it were beings apart, so he should let it go.

But something in its almost audacious perkiness fascinated him. It pleased him vaguely to hold this little bundle of life in his big, rough hands. His mother had told him to release wild animals when he was young.

He let it fly around the room watching its wings beat blindly against the whitewashed stone of the tower. He opened the window suddenly and shut his eyes; when he opened them the bird was still in the room. He tried to send it out of his window but it was scared of the light and would not go.

Exercise 6

He hated that darting stare fixed on him. He took the bird on his hands and delicately strangled the thing.

He stopped suddenly and was horrified—he left the room.

EXERCISE 7

Raymond is a likeable boy of fourteen, in a fourth-year 'B' stream but his writing is poor, and his output thin. The first poem he writes in his book is this: compare it with **B**.

[A]

Fear.

Hwas I walked down. the dark lane.
I fell a shiver go up my spine.
I thought of only the ground in front
of me.
Not the fear behind. ✓

[B]

Like one, that on a lonesome road
Doth walk in fear and dread,
And having once turned round walks on,
And turns no more his head;
Because he knows, a frightful fiend
Doth close behind him tread.

(Coleridge, from *The Ancient Mariner*)

(Raymond had never read *The Ancient Mariner*.)

EXERCISE 8

To continue with Raymond: it is to be hoped that Exercise 7 has convinced you that despite his scrawly output Raymond is inwardly very much a child still, and has deep things to say, poetically, though in simple poetic symbolism. You find out that he is illegitimate: discuss the symbolism of the rest of the work in his book.

It contains a poem:

The baby.
As my baby lay in my arms.
I Know it had lots of charms.
His big bule eyes they stare at me.
And I rock the baby to sleep soft soft ✓

Another that didn't quite come off:

The ORPhan.
I am. an orhan. I live in the
heged I live on scraps and bits of.
waste I mix them up to make a.
surper paste.

A synopsis for an 'opera':

Synopsis. ~~OPERA~~
This is a story of a long lost.
love it tells the tale of two young
people. Their names are Hans and.
yellowsinger. Yellowsinger is a
lovely! princess. Hans is a gypis.
They meet. in a market squre.
where he is playing a harp.
She came up to him and.
said . I want You to play at my ball.
why pick a scruffy gypys like
me.

Exercise 8

List of characters—he calls them 'complications'!

Complications

Hans a gypsy from thee, next village

yellowsinger a beautiful princess.

Prince, he is a Jeously sort of person

King. a fat stubby man.

Queen. She is a wild person.

maid. Who. help the princess.

A first sketch for the dialogue:

Princess Why you play beautiful on your harp

Hans Thank you Princess. would. you like me to play a tune for you

Princess yes I loved to hear you. you play me Greensleaves.

Hans. Now my princess I have plaved your tune. I must go my Mother will be cross.

Princess] Oh! don't go.. but I see you
you must wont I see you again.
my love.
Hans] .Princess you called me.
my love. Oh princess I love you.

Princess.] come here. (She kisses him.
on his head then he takes her in his arms. Then
the prince comes. in).
Prince] what is this.
Princess] Oh nothing I a sure you.
Just a good bye kiss.

Hans] I think I must go now.
Good by. Good by.

Prince] Just don't forget its me.
your marring not that gypsy.
Just dot forget.
sit II.
princess. meets Hans in the court yard.
Then The prince comes up a stairs arow.

Prince Ah so you meet again.

Now look here I know you like the. princess but you Just keep away from her all I will thill you.

Hans you think you will.

Prince

—this tails off.

What steps would you take (see Exercise 9) to encourage Raymond to go on with his 'opera' or with the following 'play'?)

A dialogue in a coffee bar. (J.A. is the proprietor. K.P. is a girl. The other characters are Ted 1, Ted 2, Ted 3 and Ted 4. 'Wog' is Ted 2.)

J. A. yes what can I get you.

K. P. well you could find a. boy for me

J A could I well their vs. a grouh of Teds over there.

Teds. Hia doll. you have a. nice pair of legs. ~~have~~

K.P. Hami I

Ted(4?). ~~Wait~~ a night out baby.

Ted(~~1~~2) Wit up stoe is coming out with me. no this will come out with all of us.

SEAN 2.

Shall wie go and. see wait the ~~Wlter~~ sun.

KP. yes that would be. nice. what did he.

~~K~~ ~~Ted~~. if you come with me I wile demerdrate to you.

T.P. Now that would be nice - Where shall we go.

TED 2: Now That is a proplem HA I know we will go. to my digs.

Sean III.

J.A. Hello. boys have a nice night.

Teds I did not. WOG took her

Exercise 8

K.P walks in
TEDS you look. fatter.
WOG didn't I tell you she is.
going to have a baby. u..

The exercise book ends with a 'song':

This grass ~~on~~ is greener on with
I stand.
So come my love and take
my hand
Let's take a walk. in.
the evening, breeze and walk.
under the those darkend trees.
The nightingale sings its.
song. Its such a bird it never.
goes wrong.

EXERCISE 9

(see above, pp. 11–14)

Do you think you can make anything of Raymond's limited gifts? If so, to what plays or operas would you draw Raymond's attention? Or how else would you encourage him to write?

EXERCISE 10

Discuss the symbolism of this poem:

The Brook

How wonderful is the brook
I love it with all my heart,
It gurgles in and out with pebbly beds
Trickling down the mountainside, bubbling and spitting

Jumping and springing over jagged rocks
Splashing and dashing beneath miniature bridges
Sometimes it hides in the grass
Then suddenly springs out in a scurrying waterfall.

The brook is young when in the mountains
But as it journeys through the bracken
It gradually changes from a beck to a stream
Then from a stream it becomes a beautiful slow, sophisticated river,
Winding slowly and gracefully and gently curving
Through villages, marshes, and fields of grazing cows
And then at last it grandly and still slowly
Mingles with other brooks and becomes a beautiful glimmering lake.

Yes I love the Brook
I have seen it in many tempers
When angry and wild, and when gentle and cool
Yet I like it always, for, in any temper.
It is still my brook. (Girl, 2nd year, grammar school)

EXERCISE 11

Evaluate this poem by Janet, a grammar school sixth-former. What do you say to yourself about it? What is it about? What do you say to her? What do you do about following this up by other literature?

Snakes and Ladders

My life is a game of snakes and ladders,
There is no set pattern; every move I make
Has a result, a beginning an end,
And is scrutinized by those set ready to pounce,
To condemn, to ridicule, to tear to pieces.
Every day is spent rushing up ladders of nonentity
And crashing down snakes of reality,
Like black stone power-stations,
Or a forgotten thanatoid building of desolation,
Blocking spoiling, deliberately concealing any pleasing view.
Behind them, the view of which I crave for,
Like an addict craves his drugs.

Sometimes I come to a ladder:
A visit to russet Hyde Park in October,
Praise from my teacher,

Exercise 11

A new Presley record.
An excursion to a theatre—
Selfish things, but what a joy they bring to me
In those precious moments before I am hurtled back to reality.

Dear God, will I ever be allowed to pass into womanhood,
Into an existence of responsibility,
Of happy living, of a husband and children?
Or will I be struck down,
Blinded by that unquenchable terrifying threat
That hangs over the world like a heavy black blanket of destruction?

Are you going to allow me to know, to feel,
To experience cold, hard-living death by radioactivity?
Am I ever going to bring up children
Without the fear of mocking them?
To bring them into this red-hot world
Sitting on an active volcano?
Inside me there are endless voices
Cawing in triumph like crows black and ugly,
Crying 'Destruction!' 'Death!' 'Uselessness!'
And asking one question—the vital question:
Will I ever be allowed to grow up?

EXERCISE 12

Discuss the various processes of symbolism, projective identification and other phantasy uses of the animals in the following pieces. Discuss the quality of language and where you think it reveals such processes. Say what literature (poems and stories) you would give the children.

[A] *A Rat*

A rat on my desk
I fix my gaze on it with an air of panic
I sit up and my chair crashes to the floor.

All the time the undesirable creature is staring at me with its small evil eyes, and seemingly sneering at me. Glad to see my displeasure, gleish evilnesch.

His head is large, and the nose, eyes and ears remind me of someone who is totally unreliable and wicked.

In strong contrast to his head being large, his body is small, with an enormous hump protrudes between his brittle shoulder blades.

With fur that is covered in equally revolting fleas, and smells of stale food. The colour being unrecognisable because of the filth of ages.

And still it continued to stare at me in evil pleasure.

It suddenly started to move towards me with short, hopping movements, and as it moved it uttered short human-like screams.

In a human these screams would mean terror, but his screams were evil.

It came upon my hand, and resting its obnoxious head on my hand, and with a final sneer sinks its fangs into the back of my hand.

And all the time continued to stare at me with pleasure.

(Girl, 3rd year, secondary modern school)

[B] *The Frog*

Suddenly with a shudder of horror, I saw it. It had a sack below its frowning mouth the colour of a milk bubble that bulged in and out, and from time to time it uttered a low croaking belch. It squatted on the slimy edge of the little pond where I had been fishing and stared hypnotically with its great humped eyes. I took my rod and slapped desperately at the frog and it flopped spasmodically on its humped back. Little red and green veins vibrated beneath the translucent white skin on its round stomach. The monster grunted and jerked back to its feet while I drew back into the weeds. Then it made a flying leap at me and bit me on the calf. I refused to take any more of this torture and so turned tail and ran splashing to my father.

(Girl, grammar school)

[C] *Spiders*

Most people hate spiders and scream when they see one, but I like them. Our house is very old and has a lot of spiders in it. One day I went in to get my bath. I went to the taps and was turning them on when I saw a spider. I quickly turned the tap off and picked it up. It stood there quivering. I had read somewhere that if you stroke them with a soft brush you can charm them. Then and there I decided I would try it. I found an old soft toothbrush and started to brush it gently. It just stood there and I was delighted, it seemed to be working. I sat down still stroking it. Suddenly it stopped quivering, turned round and started walking, well it wasn't exactly a walk more of a hop I would have said, anyway it began to move. It went down my arm and off my finger out of the bath. It walked down the side of the bath and disappeared onto the floor. I watched it with regret. For once in my life I had owned the confidence of an animal. I was tranced and walked downstairs without having my bath. (Girl grammar school)

[D]

I have always been absolutely terrified at the sight of a spider. I always used to think that a spider would come out in the dead of night and eat me very, very slowly until he grew very fat and then burst and out I would come, This of course was when I was small but still the horrid nocturnal creatures frighten me. My Father told me that once he had been bitten by a spider when he tried to throw it out of the window. That is why he always uses a handkerchief now. I remember once when I went up to bed on a summer's night. I looked under the bed and other furniture before getting into bed. Suddenly I felt as if someone or something was watching me. I looked round and there to my complete horror sat a large hairy spider. He began to move furtively along the skirting board. I screamed and jumped on to the bed as it was the nearest thing off the ground. The spider began to climb the wall, but dropped just near the door. I knew the spider was not poisonous, but I was scared it would bite my bare toes if I jumped to the ground. I shouted for my father for what seemed ages (it was only about 4 minutes) until he came, duster in hand, to remove it from the house for ever.

(Girl, grammar school)

[E] *Spider*

I wake up and look around my web and there again I feel the surge of disop- ment go thraw by buitful scaly black body once more I shall have a hungry morning for my web has been asleep. I wash myself but still I feel the pain of hunger, so decending down the headge of my web I walk under a human made door bad ugly stupid fat cretures humans are.

I climb under the unto a mass of soft green cottong wool which is called a rug and Oh! it takes so long to ride threw So I climb up a wall and under a crack at the top of the door then I decend by my web I hear "Jim! Jim! Help me theres a horrible fat black spide help! and as I look a mass of black runs out the door I think that I don't like thes fat rude cretures humans.

(Girl, 2nd year, independent school)

[F] *The Bat*

I returned to my room at dusk. It was a warm evening with a cool breeze stirring the trees and rustling through their rich foliage. I swung the door open noisily and barged in. In the corner a tiny squeak resounded followed by a flitting of panic-stricken wings. A small bat had come into the room thinking it to be a quiet place where it could rest. On detecting my presence the bat began to fly in wild circles squeaking insanely in its very high-pitched voice. If flew towards a wall then turned suddenly away towards the window panicking, foolish, afraid. It skimmed through the air in a frenzy of terror then quiet suddenly it hit the window pane; a small thud. The tiny creature flapped desperately and then slowly sank to the floor beneath the window and remained squatting there palpitating from exhaustion and shock, cringing from my presence. It seemed almost ashamed of its own insignificance and the horror with which its species was connected.

The small creature trembled. Its soft brown fur lay close against its body and it had wrapped its soft translucant wings around it in a protective shell. Its black pearly eyes stared, unseeing out of its mild face and its ears remained still, listening, straining.

I approached the creature as quietly and gently as I could. The poor creature's body convulsed in a fit of terror. I put my hand out and it flitted feebly. I clasped it gently but firmly in my hands and lifted it. Its warm body jumped and then seemed to relax to know that it would be free to live its small existence hated by humans and other animals, despised by the day.

(Girl, grammar school)

[G]

THE DEAD WEASEL

A red object lays on the ground
ahead
I think it's a weasel, dead!
It lays next to a patch of
grass
(~~Flys~~) Flies skurry off as I pass.

Ticks and fleas ~~crawl~~ crawl over
him

His eyes are faded and dim,
Red with blood is his throat
Which spoil his red-brown coat.

Compare this, by a child in the first year in a secondary modern school, with the following:

The Gallows

There was a weasel lived in the sun
With all his family
Till a keeper shot him with his gun
And hung him up on a tree,
Where he swings in the wind and rain,
In the sun and in the snow,
Without pleasure, without pain,
On the dead oak tree bough...

And many other beasts
And birds, skin, bone and feather,
Have been taken from their feasts
And hung up there together,
To swing and have endless leisure
In the sun and in the snow,
Without pain, without pleasure,
On the dead oak bough.

(Edward Thomas. Two stanzas have been omitted)

[H] *Milking a cow*

I get up and early set out
To get ready for milking my little cow Betsy
I open the gate of the green pastured field.
And gladly I let her walk proudly in to the milking shed.
Her coat is of the finest black hair wich I brush down very morning hour.
She has a pretty face with lovely blue eyes,
and eat, cow cake, crush oats, and lovely rich grass.
I pick up the chain which I sometimes chain up.
I put the stool down in a comfortable place and pick up a bucket and start to milk.
In half an hour I have a bucket full. I give some to the kittens, the baby pigs, and a rather small calf.

EXERCISE 13

In a sense this prose poem is a joke: has it any deeper meaning?

The Merciless Killer

It ate away the paper slowly at first, then accelerated into its full mercyless speed devouring every inch and turning it into the colour of death. That black miserable and sorrowful colour.

It was once a thin clean sheet of paper smooth and fresh smelling. Now it is a burned lifeless fragment of material, dirty and fragile, the crumbles when ever you touch it. (Boy, 4th year, secondary modern school)

EXERCISE 14

The Headmistress of the school in which the following piece was produced said, 'Yes, it is very good, but it was a pity it was ever written'. What do you think?

Saturday Nights

I sit in the coffee bar watching the dim, orangy-yellow lights gleaming thru' the haze of cigarette smoke. They remind me of something but I am not sure what. The atmosphere is thick and heavy, and I feel lazy, and withdrawn from everybody around me. I can hear the babble of conversation without hearing the words. I do not want to hear them. I can see a blur of faces in a dream-like way, and I sit half-asleep thinking of nothing in particular. Suddenly a piercing voice demands 'Will you take your parker's off please!' I come back to the present and see the boss-eyed waitress standing in front of me. She turns on her heel and walks off and I relapse into a daze. I am watching the yellow light at the end. It is barely visible through the smoky atmosphere. 'Take your parker's off *please*.' This time with more emphasis. There is a sudden scuffle of chairs and everyone stands up. I cannot be bothered to go out into the cold. Before I know what has happened I am downstairs. I shiver with cold, everyone is cold, the scooters start up, I am on the back, and now we set off.

The scooter wobbles slightly from side to side. I am cold. I turn round and see lights everywhere behind me. The scooters are all ready to go. I am cold. There is a sudden outburst of noise. I am frozen. Then with a roar of engines we are off. We are in the middle. We overtake the scooter in front, we are overtaking the next, and the next. We are in front. I can feel the wind rushing in my face. My head is throbbing. Faster and faster we go. The wind has blown all my hair back. My eyes are watering. The blood is pounding in my head. My eyes are streaming. My ears are getting cold. I put my head down and the wind rushes over my head. A scooter has come up and overtaken us. We go faster and come up beside it, we are side by side, we are in front. I feel exhilerated, I feel like shouting, I feel happy. We are well in front. I think we are doing about sixty-five miles per hour. I wonder if my eye-liner has run? I expect so. I do not care. I put my hands in my pockets and lean back. We are travelling along steadily. Suddenly we slow down, the rest catch us up, the scooters quiver impatiently and the engines roar noisily. Silence. It has become quiet. The engines have stopped. We have arrived. I am getting off the back. I am standing on the pavement. All of a sudden I feel very tired, and cold.

(Girl, 4th year, grammar school)

Compare the evocation of a particular mood of isolation in *Saturday Nights* with this poem:

In a Foreign Hospital

Valleys away in the August dark the thunder
roots and tramples; lightning sharply prints
for an instant trees, hills, chimneys in the night.
We lie here in our similar rooms with the white
furniture, with our bit of Death inside us
(nearer than that Death our whole life lies under);
the man in the next room with the low voice,
the brown-skinned boy, the child among its toys
and I and others. Against my bedside light
a small green insect flings itself with a noise
tiny and regular, a 'tink, tink, tink'.

A Nun stands rustling by, saying good night,
hooded and starched and smiling with her kind
lifeless, religious eyes. 'Is there anything
you want?'—'Sister, why yes, so many things:'
England is somewhere far away to my right
and all Your letter promised; days behind
my left hand or my head (or a whole age)
are dearer names and easier beds than here.
But since tonight must lack for all of these
I am free to keep my watch with images,
a bare white room, the World, an insect's rage,
and if I am lucky, find some link, some link.

(Bernard Spencer, Collected Poems)

and with this:

To the east of my upstairs drinking-room there grows
A peach-tree whose leaves are brushed by the grey mist.
That tree I planted with my own hand;
I have not seen it for almost three years.
The tree by now must be level with the room,
And still I am no nearer to getting home
My lovely daughter whose name is P'ing-yang

Plucks the blossom, resting her weight on the tree.
She plucks the blossom, but cannot show it to me;
Her tears fall; they are like a flowing spring.
My little boy is called Pai-ch'in;
He is younger than she, but his shoulder touches hers.
The two of them are walking underneath the tree;
There is no one to stroke their hair, to show them love...
(Li Po, Translated by Arthur Waley)

EXERCISE 15

Compare this story with Chaucer's *Nun's Priest's Tale*. Discuss the symbolism, and its language. To what literature would you turn the writer's attention next?

The Cock

In a small yard at the back of the house the young cock grew to a certain splendour. He learned to crane his neck and crow like the other birds.

Now he was still tipping his head, listening to the challenge of faraway unseen cocks in the unknown world.

Black and orange, white chops, bright eyes, ruffled feathers, watching and listening with half-seeing eyes.

Looking on life with a flat, brilliant gaze, pert and alive, strutty and proud.

He surveyed the small world around him with aloof indifference, and yet majesty. He seemed still, yet rocked slowly, backwards and forwards while the hens fussed about him.

Now and then he would peck at the grain at his feet or make a flurry at a passing hen, but generally that day he kept still, as if he knew something.

Towards evening, the hens dispersed a little and the peasant farmer emerged from the back door with a stranger. A stranger in tweeds, and gum boots. With his feet the peasant cleared the yard, leaving the cock in the centre. Then they drove him to a small barn, bordering the yard on the left. The barn where he had made his first conquest.

They pushed him into the dark room, and one of them grabbed him. He'd seen his father enter here, and never come back. His prideful heart knew no fear only curiosity.

They carried him to a wooden block laughing and exchanging pleasantries with each other all the time.

Only when they held his neck down did he feel the slightest apprehension.

Then there was a swish and a glint, idly he wondered whether he would have time for an extra feed before being locked away for the night.

Thud! the chopper fell. (Girl, 4th year, Grammar school)

EXERCISE 16

This piece is by the same boy as Exercise 6. From his language, try to say whether you think he identifies with the protagonist. What do you say to yourself about him and his work? What literature would you give him to follow up?

The Unaccepted One

They were coming home from school, one of those parties of school-children who talk incessantly from the sheer abandon of finishing school. All were alike, all reflecting the laughs of school life. But there was a difference—one face was different; it smiled like the others, but it held behind it a deep-seated resentment or fear—Of what?

Philip Ruston had had an accident a month previously, a shattering defeat for such a sensitive child. For now he had to be helped about on his crutches, he no longer joined in all the fun, all the excursions...

'It's swimming again tomorrow. If we have it.'

'Yes,' Philip hated swimming. Although he had never excelled himself in it, he had loved that soothing green water. Water which accepted him—enveloped him. But now swimming was unsuitable, and the echoes in the baths mocked him, screamed at him.

'Yes,' he said; it was swimming.

'You might be able to try it later, if—if you're better that is,' ventured one.

'D'you think so?' Philip's soul screamed at the thought—he was impure, too impure for water. They said his brain had been affected, they said he was unnatural, they said...They said! They never liked me at the hospital, not even his mother had understood. She said he would be able to behave normally.

'Come on, this is our stop!' someone shouted. Philip tried to rise—but dropped his crutch. They tried to raise him but failed. Philip fell back into the seat.

'Oh, hurry up, can't you. We'll miss the flipping stop.'

The bus came to it and most of the boys jumped off leaving only one with Philip. He laughed and said he would be late; then he bent to help Philip up. But he stopped as if disinclined to touch Philip who saw his eyes, grunted and stood up climsily. The next stop was reached and they both dismounted.

They parted and Philip limped across the street to his row. On the way he met the woman who kept the delicatessen; she looked away. That was the boy who was mentally unblanced; she knew what that would mean in later life, but all he saw were hard impassive faces, they screamed at him that he was mad, mad! mad! 'Oh no!' they said, 'he couldn't pretend to be normal, he was mad all right.'

And Philip was convinced because they said so. Proof? Well the hardness, the sameness. It hadn't been like that before! Look! the clouds never stop, always rolling. Yes, he was mad. An end! Put an end to it. Everything was laughing, laughing, suspicious.

The front of the lorry came nearer, there was his soul swallowing himself. The radiator yawned, it accepted him.

And the pain was nothing—as was he; but the clouds still rolled.

EXERCISE 17

Jack, a fourteen-year-old pupil in one of the lower streams in a London comprehensive school, got his brother to type this poem out for him. Discuss his imagery and style. Evaluate the poem and say what you will do about it in class:

```
Ans some dark night when the moon is bright, and death
stalks on the dale: I see that room and I know real fear
real fear. My hand shake and my musles tighten and the
veils of time just drift away, And horror gasps in quiet
dismay. And the blood drips like a brilliant dye and stains
the floor a brilliant red, and their is no-One to speak to me
of life, love and liberity and hate drops in where once
was love. And i seach in that room for one speck one speck
of hope to light the doom. But none comes and none ever will
and i'll live in this enternal hell where no man lives,
where no man loves, where no man lays, where no man dies.
But where I'll spend enternatiy, and I think of things that used
to be. Of days gone by of memeriors that still ponder on
my lips. But bloodstill runs on the floor and death still
knocks on the door. And I wonder if in death I'll find
peace like I had once before IF YOU Dont like the END.
(on that cold dark and dismall moor a long long time ago.)
```

EXERCISE 18

Here are three more poems by the same boy. Compare the imagery and symbolism, and say to what other poetry you would now draw his attention.

[A] *The Whirlpool of Life*

If you go there one night, like that young man long ago,
And look, like you must look, on the whirlpool, the whirlpool of life,
When he looked his face turned white,
He clasped his hands, he stumbled back,
And dropped the oar.
He fell down on his knees and prayed
Like he had never prayed before.
For all his life, for all his life he had never prayed before.
But now he prayed, he prayed to God.
He might be saved from what he saw.
The sweat poured from his brow.
A tingle ran up his spine.
He clasped his hands, His nails pressed deep, He pierced His skin,
His body weak.
He pressed them deeper, deeper, past the veins.
His blood poured grotesquely like waterfalls of pain
And dripped on the floor like drops of rain
And mixed with the sweat and made puddles, puddles formed from pain.
He turned a sudden gaze up to the moonlit sky,
He seeked, he searched, he wondered why,
He turned to the banks, the moonlit ropes.
He grabbed them to keep death out that he might live.
But Death came tip-toeing in, in veils draped black.
His hand shone like ivory as one cloud passed over the moon
A beam of light caught his hands, reflected soon,
And that young man could see they were but bones
Hands of death, feet of doom.
It lifted its veil dark as night, he covered his face.
In one last effort he pushed and tore with bloody hands and arms a sore.
He grabbed his throat with one last deep gulp, he died from shock, they say.
They found his body by the castle moat,
And if you got there you will see a lonely willow tree,
And these few words, some say, were writ by he.
'Can you outrun destiny, can you outlive fate?'

[**B**] *One Day*

Why in God's name do we have to do
What we don't want to do?
Why strive and shout to get out of this endless rut?
Why does it seem to me and you
That everything we ever do
Is what we don't want to do?
One day, one day I'll sit here and stay
And do just what I want to do
And then, and only then I'll feel
That I've done what I ought to do.

Compare the following:

There is no point in work
Unless it absorbs you
like an absorbing game.

If it doesn't absorb you
If it's never any fun
don't do it.

When a man goes out into his work
he is alive like a tree in spring,
he is living, not merely working...

(D. H. Lawrence, *Work*)

We all gotta do what we gotta do
We're gona sit here and drink this booze
We're gona sit here and have a tune
We're gona stay and we're gona go
And somebody's gotta pay the rent...

(T. S. Eliot, *Sweeney Agonistes*)

[C]

It was a cold wet night.
There was a breeze in
the air.
As I run along the road as
fast as air my feet a-pounding
my toos a-pattering
the rough rock tore my feet
to ribons. My bodey tire-d my
musiles taught,
my head a turning,
my body yeaning,
my has hang limp all life wire
dron.
My heart a pounding
my feet a pattering
past the place of no retern
On, on where none could come,
Faster faster to the place where
all life was gone.

EXERCISE 19

Discuss the meaning of this poem. It came from Robert, a rough, rather well-off fifteen-year-old, in 3 B in a secondary modern school.

One day a man killed me.
I have been looking for him.
All my life.

I am a ghost how that me.
I found him with my mummey.

I killed that man
like he killed me

he die on my.
Mummey nee.

EXERCISE 20

Discuss the following short story by a girl of fifteen in terms of its symbolism (i.e. as if it were a Greek myth). What do you think is the significance of the two names 'Clarissa' and 'Clare'? Point out places where you would commend the language used.

To what literature would you direct the author?

Exercise 20

Clarissa and Ruth

I walked sorrowfully down to the river, thinking, 'Ruth doesn't love me. I suppose Dad does in his way. And I know for sure he married Ruth for my benefit. It hasn't done me much good though.'

'Oh, why did he have to marry her? And why did Mum have to die? Oh, well, I suppose I shall have to make the best of things.'

Clarissa walked on along the river bank until she came to the Vicarage Meadow. She stopped suddenly, and stared across the meadow. The fair had arrived. The fair had never before been to Goldmill, the little village where Clarissa lived. She decided then and there that she was going to it. She had never before been to a fair. The clatter, bustle and busy-ness of the fair people excited her. And she skipped back along the river bank, travelling as fast as her feet could carry her. She reached her home and burst in at the door.

'Daddy! Dad!' she cried, 'Where are you? The fair's come! The fair's come! You will let me go won't you? Please, please let me go!'

She danced into the sitting room and came face to face with her stepmother.

'What do you mean by shouting about the house like that, you little tomboy?' she asked strictly.

'But the fair's arrived, Ruth,' Clarissa said.

'I don't care what has arrived. It gives you no reason to tear about like that.'

'Oh, but Ruth...'

'And don't "Oh but Ruth" me, you insolent child!'

'I am not a child. I am thirteen years old, and I think you're hateful.'

'Go to bed this instant. I am not going to tolerate you any longer.'

'I'll go to bed gladly. Anything to get away from your ugly face. Why couldn't Dad have married someone nice? I hate you! I hate you!'

At that moment her father came in. Clarissa turned and rushed out through the door, nearly knocking her father over. She tore upstairs banging her bedroom door. She lay down on her bed sobbing, 'I hate her, I hate her!'

Downstairs Ruth was telling her husband how rude Clarissa had been—and exaggerating rather a lot. Tim, Clarissa's father, knew she wouldn't act as badly as that. So he made up his mind to go up and speak to her. But as he was walking out of the door Ruth screamed at him, 'If you go up to her I shall leave you, and I mean it!'

She also rushed up to her room.

Tim sat down and thought. He didn't really want to lose Ruth, and thought that it was only a passing phase on Clarissa's part. So he smoked his pipe and got on with his book.

Upstairs Clarissa had got over feeling sorry for herself and only felt malice for Ruth. 'I'm going to the fair, whatever they say,' she thought.

At eight o'clock that night nobody saw a shadowy figure climb out of the bedroom window, crawl down a facing tree and run swiftly across the fields.

At ten o'clock Tim walked slowly upstairs to bed. He stopped outside Clarissa's bedroom door and listened. All was quiet. He walked into his bedroom and softly closed the door.

Clarissa arrived at the fair at about a quarter past eight. She could see over the fence into the fairground. The coloured lights danced up and down her face. She could see the merry-go-rounds turning, and the happy faces of the children going round with them, shouting at their parents waiting below. Everyone looked so happy she couldn't help forgetting her previous experience with Ruth. Her only thought now was to get into the fairground. She walked round the fence of the fairground. There was no gap she could see. So she went to the opening. Just then she saw coming a woman with a herd of children crowded behind her. An idea came to Clarissa. If she attached herself to this woman while she was walking through the gangway...

'I'm sure he won't bother to count the children!' Clarissa thought.

She stood at the entrance entranced. Slowly she walked forwards towards a dazzling display of coloured lights decorating a toffee apple and candyfloss stall. She walked round, her mouth watering as she looked at the apples literally dripping with toffee. She wished she had got enough money to have a go on the roundabouts and other things. But she knew she was lucky to get in, let alone anything else. She wandered round. She thought, if only I could run away with the fair. Just as quick as the thought came into her head it left it. But a few minutes later it came back again and wouldn't go away, although she tried to make it.

'But why shouldn't I?' she said to herself. 'They don't want me, let alone love me. Yes, I'll run away with the fair.'

Then another thought crossed her mind. 'Perhaps they won't want me? Oh, they must want me. Well, I'll run away without them knowing. Yes that's what I'll do.'

And so Clarissa resolved, 'I'll wait until dark and slip in one of the caravans and hide. Yes, that's what I'll do. Now all I have got to do is wait until dark.'

'I'll find a caravan all ready,' she thought.

There was a lovely bright red and yellow one, and, as Clarissa always liked bright colours, the caravan immediately attracted her attention. She got a box and looked through the window. It was entirely empty. She crept up the steps, opened the door and peeped in. She gasped in surprise, for everwhere was spotlessly clean and tidy and bright. The china was very dainty. As she looked at the bed Clarissa suddenly realised how tired she was. She went up to it, looked at it, and then flopped on it and went to sleep. It was two and a half hours later when the owner of the caravan came home.

She was a young woman aged about twenty. She grasped in surprise as she saw Clarissa lying there. She woke her gently and asked her what she was doing.

'I am sleeping in this caravan. Does it belong to you?'

'Yes, it does. What is your name?'

'It is Clarissa. I live down there the other side of the hill. I want to join the fair and live with you and work with you.'

'But won't your parents be worried about you?'

'No—they won't worry. They don't love me at all, so you needn't worry.'

'But I'm sure if you went back you'd find them very worried.'

'Oh, I don't think so. Dad might be a bit worried. But Ruth will not worry. She'll probably be glad.'

'Oh don't be silly: nobody could not want you!'

'Ruth could. You know, I think she hates me.'

'But why? Surely you don't mean that?'

'Oh, yes, I think she does. But only because I'm my father's daughter.'

'Oh, I see—she's jealous of you!'

'I don't know. But she certainly does dislike me.'

'Do you dislike her?'

'Yes, but only because she doesn't love me.'

'Well, I'll come home with you and see what they say.'

'Oh good. I know Dad will like you.'

'We'll see.'

An hour and a half later they arrived at Clarissa's home. Clarissa's father tore to the door and Clarissa ran into his arms. She noticed that Ruth stayed back in the hall and didn't come out to see her. She looked sorry that Clarissa had been found. Clarissa introduced her father to her new-found friend, the gypsy whose name was Clare. Tim was pleased to see her, but Ruth disapproved, Clarissa could see. Clare came in and had some tea. Tim was talking to her all the while and Ruth was forgotten. She was getting crosser and crosser. At some time after midnight Clare left. After seeing her out, he came back and asked Ruth if she liked her because he thought she was very nice. That did it. Ruth went blue in the face and let it rip.

'I know you like her better than me,' (Pointing to Clarissa)'—me, your wife, who was married for convenience to be a mother to that!' she said, pointing to Clarissa again.

'Oh, but Ruth...' Tim protested.

'And don't "Oh but Ruth" me,' she said. 'Don't think I don't know you meant to ignore me tonight. Well, you've ignored me once too often. I am finished. Done. I shan't give you a chance to ignore me any more. I am going. And it's good riddance to you both.'

Then she went.

And Clarissa could see that deep down Tim felt pleased. And so they both walked up the stairs to bed. Tim said to Clarissa, 'You will have to invite Clare to tea one of these evenings. I like her.'

EXERCISE 21

This story is by a boy in the first-year 'A' stream of a secondary modern school.

Discuss its poetic meaning.

What will you give him next to read (or what will you read the class, to match this pupil's interests?)

The Giant grasshopper 5.5.60.
There in a town called mean
lived a family wich was selfish
and bad they had ten in there family
Mrs Rotten and Mr Rotten and eight
boys Jim, Tim. Slim, Bim, Jeff, cliff,
seff and Jaff. ~~O~~Who all were very
selfish, till there came the gaint
grasshopper, Well the grasshopper wasn't
real it was three men in One big
costume ~~to~~ they were good men ~~au~~ who
had ~~once~~ ~~onec~~ one time saw ~~ha~~
how mean and selfish. First
Jim had ~~lad~~ laid a trap fore the parson
in the grave ground, he had taken the
coffin out of the ground, ~~dn~~ and ~~on~~ covered the hole with thin ~~stik~~ sticks with

he sprinkled over with dirt and the set flower's in it. When he had finsihed it looked like an ~~or~~ flower bed, but all the ~~td~~ time the thee men ~~do~~ in the grass hopper suite had been ~~wal~~ watching him and said in a loud voice "Why have you made the trap? Jim was so serprised that he stumbled ito the trap and broke his neck and died. The Three men were sorry but knew it was his own fault so they forgot about it. But when the family found out the father stayed at home and the boys and Mother went to look for his killer. Then they ~~her~~ herd the men talking. "That's the killer's those three men shouted the mother!" "Rush them Shouted Mother But they didn't have a hope because the Men ~~a~~ had ~~Pistal~~ Pistols, and the Rotten family only had knives. There was a ~~treror~~ teror of screams and Shots. and Bangs. And then there was a Crash and a One of the men came flying through the door with a knife in his back,

EXERCISE 22

Here is a folk-tale from the Angas people, told by a Nigerian student. Discuss its fairy-story-like symbolism.

When I was still young my blind grandfather often told us stories; this story is one of the most famous among my people.

Once a hunter and his son broke in, unintentionally, upon a witch, who sat in her hut feeding her many mouths, which were about ninety-eight in number.

When the witch saw that the hunter and his son had discovered her secret, she was extremely angry, and decided to revenge herself. She transfigured herself into a very beautiful maiden, and went to the hunter's house.

On her arrival the lads of the village gathered round her each hoping to speak to her about marriage, but she was only interested in the hunter and his son. Therefore she put her vessel on a stone. She told all those who were interested in her to throw a stone to see if they could knock the vessel over. She promised to marry whoever did so.

The hunter warned the boy not to participate in the contest. The others tried very hard to knock down the vessel, but none of them was successful. At length the hunter's boy took a handful of gravel and threw it jokingly at the stone. To his amazement the vessel fell before the stones could reach it. The girl sprang up, gratefully kissed the boy, and so married him.

After some years they decided to pay a visit to the girl's parents. On the night before they set out, the girl asked him many questions. She asked him to tell her the name of their previous king who was reputed to be very strong and brave. He did not tell her, because it was illegal to pronounce the king's name. He therefore told her indirectly in this famous verse...

The brave, for sure, sleep deep to-night,
When the moon is bright, and the wind in the trees,
But cowards have much ado to sleep,
Though the young lie often unconcerned.

When the day is bright, all things sing,
All with hoe and shield on shoulder dressed,
But our brave king, unknown, goes always empty-handed.
The greatest is this king who ever lived among us.

The woman seemed still unsatisfied, and asked more questions. She asked him again to list the names of all the things into which he could change in order to save his life when attacked by a wild beast.

He told her that he was able to change into a whirlwind, into a lion, and into many other things besides but when he began to name a butterfly his father stopped him when he scarcely had had time to begin the first syllable.

On the following day they set out on the journey cheerfully together. They arrived at the woman's former hut as the shadows were lengthening. The woman deceived her husband into believing that her parents house was still very far away, and that they would have to sleep in that hut till the following day. The man agreed, and she prepared a sleeping place for him on the ground. He was so tired that he fell asleep as soon as he lay down. Meanwhile his treacherous witch-wife left him and went out to plot against him.

As he was sleeping a snake fell from the roof and warned him about the evil woman. He was very confused and frightened by this, but he mounted his horse and rode away. He had not gone far when the woman saw him and called after him to wait and collect his clothes, but he paid no attention to her. Within a moment she was near him, and had cut off three of the horse's legs. But the horse did not stop. She cut off the last leg, and the horse fell.

The man changed himself into all the things he had told the woman, and she also changed into them. At last he changed into a butterfly, and was saved, for the woman did not know what he was, since his father had not allowed him to complete the name.

EXERCISE 23

Compare the following passages.

What do you think the animal is a symbol of, to each writer?

[A] *Death at Dusk*

Dusk was falling and I was sitting high in the branches of a knarled old tree, when looking down I saw, coming out of the shadows of the jungle, a beautiful male lion with a dusty but still gleaming mane of a dusky gold colour. He was obviously going to the water hole for a drink. As he passed under my tree, I could hear him panting painfully and noticed a great jagged wound down his side. You could see he had been in a fight just recently because the blood was still trickling down his side into little puddles in the dry dust. He was also in great pain as he was moving slowly and carefully; and every now and then he gave a snarl of pain. He began to drink feebly and gave gasps in between every mouthful, and I could see he was losing strength fast. Suddenly he sank to the ground but he did not stay there long, he again tried to rise up; as he sank to the ground he let out a roar which although he was dying sounded and resounded through the dark jungle. A few seconds later he got an answer which came faintly through the dusk. At this he gave a moan and sank for the last time with his head laid down in the mud and slime at the edge of the waterhole. The warm breeze faintly stirred the leaves of my tree. He was dead.

(Girl, aged 11)

[B]

They were driving slowly along the high bank of the stream which here cut deeply to its boulder-filled bed, and they wound in and out through big trees as they drove. Macomber was watching the opposite bank when he felt Wilson take hold of his arm. The car stopped.

'There he is,' he heard the whisper. 'Ahead and to the right. Get out and take him. He's a marvellous lion.'

Macomber saw the lion now. He was standing almost broadside, his great head up and turned towards them. The early morning breeze that blew towards them was just stirring his dark mane, and the lion looked huge, silhouetted on the rise of bank in the grey morning light, his shoulders heavy, his barrel of a body bulking smoothly.

'How far is he?' asked Macomber, raising his rifle.

'About seventy-five. Get out and take him.'

'Why not shoot from where I am?'

'You don't shoot them from cars,' he heard Wilson saying in his ear. 'Get out. He's not going to stay there all day.'

Macomber stepped out of the curved opening at the side of the front seat, on to the step and down to the ground. The lion still stood looking majestically and coolly towards this object that his eyes only showed in silhouette, bulking like some super-rhino. There was no man smell carried towards him and he watched the object, moving his great head a little from side to side. Then watching the object, not afraid, but hesitating before going down the bank to drink with such a thing opposite him, he saw a man figure detach itself from it and he turned his heavy head and swung away toward the cover of the trees as he heard a cracking crash...

(Ernest Hemingway)

[C] *Mountain Lion*

Climbing through the January snow, into the Lobo Canyon
Dark grow the spruce-trees, blue is the balsam, water sounds still unfrozen,
and the trail is still evident.

Men!
Two men!
Men! The only animal in the world to fear!

Exercise 23

They hesitate.
We hesitate.
They have a gun.
We have no gun.

Then we all advance, to meet.

Two Mexicans, strangers, emerging out of the dark and snow and inwardness of the Lobo valley.
What are they doing here on this vanishing trail?

What is he carrying?
Something yellow.
A deer?

Qué tiene, amigo?
Léon—

He smiles, foolishly, as if he were caught doing wrong.
And we smile, foolishly, as if we didn't know.
He is quite gentle and dark-faced.

It is a mountain lion,
A long, long slim cat, yellow like a lioness.
Dead.

He trapped her this morning, he says, smiling foolishly.

Lift up her face.
Her round, bright face, bright as frost.
Her round, fine-fashioned head, with two dead ears;
And stripes in the brilliant frost of her face, sharp, fine dark rays,
Dark, keen, fine rays in the brilliant frost of her face.
Beautiful dead eyes.

Hermoso es!

They go out towards the open;
We go into the gloom of Lobo.
And above the trees I found her lair,
A hole in the blood-orange brilliant rocks that stick up, a little cave.
And bones, and twigs, and a perilous ascent.

So, she will never leap up that way again, with the yellow flash of a mountain lion's long shoot!
And her bright striped frost-face will never watch any more, out of the shadow of the cave, in the blood-orange-rock,
Above the trees of the Lobo dark valley-mouth!

Instead, I look out.
And out to the dim of the desert, like a dream, never real;
To the snow of the Sangre de Cristo mountains, the ice of the mountains of
 Picoris,
And near across at the opposite steep of snow, green trees motionless
 standing in snow, like a Christmas toy.
And I think in this empty world there was room for me and a mountain lion.
And I think in the world beyond, how easily we might spare a million
 or two of humans
And never miss them.
Yet what a gap in the world, the missing white frostface of that slim yellow
 mountain lion! (D. H. Lawrence)

EXERCISE 24

Discuss the symbolism of this piece (quoted from *The Excitement of Writing*).

The Baby Bird

Once upon a time there was a little baby bird and he was a little rascal in the nest. He fell down down down flat on his bum, and he went looking for his mother, and he cried and cried till his mother came.

(Girl, aged 7, a slow learner)

2 *'Sincerity' and 'Realism'*

Even though we recognise that children are capable of using poetic symbolism unconsciously, the problem remains of telling when they are really 'working from the unconscious to the conscious'—that is, when they are being sincere *artistically*.

There are other problems, as in adult poetry and fiction. Sometimes a child's piece is real because he is recording a genuine experience, an 'outward' one. At other times (as with the fire poems in Exercise 2 above) he is recording a real inward experience. At other times a child, while being perfectly sincere, is exploring an experience he has never had; the author of *The Dead Weasel* in Exercise 15 had never seen a dead weasel—but his poem is still very real, because he is sincerely pondering death.

Children need to imitate, to take up postures in mimicry and to borrow voices: so, we can't urge 'sincerity' on them in the same way we expect an adult writer to be sincere. Yet there are forms of sincerity and realism we can commend by example. Of course, in such matters there can be no 'right answers'!

EXERCISE 25

Distinguish between the kinds of writing here, by the same fifteen-year-old pupil (quoted from *The Excitement of Writing*). How do you think writing the poem helped him to write the piece on the science of optics?

[A] Blackness in its darkest form
Creeps over all that dwell on earth,
And fills each separate being with a fear
Mysterious, overpowering and unfathomable.
The darkness hides away in deep oblivion
All things that daily give confidence.
In daylight unperturbed we walk in leafy woods,
At night fear secretes itself in us.
Mundane things become silent ghosts,
Haunting our fearful minds.

Every shadow, every rustle, is a spectre hidden
In the depths of darkness.
Imagination plays his tricks and fear impedes our way.
But sleep locks out all thoughts of fear
And cheats him of his victims.

[B]

The retina is a light sensitive coat which lines the inside of the eye behind the lens. It is made up of nerve cells and nerve fibres.

There are two kinds of nerve cells, rods and cones.

(*a*) Rods—are stimulated by twilight.

(*b*) Cones—are stimulated by daylight.

In some animals there are more of one sort than of the other, e.g., night animals such as owls have more rods than cones. Cones are thought to be responsible for colour vision. It is believed that they are stimulated by the three primary colours: red, green and blue.

The image formed on the retina is inverted and diminished. The fibres transmit impulses from the nerve cells to the brain. The nerve cells convert light stimuli into impulses. The fibres allow impulses to pass along them to the brain. All the fibres meet to form the optic nerve which ends in the brain.

EXERCISE 26

How do you think the writing of the piece below on obfuscation **A** helped the same grammar-school boy write about the nitrogen cycle **B**? (The pieces are quoted from *The Excitement of Writing*.)

[A]

The thick blanket smothered the dead city, silenced the void streets, threatened the lonely traveller, as I hobbled home one foot on, one foot off the pavement, kicking a rusty tin can into the mist before me. The minutes passed. I should be home soon sitting in front of a roaring log fire, and daring the choking smog to attack me there; but this was not our road or our house, was I lost? My feet were still savagely cleaving the fog, was I lost? Was I lost? My heart beat rapidly. I turned to run but a strange force compelled me onwards, ever onwards.

I was stopped by some invisible barrier, and then the magnetic sensation ceased. Of my own free will, I stumbled forward into a cobbled street quite deserted, but obviously inhabited yet with a stale, humid air. Directly in front of me stood a decrepit old shop with tiny green hammered glass windows and a frail wooden door with a greasy glass panel. Above the door was written one discernable word 'Antiques'.

[B]

Nitrogen is found in quantity in the atmosphere, and, therefore, the nitrogen cycle starts with atmospheric nitrogen. This free gas is 'fixed' by nitrifying bacteria and lightning to form nitrates in the soil. In the lightning method, oxygen and nitrogen are combined by lightning during thunderstorms, producing nitric oxide and finally nitrogen peroxide. After this the nitrogen peroxide dissolves in rain to form a solution of nitric and nitrous acids, which are washed into the soil. The nitrates of the soil solution are then absorbed by plant roots to be used to form proteins and protoplasm of plants. This process is called protein synthesis. Atmospheric nitrogen is also 'fixed' by nodule bacteria on leguminous plants, and directly forms proteins and protoplasm in plants. Plants which are eaten by humans and animals help to make proteins and protoplasm in humans and animals.

EXERCISE 27

Here is straightforward 'realism'. Discuss any underlying subjective preoccupations which you could seize on for imaginative work.

How would you follow up the piece with creative writing and literature work?

Extract from a climbing log

25.2.61 Saturday N.W. Gully Stab Caire NemBeith Bidean
Blizzard Conditions

We were up at 7 o-clock and arrived at bottom 8.30 PM. We went up the path to the corrie. Five of us went up the N W Gully 900 feet We had to cut steps in the snow all the way up when we got to the top we came to a dead end It was a small cave. There was a tunnel which was supposed to go right through but it was buried under the snow. Mr Paterson dropped a mitt and had to absail back down for it. We then climbed back down the gulley about 20 ft and then climbed up to the top, the climb was hard Because we had crampons on. The party then went up round the back of the hill. The mist was very thick and we had a job reaching Bidian. After that the rest was easy we went down the narrow ridge till we came past the church door and diamond buttres. We then walked back down the corrie. Every so often we had to knock the snow of our crampons the Weather was now at our back. We took of our crampons at the bottom of the corrie and walked back to the school bus We had to give the bus a push to get it reversed. We come back to the the Hostel after 10 hours of climbing.

GRADE MODERATE to Difficult

Party Mr Paterson Mr Brown D Simpson S Matyssek M Smith
Weather windy Snowy Misty

His postcard home:

Dear Mum we are having a great time today we climbed a 3,000 feet high mountain. We have seen lots of herds of deer and there are a lot of good views. There were only three of us that climbed the mountain it was the one that the climbers were killed on but we are all right. Murray.

EXERCISE 28

Here are some adolescent poems (from the collection by Mr Jack Beckett, *The Keen Edge*).

How 'sincere' and 'real' are they?

[A]

Your whole mind filled to the brim
With hate, jealousy and anger.
It grows and grows until you swell
And overflows with the devil.
It burns an amber hole, black and poisoned
Through your soul,
Until anger, hate and jealousy win
By devouring your whole body up.
At last it rushes out full of poison
And deadly words.

[B]

I grit my teeth
My blood feels like a boiling sea
My hands shake and long to hit back
My eyes open wide and lower on my victim
Inside me my feelings surge
And I swallow hard
And then anger and hate as if by magic
Slowly dissolve into nothing.

[C]

I wonder why my own father
Is killing me
For a brount offering
In place of a lamb,
I am the loved one

Exercise 28

I am Isak
The son of Abraham,
I am not a lamb
Why must he put me
On a alter
And kill me.

[D]

As he holds you tight to him,
All your fears seem to flow away,
He looks at you in the silvery light
And kisses your tender lovable lips.

He talks of love, and says when we
Grow up that he will marry me,
Then we will have children of our own,
And when they grow up they will be like us.

How soft he seems to kiss your lips,
He feels so soft and tender,
But when he leaves you of a night
You feel so lost without him.

EXERCISE 29

Discuss the sincerity of this, stanza by stanza.

A secret Place.

There's a place that I know
A secret place
That (f) no body Know's of
But me that Know's of it;

I go there when I'am lonly,
And when I'am sad
It makes me happy,
And glad that I'am alive.

There's a stream a silver stream
That bubbles (of) over stones
Just were I sit there's a
Water full the fish jumpover it.

The trees tower over head
And when the breeze comes along
It rustles the leaves like a tinkle of *
And all the birds twitter for they
Are happy today.

(Girl, aged 12, 'A' stream, secondary modern school)

* The word 'song' was written on the opposite page

EXERCISE 30

Since Susan has never had anybody die in her arms, how can we call her poem sincere?

Only Sad.

Tears fell down a red rosy cheek
They fell like pearls of the sea
Eyes so sad, but twinkling
A face never to forget; so Sad.
I could see she was unhappy
I tried to comfort her
But very soon She put her arms
round me
And said, Its too late now its
all over.
Suddenly she turn white like
pure ivory
She moved her smooth hand a
little
Tears fell on my shoulder
I did not move nor did she
I knew she was heart broken
Very soon after She died
Never did I see such a face

(Susan, aged 12, 'A' stream, secondary modern school)

Compare the child's poem with this one by Emily Brontë

Cold in the earth—and the deep snow piled above thee,
Far, far, removed, cold in the dreary grave!
Have I forgot, my only Love, to love thee,
Severed at last by Time's all-severing wave?

Now, when alone, do my thoughts no longer hover
Over the mountains, on that northern shore,
Resting their wings where heath and fern-leaves cover
Thy noble heart for ever, ever more?

Cold in the earth—and fifteen wild Decembers,
From those brown hills, have melted into spring:
Faithful, indeed, is the spirit that remembers
After such years of change and suffering!

Sweet Love of youth, forgive, if I forget thee,
While the world's tide is bearing me along;
Other desires and other hopes beset me,
Hopes which obscure, but cannot do thee wrong!

No later light has lightened up my heaven,
No second morn has ever shone for me;
All my life's bliss from thy dear life was given,
All my life's bliss is in the grave with thee.

But, when the days of golden dreams had perished,
And even Despair was powerless to destroy;
Then did I learn how existence could be cherished,
Strengthened and fed without the aid of joy.

Then did I check the tears of useless passion—
Weaned my young soul from yearning after thine;
Sternly denied its burning wish to hasten
Down to that tomb already more than mine.

And, even yet, I dare not let it languish,
Dare not indulge in memory's rapturous pain;
Once drinking deep of that divinest anguish,
How could I seek the empty world again?

EXERCISE 31

Compare the following poems, discuss their preoccupation with self-esteem:

[A] *Me*

What am I?
  A boy
Why am I?
I can never arrive
At a satisfactory
  Answer
As to why
  I am.
But there must be a reason,
For without reason,
What is the point of
  Me.
Being around to eat
  Good food
And using up
Useful space.
  So,
  Why
  Am I?

(Boy, Approved School)

[B] *Written in Northampton County Asylum*

I am: yet what I am none cares or knows,
My friends forsake me like a memory lost;
I am the self-consumer of my woes,
They rise and vanish in oblivious host
Like shades in love and death's oblivion lost;
And yet I am, and live with shadows tost

Into the nothingness of scorn and noise,
Into the living sea of waking dreams,
Where there is neither sense of life nor joys,
But the vast shipwreck of my life's esteems;
And e'en the dearest—that I loved the best—
Are strange—nay, rather stranger than the rest.

I long for scenes where man has never trod,
A place where woman never smiled or wept;
There to abide with my creator, God,
And sleep as I in childhood sweetly slept:
Untroubling and untroubled where I lie,
The grass below—above the vaulted sky. (John Clare)

EXERCISE 32

Compare these poems and discuss their sincerity.

[A] *But no one cares*

The day was long.
The winds blew on
But no one cared.

All alone,
Had no home,
But no one cared.

He fought against the wind and rain
Although he had a lot of pain,
But no one cared.

The day grew old
The night was cold
But no one cared.

The stars above
Were his only love
But no one cared.

Alone in the dark
He left no mark
But no one cared.

He had feelings
of his piteous meanings
But no one cared.

In the still of the night
He felt upright
But no one cared.

He could have died,
Instead he cried,
But no one cared.

(Boy, aged 14, Approved School)

[B] *Melancholy*

The rain and wind, the rain and wind, raved endlessly.
On me the Summer storm, and fever, and melancholy
Wrought magic, so that if I feared the solitude
Far more I feared all company: too sharp, too rude,
Had been the wisest or the dearest human voice.
What I desired I knew not, but whate'er my choice
Vain it must be, I knew. Yet naught did my despair
But sweeten the strange sweetness, while through the wild air
All day long I heard a distant cuckoo calling
And, soft as dulcimers, sounds of near water falling,
And, softer, and remote as if in history,
Rumours of what had touched my friends, my foes, or me.

(Edward Thomas)

EXERCISE 33

Discuss 'sincerity' in relation to this adolescent poem. Do adolescents exaggerate in an insincere way? Or is it that their experiences are themselves disproportionate?

Lost Love

Never, never again will I follow that long trail back,
For out there Freedom awaits me to comfort and heal my unforgotten pain,
The pain which filled my heart when the only thing in my life died.

I shall never forget that God-forsaken moment,
When my brain was numbed with the truth that could not be,
When my heart collapsed with utter despair for him.

But now I realize that all must be forgotten,
The pain must fade and die, just as he,
And I must face the world to find a new and truer love. (Girl, 4A)

EXERCISE 34

Would you say these are accounts of a real incident?

[A]

It was all quiet and then there was a cry. 'I am dying', it said and then the fight began. There was death in the air and the taste of blood in my mouth. I went all cold and stiff and just stood there. The next thing I knew was another cry. 'The police are coming,' and you could hear the ambulance coming. Then all the yard was clear except for the bodies and blood all over the place and all the police around the place and now up there it still smells of death and growling with police.

[B]

It was an argument that started it off. They moved in. All you heard was thumping, screeches, scuffling of feet. In a moment it was still (no noise) just black death, blood on his head. One by one they moved slowly backwards. Then another screech. No pain, just lying there dying. Then you heard sirens of cars and there was a scatter, everybody running here and there. The street was empty except for the body on the ground, dead. All of a sudden there was a screech of cars pulling up and a lot of muttering of people talking. Then they surrounded the place. 3 of them were caught, I girl and two boys and then it grew quiet again. The street grew bare and empty. It was all over.

[C]

I heard a very loud row. I rushed out knocking half the group's gear over, records hitting me on the head. I didn't know what it was but a loud painful row lashed out. The crowd was enormous. The shouts of murder. Who did it? Get an ambulance!—the people's vapour of breath in the air. Suddenly a murmur of an ambulance about a mile away. He laid there—blood all over the place and groans of weeping people. The police questioned and questioned.

EXERCISE 35

Both the following passages seem to me very 'real': yet, in fact both represent remarkable stylistic achievements—one a boy's intuitive rendering of oral irony and sarcasm, the other the achievement by an adult writer of a 'boy's' idiom used for the highest artistic purposes. Compare them, paying close attention to the language used:

[A]

When ever I so much as suggest a rifel, motor bike, late dance, or a Sunday picknic I receive besides the usual enpatic no a lecture on the 'good old days'. The other times I hear about when my parents were young is when a childhood friend calls, then they recall the time they knocked the policeman's hat off or made the chinaman's horse bolt.

To find out about the land scape in those days I either ask for a rifel or an air gun, pointing out that my father received his first air gun at the age of eight, and his first rifel when he was fourteen. Yes but there was'nt so many houses around in those days, why I rember...and from there on, for the next hour or so, I hear about the time they went swimming in the Creek, of how you could read the time of the GPO clock from the corner of our street with a pair of field glasses. We live fairly close to the hills and Brown Hill Creek runs close by, there were evidently only a few houses around with miles of virgin scrub, more or less, on all sides, so you see it was quite safe to have an air rifel in those days.

From the way they talk all they did was work, and sleep, amusements were like the huge family bible, only for special occasions. Pictures were almost unheard of, although for threepence you could go to the silent movies where the pianest would like as not play jazz, or their equivalent to it, while there was a death march on, all very exciting I am sure. Dancing was for people twenty one and over, all youn people should be in bead by eight o'clock, quiet moon light walk were just not done, although they did have supprise parties where they played kiss in the ring, postman's knock, ring-aring-a-rosy and hide the thimbel, all very exciting.

Knea to neck bathers were essential down the beach nothing would do for us the creek, sun tans were unheard of, the pale look had the rage. Of course there were no motor cars, and the trams were horse drawn, it was quicker to walk to town than catch a tram although you had to look out for robbers, well almost. Once a year I can be sure of getting a lecture on Guy Fox, how for a penny you could buy a rocket, sparklers boms and pin weels enough to fill all your pockets, threepence to spend on crackers was a fortune, and would keep you at it for a week letting them off. Every sunday they went to church morning, and night, they were duty bound to join the choir, the event of the year was the Sunday School picknic where they would all get on horse drawn floats and get hauled to the picknic groonds where stale bread was served with black tea.

Of course my parents were little angels, I would be scared to go half as far as they did. But I must remember that they did not have all the amusements we have, they had to provide their own, like a piece of metal dropped on a dark night sounds like a penny to an unsuspecting passer by who would stop and strike numerous matches in order to find the missing coin. Or they would tie a piece of black cotton onto the door knocker and knock loudly. All very funny.

As you can see the old days were the 'good' old days when a penny was worth a penny, and there was none of this silly jaz or jive stuff. Bogies were unheard of, the modern youth is going to the pack, what it needs is a bit of good disiplin, the stuff they got in the old days. 'The good old days'.

[B]

Another night, when we was up at the head of the island, just before daylight, here comes a frame-house down, on the west side. She was a two-storey, an tilted over considerable. We paddled out and got aboard—clumb in at an upstairs window. But it was too dark to see yet, so we made the canoe fast and set in her to wait for daylight.

The light begun to come before we got to the foot of the island. Then we looked in at the window. We could make out a bed, and a table, and two old chairs, and lots of things around about on the floor; and there was clothes hanging against the wall. There was something laying on the floor in the far corner that looked like a man. So Jim says:

'Hello, you!'

But it didn't budge. So I hollered again, and then Jim says:

'De man ain't asleep—he's dead. You hold still—I'll go en see.'

He went and bent down and looked, and says:

'It's a dead man. Yes indeedy; naked, too. He's been shot in de back. I reck'n he's ben dead two er three days. Come in Huck, but doan't look at his face—it's too gashly.'

I didn't look at him at all. Jim throwed some old rags over him, but he needn't done it; I didn't want to see him. There was heaps of old greasy cards scattered around over the floor, and old whisky bottles, and a couple of masks made out of black cloth: and all over the walls was the ignorantest kind of words and pictures, made with charcoal. There was two old dirty calico dresses, and a sun-bonnet, and some women's underclothes, hanging against the wall, and some men's clothing too. We put the lot into the canoe; it might come good. There was a boy's old speckled straw hat on the floor; I took that too. And there was a bottle that had had milk in it; and it had a rag stopper for a baby to suck. We would 'a took the bottle, but it was broke. There was a seedy old chest, and an old hair trunk with the hinges broke. They stood open, but there warn't nothing left in them that was any account. The way things was scattered about, we reckoned the people left in a hurry and warn't fixed so as to carry off most of their stuff.

We got an old tin lantern, and a butcher knife without any handle, and a bran-new Barlow knife worth two bits in any store, and a lot of tallow candles, and a tin candlestick, and a gourd, and a tin cup, and a ratty old bed-quilt off the bed, and a reticule with needles and pins and beeswax and buttons and thread and all such truck in it, and a hatchet and some nails, and a fish-line as thick as my little finger, with some monstrous hooks on it, and a roll of buckskin, and a leather dog-collar, and a horse-shoe, and some vials of medicine that didn't have no label on them; and just as we was leaving I found a tolerable good currycomb, and Jim he found a ratty old fiddle-box, and a wooden leg. The straps was broke off of it, but barring that, it was a good enough leg, though it was too long for me and not long enough for Jim, and we couldn't find the other one, though we hunted all around. (Mark Twain, from *Huckleberry Finn*)

EXERCISE 36

Discuss the realism of this: say in close detail what you like about it.

At Court

It was on a Friday night during last summer, Tich, that is Tom Litchfield asked me if I was going up to the chippy, so I said all right and I gave him a lift on the back of my bicycle. The way up was dark and cold and the wind was nearly blowing us back. On the way back we were going slow when suddenly out of the shadows came a police woman and before we knew what had happened she had us. Then she asked us our names and addresses and said she would come back to see our parents so we told her our right names and addresses, then she said it would not matter. When I got home I didn't bother telling my mum and dad what happened and neither did Tich until a couple of weeks later I got a letter saying that I had to be at court on a Tuesday morning. My mum went sick and asked me why didn't I tell her and I said I didn't want to.

That morning I went down with my mother and met Tich with his father down there. Then the same policewoman who had caught us came up to us and said to our parents, 'Don't they both look nice when they are dressed up?' and tapped me on the face. I felt like kicking her. We got there first but everyone else was going in front of us so me and Tich had a walk round and when we came back we went in. As we were going in there was a large desk in front of us with a couple of men and women talking and two small desks on each side of the big one. Then a man told our parents to sit down while we stood up and a man read something out then said, 'Do you plead guilty or not guilty?' When he said this I tried to keep a straight face for it sounded a bit funny. I answered guilty and same with Tom Litchfield. Then the policewoman who had caught us read out of her notebook about the night she caught us. After that the people behind the desk had a little talk and I got a fine of one pound because it was my bike. Tom Litchfield got fined ten shillings. It was then about quarter to twelve and me and my mum went home with Tom and his father because he lived near us. When we got home I had my dinner and went back to school feeling a bit relieved it was all over with.

(Boy, 4B, secondary modern school)

EXERCISE 37

How do you react to this piece?

What kind of language background do you think the writer has?

A Tragic Day

A long time ago, when I was five I experienced a dreadful incident. It happened in a block of flats in Ireland.

My twin brothers were playing with a ball outside a shop when the ball rolled under a bread van which was stationary outside the shop. Not knowing the van was going to move off, Joe, one of my brothers got under the van to get the ball. The van moved off and he was crushed by the wheels. The strange thing about this was that my mother was at the hospital with my elder brother who has a hole in his heart. He was ill then and it was thought that he might have to undergo an operation. When my mother came home she said 'John is all right, he will not have to undergo the operation.' When the tragic news was broken to her, she just sat still and said God took the young son so that she could keep the older one. John was seriously ill and had not got long to live then. But he is still living now and is enjoying life to the full.

When we are talking about Joe I often wonder if this was a little miracle. One thing I will never forget is the face of the man who was driving the van, he got out of the van and fainted with the fright, also of the time the policeman was taking a statement from someone who had seen the accident, tears dripped from his eyes and made his face go all red.

Two days later he was buried and there were forty-two cars at the funeral, besides the people who walked to the cemetry. This is something which I can see a clear picture of what happened ten long years ago when I was only five. (Boy, 4B, secondary modern school)

EXERCISE 38

Compare these passages:

[A] *'Thou shalt Worship the Lord Thy God...'*

I'm late. No I'm not, its only five to eight. Thank goodness. I was late last week—I suppose I ought to get up earlier on Sundays. Still other people don't get up till late on Sundays, but its worth it anyway.

My goodness, the church isn't very full this morning. Still its foggy, I expect that most people are put off. Hymn book, collection in the box, mind the Vicar and server coming round behind me; into the seat next to Katy.

Where's the hassock? Oh I see, the hook's broken, its under the seat. Kneel down, hands together and pray 'Oh God, please help me to understand... Crumbs! The Vicar's started. Quick where's the place. Morning prayer, Evening prayer.....ah! Communion. "Our Father....." I wonder how many times the Vicar has said that. Who's that coming in late. I hope its the Vicar's son, well one of them anyway. Concentrate Linda! Confession..... what have I done wrong this week? The usual things: small lies, saying unkind things; I never seem to do anything unusually wrong. I wonder if anyone here has any dark secret. Sit up for the epistle; I wonder what Jesus looked like. I don't understand Him, one minute He's gentle and understanding, the next He's awfully stern. Stand up, kneel down, concentrate. Christopher's got a cold, I can hear him blowing his nose. Poor boy, I'll blow my nose in sympathy. I really must concentrate now. I'm supposed to be thanking God. I can thank him for my life anyway and the joy I get from it. I do really even though I compain. Oops! The Vicar's started again. I've lost the place. I know the service backwards nearly, but I like to follow it in the book.

Katy's had her hair cut. I wish that woman behind me would chant in time—she's a nuisance. That's not very charitable—sorry God. Its marvellous how this service has carried on for so long. I wish the Vicar wouldn't say 'th'universal church'. Here comes the most important part. Listen carefully now. Long silence; everyones praying. 'Oh God never let me take this service for granted'. More silence; what a wonderful calm; you never seem to get much silence nowadays.

They're going up to the altar now. My turn soon, get up; walk down the aisle; queue; wait; kneel down; no more thoughts now. Finished now. Do get up carefully and don't bump into anyone. Back to my seat and kneel down. I pray. for the first time in the service I pray wholeheartedly.

Its nearly the end now, the Vicar is giving the blessing; how quietly he comes down the aisle. We've finished and I get up. Katy's smiling at me. Where's Christopher? Gone home for breakfast I expect. Out of church now. The Vicar smiles, and says 'Good morning, Linda'. Let's hurry—I'm hungry. (Linda, 4th year, grammar school)

[B]

They halted about the door of the mortuary chapel. Mr Bloom stood behind the boy with the wreath, looking down at his sleek combed hair and the slender furrowed neck inside his brandnew collar. Poor boy! Was he there when the father? Both unconscious. Lighten up at the last moment and recognise for the last time. All he might have done. I owe three shillings to O'Grady. Would he understand? The mutes bore the coffin into the chapel. Which end is his head?

After a moment he followed the others in, blinking in the screened light. The coffin lay on its bier before the chancel, four tall yellow candles at its corners. Always in front of us. Corny Kelleher, laying a wreath at each fore corner, beckoned to the boy to kneel. The mourners knelt here and there in praying desks. Mr Bloom stood behind near the font, and, when all had knelt dropped carefully his unfolded newspaper from his pocket and knelt his right knee upon it. He fitted his black hat gently on his left knee and, holding its brim, bent over piously.

A server, bearing a brass bucket with something in it, came out through a door. The whitesmocked priest came after him tidying his stole with one hand, balancing with the other a little book against his toad's belly. Who'll read the book? I, said the rook.

They halted by the bier and the priest began to read out of his book with a fluent croak.

Father Coffey. I knew his name was like a coffin. *Domine-namine*. Bully about the muzzle he looks. Bosses the show. Muscular christian. Woe betide anyone that looks crooked at him: priest. Thou art Peter. Burst sideways like a sheep in clover Dedalus says he will. With a belly on him like a poisoned pup. Most amusing expressions that man finds. Hhhhn: burst sideways.

—Non intres in judicium cum servo tuo, Domine.

Makes them feel more important to be prayed over in Latin. Requiem mass. Crape weepers. Blackedged notepaper. Your name on the altar list. Chilly place this. Want to feed well, sitting in there all the morning in the gloom kicking his heels waiting for the next please. Eyes of a toad too. What swells him up that way? Molly gets swelled after cabbage. Air of the place maybe. Looks full up of bad gas. Must be an infernal lot of bad gas round the place. Butchers for instance: they get like raw beefsteaks. Who was telling me? Mervyn Brown. Down in the vaults of saint Werburgh's lovely old organ hundred and fifty they have to bore a hole in the coffins sometimes to let out the bad gas and burn it. Out it rushes: blue. One whiff of that and you're a goner.

My kneecap is hurting me. Ow. That's better.

The priest took a stick with a knob at the end of it out of the boy's bucket and shook it over the coffin. Then he walked to the other end and shook it again. Then he came back and put it back in the bucket. As you were before you rested. It's all written down: he has to do it.

—Et ne nos inducas in tentationem.

The server piped the answers in the treble. I often thought it would be better to have boy servants. Up to fifteen or so. After that of course...

Holy water that was, I expect. Shaking sleep out of it. He must be fed up with that job, shaking that thing over all the corpses they trot up. What harm if he could see what he was shaking it over. Every mortal day a fresh batch: middleaged men, old women, children, women dead in childbirth, men with beards, baldheaded business men, consumptive girls with little sparrow's breasts. All the year round he prayed the same thing over them all and shook water on top of them: sleep. On Dignam now.

—*In paradisum.*

Said he was going to paradise or is in paradise. Says that over everybody. Tiresome kind of a job. But he has to say something.

The priest closed his book and went off, followed by the server. Corny Kelleher opened the sidedoors and the gravediggers came in, hoisted the coffin again, carried it out and shoved it on their cart. Corny Kelleher gave one wreath to the boy and one to the brother-in-law. All followed them out of the sidedoors into the mild grey air. Mr Bloom came last, folding his paper again into his pocket. He gazed gravely at the ground till the coffincart wheeled off to the left. The metal wheels ground the gravel with a sharp grating cry and the pack of blunt boots followed the barrow along a lane of sepulchres.

The ree the ra the ree the ra the roo. Lord, I mustn't lilt here.

(James Joyce, from *Ulysses*)

[C]

'Please to bring the child in quick out of the air there,' whispered the beadle, holding open the inner door of the church.

Little Paul might have asked with Hamlet 'into my grave?' so chill and earthy was the place. The tall shrouded pulpit and reading-desk; the dreary perspective of empty pews stretching away under the galleries, and empty benches mounting to the roof and lost in the shadow of the great grim organ; the dusty matting and cold stone slabs; the grisly free seats in the aisles; and the damp corner by the bell-rope, where the black tressels used for funerals were stowed away, along with some shovels and baskets, and a coil or two of deadly-looking rope; the strange, unusual, uncomfortable smell, and the cadaverous light; were all in unison. It was a cold and dismal scene.

'There's a wedding just on, sir,' said the beadle, 'but it'll be over directly, if you'll walk into the westry here.'

Before he turned again to lead the way, he gave Mr Dombey a bow and a half-smile of recognition, importing that he (the beadle) remembered to have had the pleasure of attending on him when he buried his wife, and hoped he had enjoyed himself since.

The very wedding looked dismal as they passed in front of the altar. The bride was too old and the bridegroom too young, and a superannuated beau with one eye and an eye-glass stuck in its blank companion, was giving away the lady, while the friends were shivering. In the vestry the fire was smoking; and an over-aged and over-worked and under-paid attorney's clerk, "making a search," was running his forefinger down the parchment pages of an immense register (one of a long series of similar volumes) gorged with burials. Over the fireplace was a ground-plan of the vaults underneath the church; and Mr Chick, skimming the literary portion of it aloud, by way of enlivening the company, read the reference to Mrs Dombey's tomb in full, before he could stop himself.

After another cold interval, a wheezy little pew-owner afflicted with an asthma, appropriate to the churchyard, if not to the church, summoned them to the font. Here they waited some little time while the marriage party enrolled themselves; and meanwhile the wheezy little pew-opener—partly in consequence of her infirmity, and partly that the marriage party might not forget her—went about the building coughing like a grampus.

Presently the clerk (the only cheerful-looking object there, and *he* was an undertaker) came up with a jug of warm water and said something, as he poured it into the font, about taking the chill off; which millions of gallons boiling hot could not have done for the occasion. Then the clergyman, an amiable and mild-looking young curate, but obviously afraid of the baby, appeared like the principal character in a ghost-story, 'a tall figure all in white'; at sight of whom Paul rent the air with his cries, and never left off again till he was taken out black in the face.

Even when that event had happened, to the great relief of everybody, he was heard under the portico, during the rest of the ceremony, now fainter, now louder, now hushed, now bursting forth again with an irrepressible sense of his wrongs. This so distracted the attention of the two ladies, that Mrs Chick was constantly deploying into the centre aisle, to send out messages by the pew-opener, while Miss Tox kept her Prayer-book open at the Gunpowder Plot, and occasionally read responses from that service.

During the whole of these proceedings, Mr Dombey remained as impassive and gentlemanly as ever, and perhaps assisted in making it so cold, that the young curate smoked at the mouth as he read.

(Charles Dickens, from *Dombey & Son*)

Read the whole of chapter v of *Dombey and Son* and discuss its 'realism' and how you would convey this to the author of A.

EXERCISE 39

Helen, a girl in 3B (secondary modern school) who is restless and lazy hands in the following, having been asked to write a hymn (after having been given some good examples). What do you say—(1) to yourself; (2) to her?

Where is thy God, My Soul
Is he within thy heart
Or ruler of a distance realm.
In which ~~thou~~ hast no part..
(you have?)

let all your lamps ~~be~~ bright
And trim the golden flame.
Men strain from darkness to great light
And so to gain through hurt and pain
(do)

EXERCISE 40

Does anything make you feel the experience behind this passage is real?

<u>Sudden Death</u>

About 2 years ago their was a sudden death
a lady named Misses Johnes ~~died~~ died of what
know ~~o~~ one Knowes. she ~~wach~~ (wosh) their childrenes
hire that ~~o~~ night and her own then
she went out to Mr slad ~~to~~ the
grouser and brough some ~~fru~~ frit
for ~~o~~ the 4 children then she came
bake and torks to Mrs clarke next door
and after awill she came in and got

the children to bed the sat down and
read a book ~~cat~~ calld deat on my Pillow
She was ~~ta~~ lauging at some funny
parts. the she desided to go to bed
he slef and in the mildale of the
night she ~~wha~~ went uncoshers and
that morning dad Said good morning love
and not a sound he said it again
but know replie he got up and moved
her about and she never woke up
Mr Jones got worid and went up to the
phone and rang up the doctor but the doctor
was out ~~some~~ were so then he phone
up the hospittal ~~ab~~ the amberless came
and took he to Royston hospital and
doctor ~~m~~ Nickals said she is very ill will
have to thak her to ~~Cambrg~~ cambridg
hospital their see what is the mater
they rust her their and after 2 days the
hadet had the proper things their ~~sow~~ so
they took her to London hospital ~~the~~ Mr
Jones when to london ~~to~~ with amberless
and stayd at london hospital for 3 days
then ~~st~~ he came home and whated for
the bad or good news then on Monday morning
at 5.oclock a lady round they other side
of us and came and gave us the bad
news that she had died. and evry one
one very ~~ch~~ kind they gave us meals
and two of children ~~whe~~ went and stad
~~total~~ with some freids for a weeke ~~or~~
or two and. now ~~the~~ Mr Jones is getting
marrid again and that will. be better for
the children

EXERCISE 41

Which of the following passages do you prefer and why?

Here are two passages written by boys of 12. Which do you prefer? Give reasons for your preference and then say what you would tell the children.

[A]

We started out on a beautiful morning with a bright sky above us and a cooling south wind. Nature was in her full glory, the air smelt sweet, birds were singing loudly, squirrels scampered up trees at our approach and rabbits' tails disappeared down burrows at our presence. Lambs jumped around friskily tormenting their mothers for nourishment. Cows lay lazily chewing their cud among the buttercups. A little foal galloped alongside her mother on its spindly legs. In another field a ploughman plodded along behind his horses furrowing the field. Butterflies fluttered from flower to flower.

And so our journey went on in the presence of Nature's glory. Oh what a wonderful thing to be alive!

At Langham we refuelled ourselves and continued our journey.

[B]

Turning the last bend we came to a halt by the river. The village at this time of the year is so unfrequented. Even so, a number of small boys were dipping jam pots into the river to catch minnows. One had caught a crayfish. We propped our bicycles by the buttress at one end of the bridge, and turned round to look at the memorial cross cut in the hill. Then riding on up the opposite side of the valley, we noticed a flock of house-martins wheeling in clusters above a farmhouse. They could not have been in England long, even though most summer visitors arrived early this year. Underneath the overhang of the farmhouse roof a row of mud nests could be seen. Some hung down limp and useless; others were inhabited by sparrows; but a few remained in a fit state for the martins. The slope from then on grew steep—so much so that we stopped for a moment at one bend and rested our bikes on the bank. We were now high above the village, and even the conspicuous white rumps of the martins could hardly be seen. Where the hill was too steep for farmland, Scots pines were growing. On the move again we emerged from among them into the sunlight at the top of the hill.

EXERCISE 42

Which of the following passages do you prefer—and why? (Read them aloud first.) Pay exact attention to the language used.

[A] *Making Camp*

A broiling sun, obtrusive in the ardour of its gaze, blazed down upon the scintillating waters of the river Severn, running through a field of golden yellow corn. On the river's farthest bank a clump of tangled vegetation, in the form of reeds and bulrushes, waved their tentacles like innumerable Excaliburs held aloft by the Lady of the Lake. At the top of this bank a merry bunch of jostling, gesticulating people, myself amongst them, prepared to make camp. As if a tournament of ancient design were about to commence, white tents literally sprang up from the ground, as if of a live, vigour-filled substance. I was there, here and everywhere, helping to tighten guy-ropes, knock pegs in more firmly, and to offer the sense of security to some younger comrade not quite understanding this persistent commotion and consistent noise of excited voices from all classes of human beings. As quickly as it had got into motion, it abruptly ceased, and soon our portable oil-stove was on the go, and in the frying-pan, simmering and casting delicious aromas, the life-blood of the pan's existence—bacon, etc. fried to a nicety. Different odours from all over the camp blended, casting a feeling of self-satisfaction into everyone concerned.

Supper over, everybody decided to go for a swim, and the wet reception which eventually received us relieved us of dust, dirt and other uncomfortable feelings. Soon after, the farmer who had rented us the piece of land came to see how we were getting on, and in his familiar but peculiar country burr said, 'Well, masters, I hopes ye're enjoying yourselves.'

[B]

At first Ross and I didn't go flax-pulling with the others. We were orderlies in the cook-house instead. How it happened was like this. On the first day we had the job of putting up the tents, and I had the job of knocking in tent-pegs. It was very hard work. The earth was only about an inch thick and underneath it was hard chalk. Some of the pegs had no points on at all, and others had points that curled over. I banged and banged with my mallet, but I could soon feel the blisters coming up on my hand. But Mr Dow kept me at it. He said I was just the man for the job. Then afterwards Ross and I had a competition who could chop the most firewood quickest. It was mostly splitting logs, and Ross went straight ahead and was chopping about twice the rate I could. I got wild about this, especially as all the other boys were watching us. This chopping about finished off my blisters. I found out later that Ross had got a very sharp axe and I had got the blunt one, but we didn't change over till it was too late.

Then we had to put up the marquee. Mr Dow was getting anxious and said he didn't like the look of the weather. I just went and watched, but Ross helped. The canvas kept flapping about and they had a time of it. It was like putting up a great wall against the wind. Mr Dow got mad and shouted to Ross to hang on like grim death. He did, and when the wind jerked the canvas away the rope tore right through his hands. It was that hairy sort of rope, and was it hot! You should have seen Ross's hands. Anyhow, as we said to Mr Dow next day, we couldn't go flax-pulling with hands like that, and he agreed. That's how we came to be orderlies.

EXERCISE 43

Which of these two poems do you prefer?

[A] *Poem in Spring*

Spring is the time when lambs appear
To brighten up the winter drear
And liven every living thing;
Oh, how I love the radiant spring!

The breeze, the flowers, the windswept grass
Bend to greet you as you pass;
Great happiness and joy they bring;
Oh, how I love the radiant spring!

Solomon in glory cannot compare
With snowdrop, crocus and daffodil fair,
The budding leaves, the birds that sing;
Oh, how I love the radiant spring!

[B]

When spring is here, flowers are awakening
Insects and animals from hibernating.
Daffodils from bulbs are peeping
Which through the winter have been keeping
Their beauty, colour, stems and leaves.
The birds from their nest under the eaves.
Everything is awakening when spring is here
The cows with calves so dear.

EXERCISE 44

Discuss this poem, by a not very cooperative boy in 4B. What do you say to yourself? To him?

The DYING WILLOW 20/6/61

1) The ~~feathers~~ leaves of the willow,
Are half of them grown yellow,
Above the swelling stream;
And ragged are the bushes,
And rotting now the branches,
Of the tree ~~that~~ over the stream does lean

Soon into the stream, the tree will fall,
Slowly, slowly - away it will float,
Out of it then, the insects will crawl.
Down, down in the slowly flowing moat.

EXERCISE 45

Do you think this poem is sincere?

The Road To Disaster

I am going for a walk,
A long long walk.
I may not come back.
From this long long walk.
I am walking forever.
I shall not stop.
Every step I take
I am getting nearer
To the Road of Disaster.
I sometimes stop and think
and I never sleep a wink
as I get nearer to the Road of Disaster.
There is nothing left in the world for me.
My love I cannot give to anybody
For I don't get love from them
But I always get hate.
That's why I'm going to the Road of Disaster.
The Road of Disaster is a long long road
Which no-one has ever returned
So I am going to try this Road of Disaster
And hope that I never return. (Sonia)

EXERCISE 46

Discuss the realism of this:

School Boy's Life No Good Ho!

There is no-one for dis earth wey go say he happy proper. When I dey go for my primary school I think sey I go happy much when I reach secondary school, but where?

When I reached Vom I saw big and new boys. I begin sey de principal no de punish de big boys. Asey all be de same for am. When you do something bad he go punish you as if sey you deh for children dem school.

Sometime he, we no get enough chop to wak. We go report but dem sey na de same kind palaver wey deh for most schools. In de morning we drink akamu and tea and wak bread. When you come siddon for class you feel so-so sleep. When deh see you sleep den sey you no want know something.

Afternoon chop better and i-de hold man proper. If you want leave class na dem you go ask, 'Excuse me sir, I wan go pees.' The teacher go sey, 'Make you go siddon, you no be small picken.'

Now things don begin better small-small. We get oranges, eggs, banana as light chop, though na one-one. Nna man suffer for nineteen fifty nine. Some days na beans zalla we chop. Night own worse than morning own. De women wey de cook am no fit. When we go for bed de beans for our stomach go just leave we to sleep for sometime. At about midnight to beans go make one kind noise for our stomach as if sey na one kind old diesel lorry de pass 'Hawan Kibo', or locomotive train de pass.

We happy now for nyam deh, garri deh, fis deh plenty ris deh, and acha, de worst of dem all, den deh plenty. Wetting? De ting wey de worry we plenty be no boy go wak food if no be school own. If you no belly full you no fit take penny buy chop. Dem law don forbid am. Sometime dysentery de worry we. Our nyash de make yoyo as if sey na old bucket de leak. Everyday na complain, 'Excuse me sir, we wan go clinic'. It no be disease, na beans de vex for belly.

Some of us don ol for school and don get beard. The principal say he no go gree leave student grow beard. When bid day come deng go tell we make we go march for Veterinary ground. Na so we march for Northern Self-government, Independence, and for Republic Days. If you say you no fit march na you and langa-langa go become friends for de hot sun on de field. De staffs ma na wah na you and dem go enter three. If you no get white and white na you and the principal go enter de same trousers. Dis kind ting vex me as if no be me for tomorrow.

Deng get one kind of big bell wey bellman de ring often. I no like so de bell. Early in de morning at six de boy go come tanda for dormitory begin ring am. The sound no go leave man sleep anymore. If you no fit wake up dem go book own your name. Everything na quick-quick. Go here, go there, as if say na gandroba deh for work. Man always waka-waka pass man. Just cool, next year deh, when man go finish.

When I think proper I no fit open mouth talk. I no blame anybody for de school. Na so our Premier say. He say make de our people we de train we for schools train we well. He say any man wey no suffa he no be good man. De tings dem teach we for school na discipline. If small boy abuse you, who be you to take hand slap am? If you slap am dat day you go pack go.

Make we take tings easy. In some years we go become better people. We go live in high, well decorated houses, ride in luxurious cars, wear better clothes, and wak better chop, and marry de earth's beauties.

Make we no open eye for dis world yet. Nna o'boy man go sometimes dey. Dis time we dey as if say no be we. Make we all pray God make help we and give we long lives. Amen.

Exercise 46

Glossary

wak	eat	*ma na wah na*	the person seems agreeable, but he is not
zalla	only	*go enter three*	be in trouble
nyash	anus		
nna	really		

go enter de same trousers	be in more trouble
gandroba	warder
tanda	stand

(Aloysius, VI, Nigerian School)

3 Directness and the Extrovert Virtues

Any discussion of the symbolism of children's writing tends to give the misleading impression that all children's utterance is like Blake! We need to remind ourselves that much children's writing is straightforward exploration of *outward* experience—and that they can equally be involved in this. (See *Fourteen*, edited by D. C. Measham.)

EXERCISE 47

What are the virtues of the following passage?

An Old Man I Know

I know an old man who is very fond of walking and when he walks he seems to rock from side to side like a baby's cradle when somebody is rocking it. One of his eyes has no black pupil in it so he is blind in that eye. His skin is crinkled and wrinkled like a piece of crepe paper. He has a pipe somewhere but he never smokes it. He always smokes Woodbine cigarettes. He seems to get tired easily and is forever sitting down for a rest when he is doing something. He used to be able to play the piano but now his fingers have grown too old and stiff it makes it quite difficult for him. He has false teeth and has a habit of taking them out and running his tongue over his gums and then putting his teeth back again. One thing I've noticed though. He never takes his top set out, always his bottom set. He has lived by himself since his wife died over three years ago but he seems quite happy and still has a lot of fun left in him even after all these years.

(Girl, aged 9; quoted from *The Excitement of Writing*)

EXERCISE 48

Read this through to yourself once. Then read it aloud. What are its virtues? What literature would you give the writer?

An apple

it comes off of a tree when
you pick it is rosy red and
before you eat it makes your
mouth water it even makes
your mouth water when you
hear the name gascoyne's
scarlet. when you go scrumping
and when you get caught it is worth
taking the chance of getting
some gascoyne's scarlet apples
when you go scrumping you
have got to be carefull you
don't get caught; if you
do get caught the man will
be waiting for you next time
you go to get some
more gascoyne scarlet apples.
when I go scrumping all
I go after is apples
and plums, pear's. when you
go pinching apple you do not

'want to take to many people or
you will not get away so quick
when there are a lot of people with
you a specally little boys they make
to much noise. If you pick apples off of
the ground you have to be carfull
of the wasps of else they will sting
you and the sting comes up to a big
bump where ever it stings you.
when you are by yourself and some
one comes and you have to ~~clumb~~
climb over the barb wire and get caug
the man will probally catch you but if
someone else is with you the can ~~un~~
unhook you. Some people when
the catch you they might hit
you and said he will hit you harder
~~nex~~ next time he catches you. ~~But~~
But some people say they will hit
~~hit~~ you next time but warn
you not to come in the

orchard ~~no next time~~ again
But the children could not resist
getting some more apples to eat.
It is best getting apples from an
orchard where there are no houses.
when I go scrumping I do
not take bikes because the man
who owns the orchard might come
along and takes ~~the~~ the bikes
and if you want your bike you
have to go and ask for it
and that is how the owner of
the orchard knows that you were
in the orchard. I never take
a dark Jacket or a red one.
Because you will be reconnised
very easy because red shows
up very easy. But still to it
is worth getting some
gascoyne scarlet apples

EXERCISE 49

A teacher told the author of the following how much he liked *Carp* and then read the class *Pike*. Why?

Carp

The time was 5 am in the morning
it promised to be a good day. I dressed
and had some sandwiches for breakfast. Today
I was going to Hilton mere pond to catch
(if I could) some carp. The bait I had
made the night before was ready to be
packed. I checked to see if all my tackle
was in the bag it was so off on my
Bicycle I went.
At halfpast five I reached Hilton mere
Pond. I tackled up 10 yds from the Bank
I decided to use paste and put a piece
the size of a shilling on the hook. I
made a cast some fifteen yards near some
weeds, then I sat down and waited for
a bite. Carp are the most suspusous
fish and half an hour later I saw
a good one come up to my paste
which was floating on the surface.
It looked at it and then swam round it
suddenly it was gone only to appear
a few yards down the pond to look again

at the bait. Then he slowly swam up to it and opened his mouth and to it. He was off in a flash and going like a train for some weeds I picked up my rod and with a firm strike the fish was on, the fish was almost in the weeds I tried sidestrain this turned his head and came towards me, now I was reeling in the slack line like mad then he turned from the bank and the line which had been slack tightened. then it parted with a twang. line and float went straight into a tree.

I put on another hook, this time for bait I had on a piece of bread-crust. I cast out in the same place as last time and then sat down and waited. This time an hour elapsed before I saw a disturbance ~~round~~ my float. Then slowly it slipped away. I struck and felt the fish which was rather heavy. He had almost the same tactics. The fish went into the middle of the pond and then came back at me at a terrific pace. I was

ready for this and by the time he was
about to turn I had the line tight
he turned and headed for the weeds
he got into them so I decided to
~~try~~ hand liniens I pulled gently and
he came out very slowly his golden
side came up to the surface. I had
had the fish on for 80 minutes and it
was very tired now. I lowered the ~~land~~-
landing net into the water brought the
fish into it. I took it 10 yds up the bank
and the hook I took apt. I weighed it
and it turned my scales at 12¼ lbs
a nice carp. I returned the fish to
the water and he slowly went out
of. sight. I packed up my tackle and
went home.

[B] *Pike*

Pike, three inches long, perfect
Pike in all parts, green tigering the gold.
Killers from the egg: the malevolent aged grin.
They dance on the surface among the flies.

Exercise 49

Or move, stunned by their own grandeur,
Over a bed of emerald, silhouette
Of submarine delicacy and horror.
A hundred feet long in their world.

In ponds, under the heat-struck lily pads—
Gloom of their stillness:
Logged on last year's black leaves, watching upwards.
Or hung in an amber cavern of weeds

The jaws' hooked clamp and fangs
Not to be changed at this date;
A life subdued to its instrument;
The gills kneading quietly, and the pectorals.

Three we kept behind glass,
Jungled in weed: three inches, four,
And four and a half: fed fry to them—
Suddenly there were two. Finally one

With a sag belly and the grin it was born with.
And indeed they spare nobody.
Two, six pounds each, over two feet long,
High and dry and dead in the willow-herb—

One jammed past its gills down the other's gullet:
The outside eye stared: as a vice locks—
The same iron in his eye
Though its film shrank in death.

A pond I fished, fifty yards across,
Whose lilies and muscular tench
Had outlasted every visible stone
Of the monastery that planted them—

Stilled legendary depth:
It was as deep as England. It held
Pike too immense to stir, so immense and old
That past nightfall I dared not cast

But silently cast and fished
With the hair frozen on my head
For what might move, for what eye might move.
The still splashes on the dark pond,

Owls hushing the floating woods
Frail on my ear against the dream
Darkness beneath night's darkness had freed,
That rose slowly towards me, watching.

(Ted Hughes)

EXERCISE 50

This boy is in the bottom stream (Secondary modern school) and—the fourth year. He finds it very hard to concentrate and seems to have trouble in physical coordination. Decipher his composition below. What would you do with it?

Ram COMENTARY
Come in Lamont, over, Now,
we are at Lamont the Ferrari
are in the leeding Phil hill is lead
them Barham and Moss are four
five Moss is four and Barhom
five if you listen now you will
hear Barham going through
eeearggghbroomghoor going
very ~~fast~~ now barham the is lssee
fast then the last lap ⊙! what
herp to Moss Wow ! can
hear a car missfireing
it is Moss in his Corner he
is going into the pits
Phil hill is going round
Gatwick Corner that is
a and left hand
corner Phil hill has chage
down to three gear the car
is Siding eeeecksegggharny

sh sh sh hey i am sill her
the raceing is sill now
over to Ostwich corner
meet you there is Rychard
Bullard this is Richard Seking
there is quit a mush here
P. hil hill is quit all righ
but the racedrivers behed
him was bill and their
speectaes two five egreets
One ambulance the ferrary
were sill in the bed but there
was only one in the race.

4 *Human Problems*

The creative approach to English teaching takes the teacher into dangerous realms of emotion. These realms are always there, of course: but it is possible to ignore them, or to pretend they don't exist.

But a sympathetic English teacher in a secondary modern or comprehensive school can hardly escape the human problems he encounters, unless he is to be blind to an inhuman degree.

Creative work, being concerned to promote sympathy, inevitably brings problems of personal relationship, emotion, and morality, often severe. These problems make the work rewarding: but they can also be upsetting. They often emerge from children's writing; here the teacher is on some kind of neutral ground and this helps him to keep a professional distance.

But it is perhaps worth looking at how severe these problems can be.

EXERCISE 51

Here is an account by a coloured teacher of a school situation in a London school (from *To Sir with Love*, by E. R. Braithwaite). Do you think the teacher becomes too involved? Criticise his writing *as prose*.

I was introduced *in absentia*, to most of the members of their families and very soon I learned of the new job 'our Joannie' had secured; of the girl 'our Alf' was going steady with; of the difficulties at home since 'our Dad' was on strike at the Docks; when 'our Mum' was expecting the new baby. I was part of it and very happy to be so much a part of it.

Sometimes I'd arrive in the morning to find a small parcel of wedding or birthday cake on my desk, always addressed simply to 'Sir'; then at recess the child concerned would tell me all about it, whether it was from herself or some other member of the family. I was always expected to eat the piece of cake then and there with my cup of tea.

Pamela was always there, just on the edge of things, listening, observant and silent. She seemed to have become overnight a grown woman; her hair no longer hung down in a pony-tail but was carefully plaited in two large braids which were in turn carefully fixed at the back of her head in an attractive bun. Her grave expression added a certain dignity to every movement. I felt that I could probably help her if I only knew what the matter was, but I could not intrude on her privacy, and I decided to wait until she got over it or some occasion presented itself for me to help. They mattered to me, all these children, and anything which bothered any one of them bothered me too.

One morning during recess Denham brought a new football to me; with him were Potter, Fernman, Jackson and Seales.

'Please, Sir, will you help us to lace this up? Mr Weston promised to attend to it for us but now he says he's too busy.'

The way in which they put a request always amused me; it seemed to suggest there could be no question of my refusing. They came to me with the complete assurance that whatever the case was I'd be agreeable and helpful. There was no denying them.

'Okay Denham, let's have it.'

The girls wandered away to leave us men with our work; only Pamela remained, somewhat apart. We pumped the ball hard, and while two of the boys held it firmly down on the table I laced it up tightly. In threading the thong through the last eyelet hole, however, the steel lacer slipped and made a small wound on my finger, from which the blood slowly trickled.

'Blimey, red blood!'

Potter's large friendly face wore a look of simulated surprise, and the other boys burst into laughter at his goggle-eyed stare. Pamela moved over quickly to Potter.

'What did you expect, fat boy? Ink?' she hissed at him; then calmly, disdainfully, she walked away to sit straight and aloof in her seat.

'Cor!' Denham gasped at the sheer venom of her attack.

Seales and Fernman merely stared from Potter to Pamela and back again, wordless with surprise. Poor Potter was flushed with embarrassment and stammered:

'I didn't mean anything, Sir; what I meant was, your colour is only skin deep, Sir.'

'Quite so, Potter,' I replied, wanting to say something to show I felt no resentment at his jovial remark. 'All colour is only skin deep.'

I finished the lacing and opened the drawer of my table to find the strip of Elastoplast I kept there. I was annoyed with Pamela for the unnecessary and quite vehement attack on Potter, but could think of nothing I could do about it without worsening an already delicate situation.

The boys walked over to Pamela, who observed their approach with cool unconcern.

'What's up with youse?' Denham planted himself squarely in front of her, and stuck his jaw forward belligerently.

'Are you addressing me, Denham?'

'Yes.' Pamela watched him and waited.

'All right, Miss Dare then. What's up with you?'

'I don't know what you mean, Denham.' She was cool, taunting.

'Pots was only being funny, and you had to go for him like that, and right in front of Sir. What did you want to call him "fat boy" for?'

'He's fat, isn't he?'

Pamela's gaze shifted from Denham to Potter and traversed him from top to toe.

'I was only having a little joke and Sir didn't mind,' Potter offered, lamely, quailing under Pamela's examination.

At this, Pamela rose in one fierce, fluid motion. Eyes blazing, she stood straight before Potter and in her anger seemed to tower above him, her voice thick with emotion.

'Doesn't mind? How do you know he doesn't mind? Because he's decent about it and never lets on? Daft, that's what you are, the lot of youse, daft, stupid, soft!'

I sat down and watched, mesmerised by the concentrated anger of this red-headed Fury, who seemed to grow larger as she continued, her eyes boring into the helpless Potter.

'How would you like it if they were always on to you, fat Potter? Idiots, that's what you are, idiots! My life, the silly things you ask!' She screwed up her face and fell into scathing mimicry:

'Do you ever wash, Sir? Do you feel the cold, Sir? Do you ever have a haircut, Sir? Stupid, that's what you are, all of youse.'

'Coo, good old Pamela!' exclaimed Tich Jackson.

Pamela swung around to fix him with her eyes, but Tich quickly altered it to:

'I mean, Miss Dare.'

'Sir said we could ask him anything we liked, didn't he?' persisted Denham. He was unable to match Pamela's quick cutting intelligence, but he stood firm, trying to cope with one idea at a time.

'You shut up, Denham. Call that asking questions, always on about his colour and that? Can't think of anything else to ask about?'

As if unwilling to spare any of them she suddenly turned on Seales, who had, as usual, been playing the part of interested bystander.

'And you, you ought to know better.'

'Steady on, what have I done? I didn't say anything.' He sounded rather alarmed.

'You never say anything. You're coloured too, but you just sit back and keep your mouth shut. Are you scared of this lot?'

She was wonderful, tremendous in her scorn and towering anger: Boadicea revivified, flame-haired, majestic. Seales watched her for a moment, with a patience that made him centuries older than the virago before him.

'I really don't think they meant any harm, Miss Dare. When they ask questions they're only trying to find out about things they don't understand.'

Pamela was not to be mollified. 'Then why don't they ask you if they're so keen to find out?'

'I'm not Sir, Miss Dare, I only wish I was.'

Denham tried once more to make his point. 'Sir doesn't need you to stick up for him. Who do you think you are?'

'I'm not sticking up for him,' Pamela flared, 'I'm just sick and tired with all your silly remarks. And who I think I am is none of your business, Mr. ruddy Denham. Red blood, indeed!' She used scorn as incisively as a surgeon's scalpel.

Potter turned away, calling over his shoulder: 'Come on, fellers, let's go down; she's crackers, she is.'

They turned to follow him and had reached the door when Denham, struck with a sudden thought, retraced his steps and said in a hoarse whisper:

'Know what's eating you, you're stuck on Sir, that's what.'

Without waiting for her reply, he rushed through the door, leaving it to slam loudly behind him. Pamela remained standing where she was, mouth open, gazing at the closed door; then she looked towards my desk and our eyes met. I may have looked as foolishly surprised as I felt, for she blushed deeply and rushed through the door.

So there it was. Somewhere deep inside of me I had known it all along but had refused to acknowledge it, because, in spite of her full body and grown-up attitude, she was to me a child and one who was in my care. I could appreciate that the emotional stirrings within her might be serious and important to her—it was not uncommon for girls of fifteen to be engaged or even married—but though I liked and admired her, she was to me only one of my class, and I felt a fatherly reponsibility for her as for all the others. If Denham's remark was evidence of a general feeling about it things might be a bit sticky, but he had blurted it out so suddenly that I guessed it was merely an impulsive shot in the dark. I needed to discuss this with someone. Not Gillian, because that would mean I would have to acknowledge the truth of her warning, and I was in no mood to hear her say, 'I told you so.' Grace. Yes, she would to able to advise me in this, for, coming from the same background and stock she had considerable understanding of the problems of these girls.

When Grace returned from the dining hall that afternoon I whispered to her that I wished to see her privately, and together we went up to her classroom. She listened without interruption until I had finished; then she said:

'Well, Rick, are you surprised?'

'Look, Grace, this is no time for jokes. I need advice because this thing is quite outside my experience.'

'I'm not joking, Rick. This sort of thing happens all the time wherever there are men teachers and girl students, from the Infants, right through to High School and University. Here, sit down and let me bring you up to date.'

We made ourselves comfortable and she continued:

'There hasn't been a really good man teacher in this school for ages—I'm not including the Old Man. We've been having a procession of all types. The fellows these girls have seen here have been, on the whole scruffy, untidy men who can't be bothered to brush their teeth or their shoes, let alone do something about their shapeless ill-fitting clothes. Good God, those twerps tootle off to a training college and somehow acquire a certificate, a licence to teach, and then they appear in a classroom looking like last week's left-overs!'

In her vehemence she had risen and was walking up and down, her arms folded tightly across her bosom. Now she stopped in front of me.

'Then along comes Mr. Rick Braithwaite. His clothes are well cut, pressed and neat; clean shoes, shaved, teeth sparkling, tie and handkerchief matching as if he'd stepped out of a ruddy bandbox. He's big and broad and handsome. Good God, man, what the hell else did you expect? You're so different from their fathers and brothers and neighbours. And they like you; you treat them like nice people for a change. When they come up here for cookery or needlework all I hear from them is "Sir this, Sir that, Sir said, Sir said" until I'm damn near sick of the sound of it.'

Grace had got quite worked up as she was speaking. I had not seen her show so much emotion before.

'You see, Rick,' she went on, 'I've known these kids a long time, been teaching here nearly twenty years. I've seen many of them as nippers in their prams, so I know all about them and I like them, every one of the snotty-nosed little bastards. You've made good on this job, Rick. Only the other day the Old Man was saying the same thing to me. You treat them with kindness and courtesy and what's more they're learning a lot with you. Be patient with Pamela. She's only just finding out that she's a grown woman, and you're probably the first real man she's met. Be tactful and I'm sure she'll soon pull herself together.'

I got up and moved towards the door I had been given more than I had asked for, and I felt humble and grateful.

'Thanks for the chat, Grace, you've been very helpful.'

'Come and see Auntie Grace any time you've got troubles,' she laughed.

I was half way through the door when she said, as if in afterthought, 'I like Miss Blanchard, don't you?' I turned away without replying.

Grace was right. The emotional outburst must have released some of the tension building up inside Pamela, for in a little while she seemed to throw off some of her aloofness and bad temper, and once again entered into the community spirit within the classroom and at the midday dances. Now and then I would notice a look of worry on her face, but I could see nothing to account for it and hoped it would soon disappear altogether.

EXERCISE 52

Do you think a real incident lies behind this story? What do you say to yourself? To Jill? To the Headmaster?

Discuss these problems in relation to quality of the writing.

An eventful night

A few weeks ago I went to stay at my Auntie Joyce's for a day or so. The first night I could not sleep at all, my Auntie and Uncle were shouting and arguing downstairs. I heard my Auntie shout me and I thought, 'Good Heavens! He's killing her', and I said to myself, 'now be brave Jill, go and stop him.' So I jumped up out of bed and ran downstairs. My Auntie had a knife in her hand and My Uncle was behind her holding her arm. Auntie Joyce slashed out with the knife, I just stood there shaking. My Uncle said, 'Will you take the knife off her or I will have no ear on.' So I leaned forward and took the knife slowly out of her hand. Then Auntie said 'Tell him to get off me,' so I said 'Uncle, just get off her you mad, raving lunatic.' So he did and turning to me he said 'Are you threatening me?' I said 'No, Uncle, honest'. My Auntie ran indoors and said 'Get back to Scotland,' to which he replied 'Joyce dear, calm yourself down', which got her mad so she threw all his clothes out into the street. Then she threw a bottle at him. It hit his head, bounced off and smashed all over the road. Then he really was mad and he seized my Auntie. She shouted 'Go for the police,' but I went round the back, crept up behind him and brought the poker down on his head. He fell to the floor cross-eyed. My Auntie said 'You've killed him.' I fetched some water and threw it over his face and as he came round he said in a stutter 'What happened?' I could not help laughing as we took him back into the house. By the time we got to bed it was ten past five in the morning. The next morning when everything had been straightened out my Uncle said 'Joyce you had better tame your temper, you'll be killing me yet,' then he looked at me and said 'Well at least your niece sticks up for you.' After dinner I went home and told my father about it and he said 'You won't go there again, your Auntie is a nutter.' Oh! I never did find out why they were arguing.

(Jill, secondary modern school)

EXERCISE 53

What are your reactions to this—written by a very unco-operative boy of 14 in a 'B' stream, in response to a request to write a 'Blues'?

Come on, and Sigh with me
I have a mind which is ~~blurred~~ confused
I am sick, ~~sick~~ sick in the mind.
so hear who I have been used.

EXERCISE 54

Read this story (by a girl in the second year 'A' stream of a secondary modern school) and answer the questions below.

The ~~[illegible]~~ Unhappy Holiday.

Peter and Joan, where going on holiday with their freinds, Jack and Jill who ~~whose~~ were twins, ~~both~~ all the children where 13 except Peter who was 14. Peter and Joan were so excited that they forgot some of their things such as the bars of soap wich they brought at the nearest local shop. And they joined up & with Jack and Jill who were wating for them at the stile, before going on their way.

They climbed over the stile and went on a trodden down footpath which cut in half down the field and they all talked and laught as they went along. The two boys ~~[illegible]~~ sleeping in one tent and the two girls in another.

Exercise 54

When they had settled down for the night, and in the morning Peter woke early and he lit the fire to fry the breakfast on and after he had down that Jack woke up and got up later they had fried the ~~breakfast~~ the two boys had ~~hat~~ to wake the girls up as they over ~~slepted~~, slept. Later on it began to rain, thunder and lightened and Jill was very scared she kept crying and screaming untill she was gasping for breath. where she was so exhausted. Later on she was still the same the, children were all sooking wet so they decided to pack up their things and decided to go home they walked over the fields and Jill got her ~~Mac~~ Macing-tosh torn to thread on the nail on the stile which was not there when they first started out, but later on still wet and socked they got home and they were so unhappy that their parent promised them another holiday on their own. But the children still decided to go on a-nother holiday, of course a camping one which I hope will not be wet, But when they go they had decided to take their parents. with them so they will not be frightened.

THE END.

My Character

I am a girl.

I am 5ft 4ins. I have brown hair blue eyes. My hobbies are hairdressing and Cycling.

(1) Why do you think does Averil change 'Excited' to 'Unhappy'?

(2) Why does she point out that the 'boys were sleeping in one tent and the two girls in another'?

(3) Discuss the possible reasons why Averil makes her characters take their parents with them on their second camping holiday.

(4) In Averil's next piece you detect that she had written 'I am a girl. I am. But I will not prove it' and then crossed it out'. What do you say to yourself about this? (Do you say anything to her?)

(5) Compared with her other stories this one is not very interesting (see her work in *The Secret Places*, pp. 24 and 58). Account to yourself why this should be so—what has gone wrong? Then say what you would do about this, including what you would say to Averil.

(6) What points of expression could you discuss in class from this story?

(7) What story or chapter or book could you direct Averil to read, to help her write a better story?

EXERCISE 55

The following piece of short story is poorly written and contains a strange mixture of conventionality and suggestiveness. Discuss how you deal with this: it is a common experience for teachers of secondary modern school children, and cannot be avoided, if children are to be encouraged to write freely.

A date in a lane

One day I was walking down
the Steet and as she went
down the lane she met a man
and is name is Peter Hicks and her
name is susan and he made
love to her and. she said Peter Stop
it you are not to do that my mum
well come and see you in a Tick
and then you can [illegible]
with your hand on my back and then
you Can make Love and then
they got engager, he buy a ring
of gold and her mother was
so glad. and then they want
to the Pictures and he said
well you marry me and she
said it to soon to be married
yet, all then we well get married
on April the 21st is it all right

to get married then so she
said all right it is all right
to marry him then So I can
marry him on April 21st yes my
dear yes my dear you can I am
glad that you are glad. So
she married him in the End.

EXERCISE 56

What do you say to yourself about this piece from Kenneth, aged 14 (in a 'C' stream, third year, secondary modern school)? What do you say to him?

The Kidney man

one day a man kill a woman. and cut
Her kidney out and eat chem. nexe
day. He kill a another woman. and cut
Her kidney out and eat chem. ond
made a awful mess. He wos called
the vampire. He hab ca horrible. ceeth
91 Thursday janvory 9161 a wamon wos
Kill. and a kidney wos missing.
it wos getting seriaws. nexe thay
Find che Body was on marshiadn
and Foodprints in ca swamp.

THE END

EXERCISE 57

A little boy, of 13, hands in the following story. You are picking out stories to read aloud to the class, and you have to decide quickly whether or not to read this out. Discuss: (*a*) what you say to yourself privately; (*b*) what you do.

~~Falling~~ In Love.

Dick was writting outside the cafe for Julie. He could hear the sound of the juke box in the distance, and the clanging of cups. He saw Julie comeing towards the cafe. She had dark hair, and blue eyes, she was very attractive. She wore alot of make up. Dick was tall, and he had dark hair. He wore pointed shoes, blue jeans, and an Italian styled jacket, blue shirt, and a dark tie. He had sideboards that came halfway down his cheeks. Julie came up to Dick, she was very sexy Dick said, "Shall we go in the cafe?

Julie said, "No it is too stuffy in

there, let us go into the park, it is a nice moonlight night." So Dick & put his arm round Julie, and Julie put her arm Dick, and they walked through the park. They sat down on a seat, which was under a tree near a pond. She had lovely breasts, and a good figer. He said, "Julie I love you veiry very much."

Julie said, "I will always love you." There they were siting on the seat, kissing and cuddling. He put his hand behind her back, a started to undo her brassiers. She t slapt him on the face real hard which made him jump back. She said, "I hate you for that." Dick was very angry, and said, "I hate your liver." She marched off in a rage. Dick was very sad, and he went back to the park were he had parked his Norton. He was mad, started his motor bod bike, & pulled away very fast. He was travelling down the high street at 8X5 mls m.p.h. he must of gone mad, he took a blind corner at 60 m.p.h. crash, he hit a pig lorry, with a head on colishon. He was kill at instently, blood trickled down the road from a gash, in his head. Julie heard that Dick had been killed that night, she burst into tears, because she thought it was her fault, she could not sleep that night. He had gone, but her love for him still remained.

EXERCISE 58

The boy who wrote the poem in Exercise 19 hands in the following: what do you make of this?

The HILL

on top of the hill.
I had to take a pill.
I swoll it Down,
and hit Her on the Crown

In and out
In and out
the little girl began to shout.

it was very windy
I was very windy
I fell in a hole
and landed on a mole

In and out
" " "
the little girl began to shout

when I got up it was so Dark
And I ~~here~~ heared ~~and~~ a Dog Bark
A little girl ~~oh~~ with her Dog
came out of the dark, Dog.

In and out
" " "
the little girl began to shout

The little girl with hair so fair
But she had nothing to wear
She was shiving she was so cold
And her hand she had some gold

In and out.
In and out.
the little girl began to shout.

the gold was not
~~tal~~ and ~~her~~ she was not
so I got out of the Isle
And ~~oh~~ went home
THE END

5 *Deciphering*

Once the point of a 'creative' approach to children's work has been grasped, a teacher becomes concerned with the germ, the gist of a piece—its content, *first*. Of course, matters of spelling, punctuation, layout and handwriting are important.

But the most important thing to get is the message.

The first appearance of the work of less able children is discouraging—and to some student teachers, shattering! The following exercises should help to show that the problem of deciphering is at one with the problem of 'getting the message'. (See also Exercise 50 above.)

EXERCISE 59

Notice the extraordinary difference between the two forms of handwriting in these two facing pages of a girl's book (3 B in a secondary modern school)—and the difference in content. What would you say to yourself if you were reading this child's book during a marking session? What would you say to her? Note how the content reveals a dissociation between the school child and the out-of-school child.

girls said that when they
got free if they got free
they would tell the police
The men whipped the
girls and made them
work their fingers to
the bones.
When the girls did

not arrive home their
mothers phoned the polic
this called for a great
serch and all the
area of Flossy village
was combeat for the
kidnappers
Every 16 hours
the girls were whipped
and tolp them
if they didnt do as they
were told they would
be tourched. They
would hang by their

NODDY_

One day as noddy was going down the road in his car and as he came to the corner he nearley knocked over mr. Plod the Policeman.

arms so that their feet would
not touch the ground.

EXERCISE 60

The following story was written by George Green, the bottom boy in a 'D' stream, in an examination. It represents some 200 of the 2,000 words he wrote in two years.

Translate it and make notes on it, then say what you would say to George.

The Sick Sow.

won day The Sow was. Sick and the. old. frm went four the vethn.
and the old Sow whdit not hethn on. ifonits and the old
frm sedsto vethn the old Sow is on. hethn so then
vethn. sedn to the frmh 1 wilh Kurah and. See. the
lod. Sick. Sow Sedn. the Vethn and the frmh. webt two
see the lod Sick. Sow. and the vethn and the frmh.
S.ee. lod fat Sick. Sow Stbts the frmh and wents at the
frmh and not the frmh outt the beg fat Sick. Sow
went and. ladta down the frmh. wents two with the
big fat Sick. Sow and Saiw belhlsiy and the frmh.
wents in he house and he. Sat down. and.
he. bav he. and. Sick. Sow went. two ladts
down and the vethn wents and the vent. see.
wat is nont wys. and. the Sick. Sow wents.
to seph and the vethn wents two the
frmh haise and Sick Sow. the Vethn
to the frmh and the vethn sidn two the old big fat
Sick Sow is a seph. and the sick. sow not the vethn and
frmh run. and run up. Sectirs and. the sick sow went
to the Pigs house. and ladh. down. and wents Seph.
and the frmh hot vetin and. went to —
and. frmh weth to See Sick. Sow and.
he puth whits and Sick old Sow wok up and old Sow
is beth. the AND

Deciphering

Discuss how you might get these poems and passages over to George.

[A] *View of a Pig*

The pig lay on a barrow dead.
It weighed, they said, as much as three men.
Its eyes closed, pink white eyelashes.
Its trotters stuck straight out.

Such weight and thick pink bulk
Set in death seemed not just dead.
It was less than lifeless, further off.
It was like a sack of wheat.

I thumped it without feeling remorse.
One feels guilty insulting the dead,
Walking on graves. But this pig
Did not seem able to accuse.

It was too dead. Just so much
A poundage of lard and pork.
Its dignity had entirely gone.
It was not a figure of fun.

Too dead now to pity.
To remember its life, din, stronghold
Of earthly pleasure as it had been,
Seemed a false effort, and off the point.

Too deadly factual. Its weight
Oppressed me—how could it be moved?
And the trouble of cutting it up!
The gash in its throat was shocking, but not pathetic.

Once I ran at a fair in the noise
To catch a greased piglet
That was faster and nimbler than a cat,
Its squeal was the rending of metal.

Pigs must have hot blood, they feel like ovens.
Their bite is worse than a horse's—
They chop a half-moon clean out.
They eat cinders, dead cats.

Distinctions and admirations such
As this one was long finished with.
I stared at it a long time. They were going to scald it,
Scald it and scour it like a doorstep. (Ted Hughes)

Exercise 60

[B]

Outside the inn, the gentleman of the road sat down under the hedge and drank again. He would have liked to do a little more dancing with his new boots that night. He drank again, staggered to his feet and leaned over the dairy gate, looking towards his son's home. The dark cowsheds slumbered under the stars. A hungry grunt came from a pig.

The warmth of the tramp's feelings made him unbutton his coat. It was the only upper garment that he had. His coarse hairy chest received the cool night wind. Mr Tasker's father tilted up the bottle and drank.

The autumn wind moved about the fields. The church owl flying homeward with a rat in its claws was aware of a man crossing her path. She passed to the right instead of the left of the vicarage.

Mr Tasker's father, bottle in hand, staggered across the meadow. His happiness was complete. He belonged to the élite for whom the world is made. A black shadow crossed the cow-yard and slunk under the wall.

Leaning over the yard gate, he finished the bottle and held it upside down. Two drops of spirit fell into the straw. Mr Tasker's father had never felt so complete a happiness before. Why should he not go in and smash the head of that huge black sow with his foot? It would be a pleasant early morning sight for his son. He unlatched the gate and entered.

A dark beast crouched under the wall, ready to spring. The huge sows lay sleeping. Others of the gods lay about in the soft dung. There was not room enough for so many in the sties.

The tramp raised his foot to kick. The other foot was unable to bear his weight. He lurched forward, staggered, and fell. A wolf-like shadow sprang from the wall and had him by the throat. A beast's cry—and silence. The teeth of the dog gripped deep. It had not forgotten the smell inside the felt hat, torn bits of the hat were still in the bottom of its tub. For five minutes it held on. Then it let go the body, and curled up at the end of its barrel, sniffing angrily at the pieces of torn felt. As it passed the largest sow, the dog moaned. It was a way it had, to moan in the night. It moaned like a beast in pain.

The two sows raised their snouts. They grunted greedily at the stars. They smelt blood. They had been taught by man to devour carrion. A day or two before they had torn to pieces the carcass of a cow that Farmer Dane had sold to Mr Tasker for five shillings. The largest sow struggled to its legs and sniffed. Was there still some cow left? She moved towards a dark object that lay in the straw, and from whose throat blood oozed. The other gods were roused. They had no desire to be left out of the feast. The tusks of Mr Tasker's lately purchased prize boar were quite able to break the outer covering and the inner skin of a man.

That last cry, of the father, did awaken the son. Mr Tasker heard a noise in the night. He thought for a moment about the little pig that he had got for nothing, and fell again into a sound slumber.

The hare died in the gin. The owl tore out the bowels of the rat.

A friendly feeling towards the world awoke Mr Tasker early the next morning. Besides the recollection of the little pig, he felt sure that something had been about in the night. At 4.30 he carried his lantern into the yard and saw his father, or rather what his gods had left of him.

Mr Tasker had never suffered from nerves. He dragged his father into the corner where the cow had been eaten. Fetching a fork he covered up the remains of the man and of the cow with dung.

(T. F. Powys, from *Mr Tasker's Gods*)

[C] *Bowling for a Pig*

One of the first things we did when we came to this village
Was to visit a Fête in the Rectory Garden,
And there were some kale-pots, with numbers and large holes
Into which you threw tennis-balls; and nearby in a crate,
Like a shivering maiden chained to a rock
(Except that she wasn't shivering, but scratching herself daintily)
Was a piglet, in a long crate, strawed and bristly,
Rubbing her silver-haired flank on the silver-haired wood.

I bowled for this pig, determined to show the village
I was no town fool unskilled in the hand.
Two and sixpence I spent, raising my score to thirty,
And the piglet was mine. We cleared out a stable—
Sharp irons, unstable log-piles and rusty bicycles
Replaced by a golden thicket of crackling straw.
Then we heaved in the piglet, who snuffed, squealed, and buried.
And then, just as we thought she had died from mishandling
Or fright, dashed at us, sallying and veering away,
Just like a dog, teasing its master, to express affection.

'Henrietta' we called her, after a gentleman friend,
And Henry was pleased, and the piglet was pleased to be called
Something. She ate washing, the sleeves of shirts, or apron-
Strings that dangled. Our paddock, a mass of nettles,
Mallows and kecks of all kinds, rubble and granular
Long-rotted, muck-filled earth—this she rooted,
Driving up tunnels and earthworks, wallows and simple snuffs
From which with a 'hough!' she emerged to scamper two circuits.
Lapping the barn at a good fifteen miles an hour: then tease us,

Pretending to eat a shirt, or actually eat a shirt,
Or drag a petticoat like a ring-trophy through the mud.

And then—the meal she consumed! At first small packets,
But then this mournful pig became hollow and wobbly-flanked,
And I had to buy sacks, huge fat unmanageable hundredweights,
Which stood bulky and gross beside a smallish gilt pig,
Which later stood bulky and gross beside a smallish sad sack,
And the bills mounted. But we planned to breed,
To give Henrietta the happiness other elephantine sows
Screamed about in the night on the other side of our lane,
Breeding another litter: she must have that,
And dozens of Henries and Herberts and Harries would squeal
Round our snout-ridged paddock.

Then we thought of the cost of the meal,
Christmas came, autumn bills, the seasons of greed, and hams—
And goodwill. Then, after one bad post, I rang
The bacon works, and for a lorry. That day I left
The house by a seldom-used door, not near the paddock;
My wife hurried in and out, as people do
When someone within is grievously sick or dead—not even
Retrieving a couple of dishcloths Henrietta wound
Tastefully round her neck, then buried, then rooted and ate,
While we watched her with craven eyes, too guilty to speak.

Since autumn I'd thrown her heaps of windfalls to eat,
Red, tempting and succulent: these she'd delightedly sniff,
Hough, gamble, and toss. She loved them, and frosty days
Had been happy for both of us, winner and munching pig
Under pale blue autumn skies. Those apple baits
I employed to lure Henrietta up the ramp. One last ear toss,
A clatter of bolts, 'sign 'ere sir', and off she went,
While we gloomily ate, and hadn't the heart to confess
The misery hanging over us. What, you say, just for a pig?
Yet I've seen farmers sorrowful, at the loss of a horse,
Or even a handsome bullock. Sad at necessity.
But Henrietta! For the Christmas bills! Betraying
The prize that made my shirts armless, companion
To my small scratch-back girls? It cast a light
On human weakness. We could do this! No trust
Should rest on such as we were.

She made good;

Deciphering

Grade A in all her parts—a paper
Came in a day or two. We thought of our pig lingering
In the steel pens, no clunch to root, no washing,
No mallow flowers, no chase with angry wife,
No scratch-back children! Only the forced cake-walk,
Into some cold machine. The stun. The hook. The knife.
And then the needle-pickled bacon, clean long sides and hams
Divided and eaten throughout suburbia. Twenty-two pounds ten
Was all I had. It went. Some of it even on bacon.
She would have got too big, we rationalised. The meal
Would have cost too much for us. Yet we felt her sacrificed
To an improvidence that wrecks so many plans,
Ineffectual and sad. We were in that steel pen
With our young maiden pig.
How I'd love now to feel
The morning winner's pleasure of hearing her lot squeal,
Dashing under the straw as the half-door opens—pail
Clattering (her tenth litter!), slops and swills,
Grateful old mother sow!
Alas!
Even her carcase ticket's burned now with the settled bills!

(David Holbrook)

EXERCISE 61

What do you make of this poem?

JULY

ENGLISH
DOING A TON
~~Smoking~~

They say Doing A TON is fun and a frill
"But" w[illegible] you scpile. w[illegible] DOING A TON
you Get cente Back to Dear old mum
[illegible] datt, you Maybe livind
But if you are its No chances for you
DOING A TON

6 'Pop' and Pulp Influences

Inevitably, children's imaginations are affected by the influences of popular culture, all of it indifferent to their creative needs, and some of it destructive and corrupting.

But, while disturbed children are often upset by such influences as horror comics, most children defend themselves by a comic irony—and some can turn the modes of cheap and horrific sensationalism to their own use.

EXERCISE 62

Here is a story by a boy in 1 B (secondary modern school). What are the sources of the phantasy? Is there anything 'there'?

A figure in the library

There was a school girl in
a library and one night she whent
there and she heard a voice and it
said in a gostly way You have
only 24 Hours to live and on the 24th
hour come to the school gate So she
went to bed and she tosed and tosed in
her bed. At thes time the figure was going
to its hiding Place. At the same time the girl
was Phoning the Police and soon they arived
They told hen what to do and
on tohe 23 houn she went to bed the
24th houn had come
3 minutes had past of the 24 houn and

a panel slide back and a hand come
throug and reached her throat:
The Police jumped out and graped his
arm there was a strugel and they
pulled him out it was the person
who they had been looking for
a long time.

The End

EXERCISE 63

Here is a 'pop' ballad written by a girl in 3B (secondary modern school). What do you do next?

A Ballad.

His coloured shirts and tight black jeans
I always see him in my dreams.
His trembling lips his tender eyes.
These are the things I idolize.
His black wavey hair,
Thats sends me through the air.
The way his hair falls on his face,
And send's me into out a space.

EXERCISE 64

This poem is by a boy in 4B (secondary modern school). What do you say to yourself? What do you say to him?

SATURDAY NIGHT DANCE

As we entered the dance hall,
People were dancing,
Girls skirts were flying. as they spun around,
We sat in chairs, against the wall.

We danced a few dances,
It took away our breath, and we found
ourselfes gasping.
11:30 came we walked slowly home
Arm in arm, then that good night kiss;
It was an evening well spent.

EXERCISE 65

Is the following simply the kind of thing the author reads in *Mirabelle*? Does it have any good points? What use would you make of it? What do you say to her?

Celia's Love

As usual Celia got up and went straight to the studio where she made costumns for the actors. It was a very special day for Celia as this young boy was coming to help her with the clothes. Celia had long blonde hair with a sweet face. Then as she was busily making a hat in came the boss with this glamous boy.

He introduced Celia to the boy. His name was Derek Cousins. All the morning Celia showed Derek around the studio and telling him some of the things she had made.

'I want to do something big not just make things' said Derek.

'Why don't you try singing because you are good looking and I am sure you can sing' suggested Celia.

'I am hopeless when I sing, I will be a flop.'

'I will ask the boss about it' said Celia.

'Well' said the Boss 'it is an idea, I will get Mr Archie to hear him sing.'

But my God, he sang awfull. 'I know' said Jenny the girl I work with. 'Let him mime and we can play a record.' 'What a splendid idea' they all said.

So that is what they done. They put huge posters up all over the town, saying that he loved all the ladies. All the teenages crowded in the theatre that night. They kept shouting 'He's the kissing man.' He was tremdous hit. It was true he did love the girls and he kept on kissing them every night after the show. This went on for a long time. When Celia relized that he hadn't kissed her at but all the other girl had been she was very Jealous. Then one day as she was with Derek he told her to stopped the car in the middle of the town so he could kiss all the girls. The traffic was enormous and they very bibing their hooters. Then this fat police woman came and she 'who are you' but before she could say any more he kissed her. After a while the street was cleared again and they drove to the studio. Derek never took notice of Celia. She loved him but he would never ask her for a date. When he was singing one night she took off the needle and then Derek blushed and had to sing by his self. 'Boo Boo' the crazy girls shouted. 'He's phoney' 'We hate him' said another.

After the show Celia was ashamed of what she had done and she ran away far into the forest.

'Oh my goodness I shall never, never see him again' she cried.

'Oh yes you will,' said a voice. It was Dereks. 'Oh my dealing' she cried.

'I am sorry for what I did' Celia tried to say.

'I am glad you did that, because you are the one and only one I love.'

Derek kissed Celia and everyone could tell they were in love. So Celia was contented with what she had got and she didn't mind that he couldn't sing. She married him soon afterwards. (Girl, aged 13)

EXERCISE 66

Read and evaluate this story by a girl in 4B. Try reading it aloud. What is the source of the style? How do you 'mark' it?

The Forgotten Dream

The night club was drab and dreary in the old drab town and I was just about to give up the ghost and go. But then, just at that moment, as the clock struck ten, she walked in and the place was full of her pungent perfume which floated about in the air like stale food.

Exercise 66

She went up to a nearby table and sat down. Giving a sigh and a moan I got up and strolled up to her, knowing I would be at her mercy as soon as I looked at her. I was a private detective, and was here to investigate Rod Burrows, a night club owner's, murder. He had been murdered early last night and his body was retrieved in the early hours of the morning. He had been found with his head bashed in by a hammer and was leaning on an old stone wall which his blood made a deep red chalky colour.

As I reached the table the girl greeted me in her deep husky voice I so well knew. I sat down rather cautiously and casually said 'Hallo!' The girl looked up and, 'To what do I owe the pleasure of this visit from the oh-so-gallant detective?' The sarcastic way she put it made me see red. But her enchanting face made all the anger in me disappear as quick as it had come.

'Okay, Della,' I said, 'Give up the fooling and let's have the gen on Rod Burrows. I know you knew him and went out with him'. She looked at me and sighed with a deep husky sigh and said, 'Hm!' And got up and walked out on me out into the crowded night. All I could do was gaze stupily into my cup. I stayed at the night club a long time trying to think it all out. Della didn't seem bad, but there was something about her in an odd sort of way that seemed evil and strange and, somehow, sad. Her background was good. She had nice parents and had lived in a nice part of America. And as far as I know her life had been good and happy. Well, I gave up thinking about her and went out into the street. As I went along the side walk I felt tired, miserable, sad and lonely. And somehow sort of trapped. I had the feeling that somebody was there looking, waiting, and gunning for me.

To get back to my flat I had to go through a small side street. I walked on and on, and nothing happened. I went through the alley and still nothing happened. Then suddenly, from out of the dark and silence, came a voice, a still silent voice, like a dead man's, which said 'You thought I was going to get you didn't you? Never mind: perhaps next time? Meanwhile do yourself a favour and lay off that Della dame, she is evil, evil through and through!'

I didn't know whose the voice was, and I didn't care. All I cared about was getting away from the evil place—away from it all. Most of all, away from murders and murderers. That night I didn't sleep for thinking of it all—thinking of Rod Burrows and Della. Most of all Della.

The next day I got up late with a dreadful headache. It was Monday morning and the thought of the working day and all that dreadful business to be turned up again was too much. So I decided not to go to work that day.

I had been at home for about two hours moping around when a ring came at the door. I went to it, and lo and behold, I came face to face with Della. Her lovely face shone in at me through the open door.

'Well!' She said, 'Aren't you going to ask me in'

'I...I come in, Della'

'Thank you for the nice welcome!' she said. And her slightly amused face made me feel angry and more foolish than ever.

'Well?' I said 'What have you come for? I am busy. I don't want anyone in here.'

'H'm, it looks like it!' she said.

'You don't seem to be doing much now anyway'.

I looked up at her, anger burning in my eyes, wondering why I liked her.

'Anyway' she said '—got a bit of a fright last night didn't you?'

Loathing filled me. I exploded.

'What do you know about that?' I said.

'A lot more than you do,' she said.

I had never felt like hitting a woman before but this woman really was the most irritating woman I had ever known, and liked. If I had been a bit less curious than was good for me I would have told her to get out. But instead I offered her a seat and a drink and told her to uncover.

First of all she just sat there. Then she drawled out,

'Well, what is it you want?'

'You know what I want' I repeated, 'I wan't to know about the manlast night and how it is somehow connected with Rod Burrows and his murder'.

When I mentioned Rod Burrows I saw Della's lovely face go white. But in a quick effort to revive herself she said, 'And what makes you think I had anything to tell you about Rod Burrows and his murder? As far as I'm concerned it's just another terrible murder that one reads about these days in the paper. And about a voice I know nothing.'

She had only given herself away for a moment but that was enough: I knew it and she knew it. Della was in this. In it up to her neck.

Della decided she didn't want to hear any more. So, getting up, she said, 'Well, I must be going now. It takes quite a while you know to get back to my flat.'

'No, I don't know', I said 'Come on, Della, if you're in some kind of trouble tell me.'

What a fool I was to have said that! Little did I know how much I was going to wish I had not! To my horror Della burst out crying. To comfort her I had to put my arm around her. Now she had a chance, and Della knew that, and took it. She made up a good story (which I believed, poor fool that I was). It was about somebody named Fitz Crasfort, a man in his late fifties, with a beard, and mean-looking eyes. I had met him once, though I could not for the life of me think where. He was Dutch and although he had been in America quite a while he still talked with a strong Dutch accent. Well, it seemed this man had been blackmailing Della for a quite a while—or so she said. She would not tell me why and when I tried to get it out of her she put on another fit of crying.

Exercise 66

'You have got to help me! 'she said. 'You have just got to!'

'Della' I said 'How can I help you when I don't know what it is about?'

'You can, You can!' she cried. 'I promise its nothing wrong really, but its just...Well, you will know after it's over!'

If I had not been so mad about Della I would never have agreed. But, poor fool that I was, I did agree.

'But Della' I began 'What about the voice—this mysterious voice last night?'

'What has past, has past.' she said, and with these strange words she left me. I looked out of the window when she was going. I watched her brown stockinged legs go down the path. Then, as if by chance, I had a feeling she was in danger. My feeling was right as I was soon to discover. For all of a sudden men with masks on their faces grabbed Della from behind. Thinking myself a bit of a super-man (and also wanting a bit of promotion) I ran blindly down my path and on to the cement side-walk. I don't remember much about the attack, for the next thing I knew was that I was lying in hospital and being attended to by two very pretty nurses.

Della! I thought. What happened to her? I asked a friendly sister who I knew what had happened to her, and she said, 'What, Della, that play girl? Well all I know is that she came with you and said, 'Look after him. He's had a bit of an accident.' and, my God, you had too! Been here three days, you have—unconscious. Somebody gave you a nasty crack on the head' I thought of Della and all that talk about her being in trouble. Was it all a put up job? I thought she had staged the whole accident with those two. I thought she knew them. I thought they were all in it together. Oh, what a fool I had been! Was it all a trap to get me into hospital while they got out of the country—while I lay helpless in hospital, with a splitting headache and a lump on it as big as a walnut? I would probably be in hospital for about three weeks, and that was too long.

However, fate was to play a hand. Next morning I asked for the paper. And there, splashed along the front page was splashed MURDER OF MISS DELLA ORDURCE AND MR FITZ CRANFORT. In the late hours of Friday night. Both of which had no relatives living. This was a very terrible murder. Done by a blunt instrument.

Well, I can tell you, that really cut me up. And though I thought Della was no good I could not rest until I had got out of that hospital to look for the person who had killed her. Meanwhile, well—I had been in hospital.

There was a stranger arrived in the village and when I saw him I suddenly felt I knew him, he was so like somebody I knew or had known. The police had meantime got ahead on Della's and Fitz's murder and were able to give me quite a lot of gen on Della and him.

Della and Fitz were married, it seems, long ago, and they had had a child who had a slightly mad streak, which it seems he had inherited from Della.

So that was what I felt was sad about Della. It was a great shock to me. But I couldn't believe she was mad. The inspector informed me that the lady in question was not inconvenienced in this way. But she had an aunt that had to be put away and it had somehow come out in her little boy's generation. This was not all he had to tell me. It seems that when they had found out that their boy was, as the inspector put it, 'inconvenienced' they decided to put him away for life and Fitz killed him. It seems that Rod Burrows (who had been murdered a few weeks ago you remember)—well, he had found out about this and had started blackmailing them. Della and Fitz were pretty desperate. Rod Burrows had gone a bit too far. He had now got all their money. So they murdered him. And to get me out of the way they had staged the whole thing about the attack and Fitz. And the boy down the road called Simple Sam (who is a bit mad) had attacked me to put me out of the way—or so the inspector said.

After I had got over the shock of it I started looking around me. And one night when I was sitting in my flat wondering what to do next something struck me. I suddenly knew I had seen the stranger in town before. I had seen him in the Purple Lady, the nightclub, Rod Burrows owned. He must be his brother, for there was an acute likeness, which was not noticeable to anybody's eyes except mine.

I was about the day after, when I noticed Burrows' brother coming out of a broken down warehouse and my thoughts instantly went back to what the newspaper column said. Miss Della Ordurce's and Mr Fitz Cranfort's bodies were found at the bottom of an old warehouse which had not been in use for some time. This was the very same warehouse that Burrows had been into. I decided to follow him, keeping a safe distance away. When I had been following him for quite a way I suddenly realised that this Burrows had good reason for murdering Della and Fitz—had not they done away with his Brother? The excitement of finding that I might be following a murderer of a girl I had once loved—drove me on. We had now come to a part of the town I knew nothing of. It was rather off the beaten track and out of the hustle and bustle of America (Indeed it was like a quiet English grave yard and it had a sinister outlook). We walked on for about a mile. Burrows still had no idea I was following him. Along the track the room of a red tiled barn came into view. Burrows went up to the door, and to my surprise Simple Sam came out through it. But this time I had hid behind a nearby bush. Sam came out and spoke to Burrows. To my surprise I realised that Sam's was the voice that had warned me about Della that dreadful night some weeks ago. He knew Burrows was out to kill them then and tried to warn me. In his simple way he wanted to or else he would not have put in that bit about 'Never mind, I'll get you next time!' After a time Sam and Burrows walked off, and deciding I knew enough I ran back to the police station and told them all I knew. Well, we hatched up a plan and decided Sam was our best bet. He would be bound to give in—him and his delight for hurting people. Well, we got hold of him, and as we thought he gave in and let out all. I think he even had a delight in seeing Pat Burrows in the dock. Poor Sam he had always had a bit of a mean streak about him. Pat Burrows was sentenced to life imprisonment. Me? I went back to my lonely flat and tried to forget the whole dreadful business. By this time I had forgotten Della and all she stood for.

She was just a forgotten dream.

The end.

(Exercise for student-teachers: write a better pastiche of this mode, with a serious purpose to it.)

For comparison—the author's next story begins in quite a different style, which at least shows that she chose to write in an assumed voice for *The Forgotten Dream*:

The Ted

My story begins in a part of London's East end slums and it happened to a local teddy boy named Ted. He was a big tall boy and wore drain pipe trousers and long jumpers that were more off his sholders then on he wore pointed Italian type shoes and bright socks that nearly blinded you if you looked at them. His hair was...

EXERCISE 67

Is there anything here more than the child has taken in from women's magazines? How can you improve her vision?

She lied for Love.

Jackey was like any other girl with her good points, her faults, and her hopes and Dreams. Above all dream, for she was in Love with Tony a young man who was spending the Summer At the same sea-side resort.

Coming for a swim Jackey the water is Lovely today? Dive in and spoil my hair do? no fear not me. But Jackey suddenly changed her mind when she saw Tony in his canoe not far out. I'll play helpless and see what happens. I hope my scheme works out Tony doesn't know I was swimming champion at school. but slowly she began to swim out to sea. Tony kept paddling but didn't notice her until a shrill cry for help arrested his Attention. Hey Tony help me I'm drowning! Turn on your back and relax I'll get you out.

He's swallowed the bait. careful if you grab the boat you'll have me over the boat heeled over, and Tony Lost his balance.. There just as I feared: Leaving his craft he swam towards Jackey. Are you frightened? I'm never Afraid when I'm with you, Tony. good I'll hold

you under the chin and tow you in. Oh dear
this is Awful. but Jackey was determined to drown
rather than reveal that she could swim when she came
back to the surface she felt him thrashing around
beside her He was very worried. are you all right?
Yes I'm fine. But what about you you're Acting
very oddly.. Its nothing just a little cramp
in my right leg. It will be all right in a second.
Now. Listen carefully Jackey swim calmly. Breath
in when your head comes out of the water and
out when it goes under that way you'll get
ashore without swallowing too much. And you?
I'll be O.k soon I'll float for a moment until
this cramp wears off you start swimming.
no I cant Leave you! I told you a lie Tony
I can swim perfectly: I'll Take you back to the beach
holding Tony firmly under the chin. Jackey swam for
the shore Jackey found it easy to swim ashore
with Tony she swam with complete confidence.
thankful that she was capable of rescuing him
at Last they reached the beach. Thank you Jackey
you're an excellent swimmer. forgive me it was Just
a Joke An excuse to get to know you A

funny sort of joke However, you did save my
Life for me and for that I'm very grateful thank you
and goodbye. Tony walked away and as Jackey
watched him disappear along the beach her heart grew
Heavy with despair. any other man would Have ~~stopped~~
slapped me and with good reason! that same
evening there was a dance at the Hotel and Jackey
hoped Tony would come. she had to make him see
the truth she had to show him how much she loved
him! He Hasn't come after this morning he must hate
me oh dear! But Later in the Lounge,
Good evening miss Lifesaver! he made for the
Terrace, Tony Tony wait I must talk to you. You
don't know How difficult it is being A woman. with only
Two weeks holiday. That's it is it? Two weeks
to fish for a husband. But that shouldn't be
difficult for a girl as lovely as you and such a
good swimming. I bet you could catch any poor
fish if you really wanted to. And I thought you were
such an innocent girl I didn't even ~~dear~~ dare kiss
you! Tony you're wrong! the only thing I want is to
marry the man. I Love, to make him happy.

but a girl can't say these things to a man.
He'd think her for Ward who says she can't
what a man doesnt like is a girl tells lies
and you are wonderfully Honest and frank.
Jackey couldn't remember whether Tony kissed her
or she kissed him. all she could recall was
that they kissed for a long time, sealing a love
that was to last throughout their married life.

THE End

EXERCISE 68

Asked to write a 'blues', a girl in 4B (secondary modern school turns this poem in: evaluate it.

As I was walking down the street,
I saw a boy I'd like to meet
H is hair was fair
H is eyes were blue
The loat he wore
was shabby and gray

He stood on the corner
Looking blue
His head was bent
as though to say
What are you doing
on this day.

I walked past him once
I walked past him twice
I saw him look up
But he never did say
where are you going
on this day

EXERCISE 69

Compare the following stories:

<u>The Boy Next Door</u>

'My baby's Hot Chocolate Crazy
blared out of Maxin's radio
At the foot of the stairs
Mrs. Taylor shouted Maxines name half a
dozen times and was Just about to
turn away, when Mascine came out
of her bedroom
'There you are,' said Mrs. Taylor.
'about time look, Shirleys in the kitchen'
Mascine ran down stairs
into the kitchen, 'Hiya Shirl.'
'Hallo, where you bin burying your-
self?' asked Shirley.
'Since Joan's left I don't do much'
'What about your new neibours?'
'I've only seen a women, never spoken
yet.'
'Well she spoke to me this after

room, her names Mrs. phillips, there's her husband and two ~~g~~ kids. Jenny's 20 and John's 18.' said Mrs. Taylor.

'Really. hope the boys nice.' said Maxine.

'Come on Maxine theres a smashing film at the Baumont.'

'Just a mom. and I,ll get me ~~co~~ coat.'

'We'd better get the tickets ~~for~~ to see Cliff as well.'

The two girls went off down the street. The boy next door was looking out of a window when the girls went by, he watched them go to the end of the street and went in.

Down stairs Mrs. phillips was baking. 'Mum know who the neigbours are?' he asked.

'Yes, ~~there~~ thier names Taylor, Maxine lives at home and is sixteen. Her brother Graham is married and lives in

West Bromwich.

Next day Maxine went to work ~~in~~ at the Plastic factory. The boy next door came out of his gate, the same time as Maxine.

'Hallo!' he said. 'My names John Phillips.'

'Mines Maxine Taylor.'

'Off too work?'

'Yes'

'I,ll ~~walk~~ walk with you as I don't start work until next Monday.'

'How do you like it here?'

'I don't yet. Havint had much time to see anything or what there is to do.'

The both walked in silence They had ~~to~~ Just turned the corner leading to the Plastic factory when along came ~~Ho~~ Carole Martin. 'Oh No.' Maxine to herself.

'Hallo Maxine, got your self a new boy friend

Mascine blushed and said no.
'Well arn't you going to introduce me?' Carole asked.
'This is John Phillips. John this Carole Martin.'
'A pleasure to meet you' said John.
How I loath Carole thought Mascine.
'The pleasure's all mine. I must go now be seeing you.
Off she went her petticoats rustling with her. Why did she have to wear that lovely new dress and have her hair just perfect.
They left at the factory. Mascine wasn't at all happy and kept wishing it was time go home.
Mascine put on her old blue coat and left for home. She kept her eyes on the path, ~~and~~ when she neared her house, Mascine looked up. There were John and Carole together, they were laughing and talking.
'Hallo' she said cheerfully

'Hallo,' said the other two and began talking. Tears rolled down Maxcine's face. 'There's plenty of other boys I don't really like him.' Then she ~~bea~~ began to cry.

John had taken Carole out for over a month. Maxcine had been out with several boys in that time

One day Maxcine was coming home after being ~~with~~ over Shirleys house, when John stopped her

'Maxcine, is any one taking you out to-night?

'No,' Maxcine was surprised 'Why.'

'Well... I.; would you come out with me?

'Yes..but.'

'Okay! theres a smashing film at the Gaumont. What about it.'

'I'd love to.'

'Right, we can go at ~~two~~ 7.30.'

'I don't beleive it. It's not true. He actually asked me out.' Maxine put on her new blue dress, and white coat and shoes. She brushed her fair hair, grabbed her bag. It was a little before half-past seven when Maxine appeared downstairs.

'Bye everyone,' she said the same time as the front door bell rang. 'Have a good time, love!' said her Mother.

After the film they walked around the park.

'I didn't think you liked me' said John.

'What, I thought you liked Carole.'

'I only went out with her because I never seemed to see you.

Out side their houses, John kissed Maxine good-night. She came in with a dreamy look on her face. The boy next door was certainly alright and she smiled to her self.

'The End

Exercise 69

[B] MY BOY DIDN'T MAKE IT

Tru' as life pop romance

He couldn't help fancying her as she stood there looking in the window. She was quite a snooty-looking girl, the type that always fascinated him and made him want to pull her down a peg or two. At first he thought she was alone, but there was a boy by her—one of those nice, ordinary types.

You couldn't say that about Frank. He wasn't ordinary and he wasn't particularly nice when it came to it he'd always had to hold his own and fight for everything he got—which didn't seem too much at the moment.

He felt aggressive and wanted to take it out on this couple. He looked the girl up and down—and their eyes met in the reflection from the window.

He felt his usual sense of power when he saw her eyes flicker with interest. He was different. He knew how much power he DID have with girls.

He moved closer and stared openly at her. At first she blushed, then smiled sarcastically and decided to stare him out. The unsuspecting boyfriend looked on, realised he'd lost his girl's attention somewhere and followed her eyes.

But Frank's didn't move. He was staring insolently at her legs, and he knew just what this nice ordinary boyfriend would feel obliged to do. And he did it.

'What're you staring at then?' he said moving closer to Frank.

'Nothing much at the moment, but it might work out different.' Frank felt his collar almost choke him when the boy grabbed it. He smiled to himself. He was enjoying this.

So the boyfriend could pull a fast punch, so what? Frank received each blow and returned it almost simultaneously. The girl was beginning to look better all the time. Suddenly she WAS worth fighting for.

She tried to pull them apart, but every time her hand tightened on Frank's shoulder, he lashed out harder. Her coat and handbag fell to the floor. He was the stronger of the two, so it must have been a lucky break for the other boy. He landed Frank a right hook under the chin, and Frank felt the ground beneath him bounce. Or was it him?

The boyfriend left. What was the good of staying? His girl was kneeling by Frank, as he lay there stunned for a moment, and the look of concern on her face was pretty obvious. She couldn't stop her hands from stroking that thin, finely sculptured face. Her fingers traced the scar from his nose across his right cheek.

He walked off, forgetting he was clutching her coat and handbag. She didn't notice, either.

When Frank's eyes focused on the girl sardonically, she jumped to her feet and realised she was alone. Frank leapt up as if he'd just lain down to rest.

She couldn't resist it. She raised her left arm and swung round as hard as she could. He didn't even flinch. Before she could move again he'd yanked her hard by that same arm and made her groan with pain.

'What's your name then?'

'Patty. Does it matter?'

'What's a name? You're just a girl.' He pulled her close and they walked along a bomb site.

'I hate you,' she said quietly.

'But you're stuck with me,' he replied. And she was. He was everything she despised—but she was walking along with his arm around her shoulder. Already belonging to him.

He didn't ask her whether she minded sitting down on the dirty grass. He fell on to it, pulling her down beside him. They were silent. They had nothing to say to each other. They didn't know each other.

She didn't even ask him. He just started talking. He would make it one day, he told her—or was he just telling himself? She'd heard of him and his group, surely?

Patty said nothing. She'd never heard of him or his group or his record. So he was a pop star.

He stood up and gazed over the bomb-site as if it was his kingdom. 'I'll show them. I'll make it. They all wanted me at first. They just don't want to seem eager because they grudge the money. But I know they want me. But I can play it cool, too, you know.'

'Yes', agreed Patty. He sat down suddenly again, beside her. 'I play it cool all the time. They want me. Everyone is waiting for the chance to own me. But I'm careful, see.'

He pulled her close and kissed her. She didn't resist. Not that she could have, even if she'd wanted to.

He spoke again. Told her just how good he was in show-biz. She listened. But she didn't agree. He had the looks, but he was waiting for this great thing to happen to drop wealth and fame into his lap. This wouldn't happen, and he would never give up.

So it was clear to Patty that this boy was one who couldn't make it.

He was aggressive, he was good-looking and he had the push. But he was lacking something. The something that was needed for him to make the grade. But he didn't know this.

It all happened in one day. It was strange that out of all the girls he picked to vent his unconscious lack of confidence was Patty. For Patty was an assistant manager of some up-and-coming people.

She didn't tell him. She knew deep inside that Frank would never make it.

She was positive. But she could do her little bit for him without him knowing it.

'Funny why I picked on you.' That was all he said. But Patty understood. She hadn't once thought about her boyfriend. He'd understood, too.

Later, a week later, she arranged for an interview with a new club opening at Wakefield. She met him at the station. He was still looking suspicious—and he still didn't say he was glad to meet her. But it was as if they had an understanding.

He was a boy who was content with dreaming about being big, so maybe when he realised that he just didn't have it—it wouldn't be such a big shock.

He needed time—and someone like the girl he'd picked up to help him. He'd get over it. Lots of boys didn't make it. It was just that some boys needed special treatment.

Patty was there to see about this. Show business wasn't the only thing in the world. Her boy would make it—and make it big—on something else.

(From a commercial 'pop' magazine)

EXERCISE 70

Compare these stories:

[A] *A Tearful Love Affair*

My name is Janice Turner. I am fifteen years of age. I have only been out with one boy, but it broke up very sorrowfully. It was like this: I was at our Youth Club with a friend, I was sitting down having a drink when a Teddy-boy came up to me and asked me for a dance. I didn't like the look of him, but it would have been rude to refuse so I accepted.

We got on very well, and he told me I was a good dancer. Then, when the Youth Club had finished, I went to get my coat, and he asked if he could walk me home, so I said 'Yes.' He wasn't very handsome, but it's their personality that counts, and he had a nice one, although he looked rough outside. His name was Raymond Conboy. He walked me to the gate and asked me if he could go out with me, so I said 'Yes.'

The next morning, as I was walking to work, I saw Raymond on his motor-bike, and he stopped and offered me a lift, so I got on the back and away we went. I got off at my work and gave him a little kiss on the cheek. All that day I was in a dream. I knew I was in love, and I hoped he felt the same way about me.

At half past seven I was going to a dance with him so I had to hurry home. I had a quick tea and then got ready. Then someone knocked at the door, so I hurried down and opened it. Raymond was standing there in a lovely suit with a bunch of flowers in his hand. I told him to come in. When I was ready we went out, and there was a Taxi waiting for us.

I wondered where he got the money from all of a sudden. When we got there we had a very expensive tea, then we danced. Near the end we were having some fun when a bunch of Policemen walked in. They grabbed Raymond by the arm. I rushed forward to stop them, but they told me he had stolen a lot of money and they took him away.

Just as they were going out of the door. I shouted 'I'll wait for you.' But Raymond shouted 'You needn't bother.' I ran out crying my eyes out. A very nice boy took me home, and asked me to go out with him, but I said 'No,' and I've never been out with a boy since. So there we are, I never went out with Raymond Conboy again. (Girl, 3 C secondary school)

[B]

Whatever it was, it had got me going.

Halfway through the second feature, the time when they slip an arm around your shoulders, but all he does is scoff ice-cream and watch the film!

He didn't even try to steal a goodnight kiss.

'Goodnight, Miss Simpson...Maud. I hope we meet again.'

Don't get too excited, will you?

That was the oddest romance I ever had!

You couldn't even say I'm chasing him. How *can* I when he just stands still...and doesn't even bother to look at me!

At last I had to force the pace.

Moonlight, a quiet river...surely even *John* can't resist this. He'll just *have* to kiss me!

Correction...I just *had* to kiss him!

And afterwards...

'Don't like the look of that cloud. Do you think it will rain tomorrow?'

'What? Is that all you've got to say at a moment like this?'

There was nothing left for it...

'You're a fish! A cold, deep-frozen fish! I never want to see you again! Goodbye!'

'But whats wrong!'

How could I tell him?

'Nothing's wrong! You've just made it clear that you don't like me...so goodbye!'

Honestly, I didn't mean to be under the town clock three nights later...

And the fact he's here has got nothing to do with it! Why, I...

That's when he talked to a girl...

'Excuse me, but...but I'm waiting for someone. This is the town clock, isn't it?'

Do you hear that? Just what he said to me! So it was all a pose, from beginning to end!

Well I couldn't let another poor girl be fooled, could I?

'That's right, darling, this *is* the town clock, and I'm on time for once.'

'Oh...Um...Hello, Maud.'

Come to think of it, every girl needs protecting from types like him!

'I'm not letting you out of my sight for a moment from now on, my sweet.'

'You... You mean you *do* like me? Why didn't you say so before?'

(From the 'balloons' of a strip-cartoon story in a teenagers' paper)

EXERCISE 71

Here is an article from *Marty*, a journal for children aged 12–15, mostly girls. What is your opinion of it?

A Kiss to Remember

* It takes two to make a memorable kiss. You and him! So don't leave it all up to him. You need a little technique, too.
* Don't stare at him. You'll put him right off. Close your eyes and part your lips oh-so-slightly.
* Kiss as though you really mean it...
* ...Use the indelible kind (of lipstick).
* Soft...that's how your lips should feel under his...
* ...well, make it a kiss he'll remember. He'll come back for more.

EXERCISE 72

Here is a story by a boy in the fourth-year 'B' stream of a secondary modern school: evaluate it.

The End of Schmitt

Snatching up a jacket and straightening up on his feet he shuddered and shivered, thinking of his previous engagement with Schmitt, an old enemy of his. Then a door bell rang. Nicky went over to the door with a hard effort, but when he opened it nobody was there.

'That's queer!' Mm! Very queer'.

Still stunned by the beating from Schmitt's bodyguard Nicky still had to stumble and hobble around in his flat. Suddenly the phone rang—it was his Fiancée.

'Nicky?'

'Yes'

'When are you going to France—eh?'

'To France? Oh so I was, oh dear'.

'You've overslept again haven't you?'

'Yes, that's right, on a business trip to France, and then I have to sleep—I tell you what, I'll meet you in half an hour's time at Joe's Mobile stand.'

'Right—see you later'.

'Cheerio'.

In half an hours time Nicky and Jill met at Joe's and he told her what had really happened earlier on.

'Oh what brutes! I know we'll go to the Police Station'.

'No! I don't think we should tell the Police if you don't mind'.

'But I do mind! I mean after all its not fair. Why couldn't Schmitt do his own dirty work?'

'Look Jill! Will you please think what position you'll put me in—especially with the firm. I mean after all, just because I saved Jim Carvers life in a street fight, he has to pick on me'.

Soon on the way to the pictures, Nicky told Jill of the past day's confusion and the way he and Schmitt's bodyguard got scrapping with one another and how he had got the worst of the bargain. Later on when the film was finished Nicky took Jill home and came back to his appointment. Just as he unlocked his door and stepped in to turn the light on, an arm like a bent iron bar grappled him round the neck. Then he heard a voice;

'Hallo Brackston—we have been expecting you—haven't ve Valter?'

'Look Schmitt, I could have told the cops of you tonight if I had felt like it, only I went to the pictures because you didn't scare me a bit'.

'Yes we realised that—but you went to the pictures with a bird.'

'Yes that's right; Fiancé of mine. Why? Got your eyes on her?'.

'No, I was going to tell you that if you interfere with me again, I will have your fiancé, so you call her—killed in an accident.'

'You do Schmitt, and I'll kill you.'

'Oh well, so much for the party. I think we will visit another friend eh, Valter? Cheerio Brackston, we'll see you around some time.'

Schmitt went out, taking his friend with him.

'Don't forget to take your ape with yer'.

Schmitt's body guard turned round and stared at Nick for a second or two. Until a soft harsh order drew him back to his boss. It was alright during the night till next morning. When Nick received his paper, he noticed on the right side of the first page that there was a picture of Jill—then he read a small paragraph explaining that she had been found dead. She had taken an over dose of sleeping tablets, so apparently the case was 'suicide'.

He knew that the over-dose was Schmitt's work. So he was out to kill him. Soon Nicky went down to Schmitt's block. He turned left on Waterloo Street and sighted number thirteen—apparently an unlucky number, but just now the luck was on Schmitt's side. Then the door opened mysteriously, with a cop stepping outwards, then eight or nine others came out with Schmitt's bodyguard, struggling and punching him. Later on two other policemen followed carrying a stretcher. On it was a body covered by a rain coat. Nicky guessed that Schmitt had put up a fight and this time had lost. His crime had caught up with him. In court his bodyguard got the electric chair.

From that day to this Nicky has never been married.

EXERCISE 73

How do you respond to the morality of this story? What do you say to the class?

The ex-convicts revenge

Eddy Sharp was released from Jail after five years for armed robbery. A man named Joe Cartwright one of the leaders of the 'Scar Face Mob' had sent him to jail.

Eddy bought a revolver and some bullets. He asked all over town for the whereabouts of Cartwright. He learned that he was living on the edge of Dartmoor. So he got a job and made enough money for a cheap sports car and drove to Dartmoor. He found the house where Cartwright lived. But it had a huge wall round it with alsatians patrolling in the garden. There was an army post nearby, and one night he went under the wire and broke into the store where he found a ·303 which was loaded. He crept out and nobody saw him.

Eddy hid in the rocks near Cartwright's house where he saw a figure in the window—he aimed the gun. Something touched him. It was a beautiful girl. He asked her what she was doing. She said that she had followed him and was going to help him kill Cartwright. He aimed the gun. The man was still there—He pulled the trigger. The man fell head first through the window. He turned round and kissed her.

No one ever knew who killed Cartwright, and Eddy married the girl.

(Boy, aged 13)

EXERCISE 74

Evaluate this boy's story. What do you say to yourself about it? What do you say to the author? What literature do you choose for him?

[A] *Jungle Patrol*

'An' I tell you, no bloody 'Nips' goin' ter have my blood on his conscience if I can help it,' ejaculated private first class Green. After that we were all quiet. This was going to be another routine patrol, a trip into the stinking steam and fever ridden jungle. As we moved off down the track in single file the first man out of that fatal journey was killed. As he passed a thick clump of bushes he passed over the sights of a waiting Japanese. A sharp report, a dull groan, and he fell at my feet.

As we passed by the clearing we threw caution to the wind and walked straight out—a fatal mistake, for as the first man stepped out of the jungle cover, a squadron of jap aircraft...(*Here the story is taken up by a flight leader of a spitfire squadron*).

I saw the three 'Zeros' diving in at three o'clock and took a quick look below in the clearing. There were men scurrying all around for cover. Then I saw what I was dreading, little twinkling flashes from either wing: two men heeled over before they had a chance to reach cover. It was then we opened up. I did a band roll and went into an almost vertical dive. As I straightened out I found myself on the tail of the one which had shot the men down.

I had never before hated my enemy so much and as I pressed the trigger and the recoil of the twenty millimetre cannon sent shudders through the airplane. I enjoyed the feeling almost as if the aircraft was shaking with rage the same as I. Then suddenly there was a puff of smoke and a flash of flame. The zero switchbacked and rolled along like a sick beetle then fell with a horrible flash to earth. Then found myself thinking, 'Man proposes, God disposes...'

(*The story is again taken up by the men on the ground.*)

'Bury these two and then let's hop it', the lieutenant growled. They started off. Then a metallic ripple of gunfire splattered at them. The lieutenant dropped and the platoon dropped also.

'He's over there, sarge', one man yelled. The sergeant squinted down his rifle barrel and a shot issued forth from his rifle. A hoarse cry or mumble even reached their ears as a 'jap' sniper dropped from his leafy perch.

'Good shot sergeant,' one man said. They all got off the ground except one man who did not even stir, the lieutenant. A faint inkling of trouble stirred in the horror-struck minds. The sergeant knelt down. 'Lieutenant, sir.' He repeated it several times shaking him by the shoulders. Quietly he set him back down. In a hoarse quiet voice, almost a whisper 'He's...' He said no more. They all bowed their heads because here for once was the man they most needed, dead.

'Okay boys, bury him' the sergeant said. Nobody moved.

'Green! Carter! Bury him, or I'll break your effing necks!'

Still further along they came to an open field. 'Come on', the Sergeant hissed: they started running. They must have been trotting for a minute or two when suddenly the man at the back was no longer there. They all heard a piercing horrifying shriek. They turned round. Burning napalm was spattered all about. The man directly in front of him received a burst of this terrible stuff right in the legs. He fell on to one side and almost immediately he disappeared in a sheet of searing flame and oily smoke, and again a piercing shriek issued forth. The flames licked the next man's back and burnt his shirt of his back, burning through and exposing raw flesh. Nobody moved. All too scared. Now the sergeant looked round. He knew what was going to happen. Gunfire started to spatter toward them. One forgetting the predicament dropped to his side and that stinking filthy black flame searing and burning all in its way gushed out. Another man spun and fell to the ground with a low moan. His immediate partner was not so lucky: he received a bullet in the stomach: screaming he pitched to the floor. The sergeant, now petrified, yelled 'Clear out,—Leave him! He's past help'.

They ran back to the jungle past the charred remains of flesh that once was a human, and into the jungle. They dived on to the ground. Hugging the bare earth they looked back to where their mates lay still. But wait. A fresh burst of screaming came forth from the one with the bullet in his stomach. A gun spattered. He jerked convulsively. 'The murdering swines' Green muttered. 'Stow it', yelled the sergeant. He looked round at the remnants of his patrol—Green, Private first class,—and me.

(Boy, aged 15)

Compare this from a boy in 2B: does it have any redeeming features?

[B] *War In Burma*

In Burma there was a lot of British and American troops, and the Japanese were driving them back. So in America three weeks later 8 Dakota D. C 7's towing horse gliders took off for Burma with mustang escourts they were carrying chindit troops. The code name for the landing ground was Broadway, a small clearing in the jungle. When the Dakota's ect were over Jap territory a whole flight of Zero's suddenly appear through the clouds all guns blazing in less than three minutes one glider and one dakota were going down on fire then 8 of the mustangs retaliated and in 4 minutes dead 6 Zero's had gone down so the rest went back home. Soon a red light shone in the dakota's (meaning that they were near dropping area) then the gliders were let loose and went down then one hit a tree and burst into flames, there was no survivers then FLT Lieutenant Pitts of the RAF flashed his torch to the dakotas and then a hundred troops came down and the dakotas departed peacefully as soon as the troops had grounded they dashed into the jungle. there they radioed base

End of Part One.

Murry Mints Murry mints ect Ty-Phoo ect

Part Two

for some mustangs and hell cats to support them on a attack on a important Japanese train. The leader of the mustangs was squadren leader Masted DS.O, D.S.M. and bar and V.C. and leading the Hell cats was squadren leader Timbers D.S.O., D.S.M. and bar, V.C. and Burma star. The leaders asked for their orders. The orders were to destroy any transport in sight and especially a certain train leaving (Kinejab) at 1600 hours

7 *The Short Story*

Two examples of the competent short story second-year pupils can write ('A' stream, secondary modern school). Being so able imaginatively, such children require a good introduction to literature proper. To which writers shall they be sent? To answer this requires a sound analysis of the merits of their work.

EXERCISE 75

What are the good points of this story? What stories and passages from literature could you bring to the author's notice?

Eloping

The house number ten seemed very noisy from outside. Yes, I was right; Jenny was having another quarrel with her mother.

'Oh shut up,' shouted Jenny.

'Don't you answer me back like that, your own mother,' said Jenny's Mother, Mrs Dale.

'Oh I'm sorry mother.' She went and kissed her mother, 'I'm going out with Brian,'

'Don't bring him here!' answered her mother;

Jenny slammed the door and went to meet her true love. They were very much in love. But at 16, their parents told them to wait another 4 or 5 years. Jenny couldn't wait that long time.

She walked down the road where she met Brian. He was very good looking, tall and looked a very quiet chap.

'Darling,' shouted Jenny, rushing toward him.

'Listen,' said Jenny. 'I've had another row with Mum, I shall get killed when Dad finds out what I said to her.'

'What are you going to do?' said Brian.

'I don't know unless I run away.'

'Yes and I will be in trouble when I get home as well,' answered Brian.

'Why?'

'Well I have lost my job.'

'Brian...let's run away together.—And...' said Jenny

'And what?' answered Brian.

'Perhaps we could get married.' said Jenny. 'In Scotland.'

'Yes. That's a good idea, I'll meet you outside the cinema. Don't let your ma or pa see you...' said Brian.

Next day the couple had packed. They had about £150 with them. Brian had brought a cheap ring, and his old tattered scooter. Jenny had now started off from home to the cinema. She had left a note saying:

Dear Mum,

I've gone on a business trip. Sorry I did not tell you. Going to Scotland. Be back soon.

Jenny

xxxxxxx

She had arrived. Brian was waiting and his old scooter stood beside him. Jenny carried her suitcase up to him. She dropped them at her feet and kissed him.

'Oh, you have made it,' said Brian.

'Yes, I have,' said Jenny sadly.

They began to pack their cases on to the back of the scooter. Jenny sat on the back with Brian driving. The scooter's engine started up and then they roared away.

Later on they settled down in an old barn. They sat on some straw and talked.

'Are you happy darling?' asked Brian.

'Ye..s,' answered Jenny.

That night they talked about their plans.

Next morning they were up and they were off early, anxious to get to Gretna Green. By dinner time they were very exhausted and they stopped at a dirty grubby cafe which stood near a station.

Meanwhile Mrs Dale was worried. Her hubby had popped along where Jenny had once worked and he had asked the manager if he knew where Jenny had disappeared to. Jenny's boss had been no help to Mr Dale. But when he got home he had a very bright idea. He raced home to his wife who, when she saw him, burst into tears.

'It's no good—her boss couldn't help us,' said Mr Dale.

'But cheer up. We're going on a little trip to that young rascal Brian Hill's house.'

'Why?'

'Wait and see,' Mr Dale replied.

They got on the bus and soon were on their way to house number 108. They arrived at the house and all seemed rather quiet. It was only a damp cottage and all was to be heard was the television. Mr Dale knocked at the door and somebody came to the door—a tall dark haired man with a little moustache.

'Yes' said Mr Hill. 'Oh! it's you is it?'

'Yes, I've come to see if you can help with finding my daughter'

Exercise 75

'I'm afraid I can't help you,' said Mr Hill.

And he was just about to slam the door, when Mr Dale put out his hand and kept the door open and his voice spluttered out,

'And where is your disgraceful son, that...'

'Oh never mind,' said Mr Dale.

'Why are you picking on my son? he hasn't done anything with your daughter. He has gone to Scotland on a business trip.'

'I bet he hasn't! My daughter wrote the same thing,' replied Mr Dale.

They stood on the doorstep for a quarter of an hour: then suddenly Mr Hill invited them in to have a chat over a cup of tea.

It was over an hour before Mr and Mrs Dale went. They thanked Mr and Mrs Hill for the cup of tea and Mr Dale said to Mr Hill, 'Well be round straight tomorrow morning.'

The next morning Mr Dale was up very early. Mr Hill woke up and got ready, and went round to Mr Dale and he found him all ready with his suitcase in one hand. Mr Dale went over to his wife and kissed her. They heard the sound of the taxi as the brakes screeched.

'Goodbye! I'll be back soon' said Mr Dale.

'Goodbye find them both,' replied Mrs Dale, weeping.

The two men went out of the door, stepped into the taxi and drove off.

Meanwhile Brian and Jenny had bought their marriage licence and in 21 days from now they would be newly wed. Jenny had managed to buy herself a new costume for the wedding and Brian Had brought a second-hand suit from the £75 left. It was getting on for lunch time and Brian and Jenny had found a little hotel and had been staying there for nearly a week. And both still wished to be married.

But now, travelling on the train to Scotland were Mr Dale and Mr Hill They had become very good mates towards each other and both agreed— let the couple come home to get married, because both sets of parents had married at Gretna Green and wished they had had it in a really nice church. The night passed by. A week passed and the two parents had been looking in all the hotels near Gretna Green. Only four days were left. They came to the right hotel. Mr Dale knocked on the door and an old man came to the door. He had not shaved and his hair was grey and white with age. 'Good evening. Do you want a room?' asked the man. 'Yes please.' replied Mr Hill.

The old man showed them in and took them next door to number 2 which was Jenny's. Number 4 was Brian's, and number 3 was the two men's. They closed the door and sat down on the beds. Later Mr Dale went down to have a bath and all of a sudden Jenny came out of Brian's room. She gave a frightful gasp and ran into her room. Mr Dale was so excited that he ran back again to tell Mr Hill. Then he went to have his bath.

This happened two days later. Then the parents got to know how the two young people kept on going into each other's rooms at 9 o'clock. So one day at nine o'clock Brian was late. And Mr Dale went in instead. (Jenny did not know he was coming in).

'Oh Dad, go away, go away,' pleaded Jenny

'What! I have come all this way to bring you back.'

'But you didn't put anything in the paper. I thought you didn't care,' said Jenny.

'We do.' said Mr Dale.

'Don't we?' Mr Hill had just walked in.

What's the matter with you both,' asked Jenny, 'I thought you were both enemies'.

'We are not any more, are we Mr Hill?' said Mr Dale.

'No!'

Then Brian came in.

'Dad! Jenny! What's all this about?'

He rushed to Jenny's bed.

'Well, they want to take us away.' said Jenny.

'They can't!' replied Brian.

'Listen son,' said Mr Hill. 'You come home and get married in the church. We will give you anything.'

'Are you tricking us?' asked Brian.

'Think it over,' replied Mr Dale.

Just then the old man came up carrying the breakfast tray when the two men left the room. Next morning Jenny and Brian were waiting for their fathers to come.

They came in two minutes later.

'You tell them Jenny,'

'We have decided to stop here, and get married,' said Jenny.

'Jenny,' said Mr Dale, 'You...'

'We don't trust you,' answered Jenny.

The two fathers went off rather shaken with dismay. But next day they had got up and they were listening to the eight o'clock news, when suddenly Mr Dale gulped.

'Oh! Goodness!'

This is the message that was read out:

> Will Mr J. Dale somewhere in Scotland, please come home immediately to Sussex General Hospital where his wife Mrs S. Dale is dangerously ill. Attempted suicide is suspected.

Not five minutes later Mr Dale trembling left. He got a taxi. Mr Hill stopped to break the news to the young couple next door.

Meanwhile the couple were packing. Tomorrow they would be married!

And afterwards they would go home and find a hotel as they knew their parents wouldn't forgive them.

At Sussex General Hospital Mr Dale was sitting at the bedside, with his head bowed down. Not much hope was left.

In Scotland Mr Hill was just going to break the news to Jenny and Brian. He knocked at the door and before they could answer he went in.

'Get out, Dad' said Brian.

'Where's my Dad?' asked Jenny.

'He has gone to Sussex General Hospital. Your mother has been trying to commit suicide,' replied Mr Hill.

'No!' said Jenny and went pale, 'I must go.'

'I thought you would' said Mr Hill.

At the hospital Mrs Dale was feeling better and was able to talk.

'If only Jenny would come back I know I would get better,' said Mrs Dale slowly.

'She will come.'

Two hours later Jenny had arrived and just before she came, Mrs Hill had arrived.

'I'm sorry Mr Dale. I didn't know he was like that,' said Mrs Hill.

'If only Jenny was here,' said Mrs Dale, who had heard them talking.

Jenny had arrived. She stopped outside the ward and peeped through the glass in the window.

'I daren't. I must,' she murmured to herself.

She boldly pushed open the door and ran to her Mother's bed.

'Mum' she said.

'You have come,' replied Mrs Dale. 'If I don't live until you get married, I hope you will be as happy as I am with your Dad.'

'Mum, don't say that. I am not getting married till you are better. Brian and I are not ever going to get married.' said Jenny feeling satisfied with herself.

'Why?' said Mrs Dale.

'We are just good friends.' said Jenny. 'I am not marrying him'.

Three months later their friendship had still continued. But although Jenny liked Brian he got married to a very nice girl. And Mrs Dale recovered. Both parents were very upset about their teenage children. But it couldn't be helped as Jenny died very unhappy in a road accident, which brought more agony to Jenny's parents, and to Brian's parents as well who kept in very close touch with them.

THE END

(Averil Wright, aged 13)

EXERCISE 76

What is the symbolism of this story? To what short stories and chapters in novels would you send the author?

The Gang round the Corner

'Hello dear,' said Janet's mother, as Janet stepped in the door, just coming home from work.

'Hello mum' replied Janet flopping on the settee.

'John has just rung to say he can't make it tonight', said Mr Wilson.

'That's the second time this week,' replied Janet, throwing her coat on the table.

'Janet! Is that the way you treat your new clothes?' asked Mrs Wilson.

'I'm too tired. I'm glad John is not coming, so I can have a walk.'

You said you were looking forward to that dance tonight,' said Mrs Wilson.

'Well, its no good being happy now', said Janet.

'Well....' began Mrs Wilson.

'Oh, shut up Mum,' said Janet

'I'm going up to my bedroom', she said, picking up her coat and slinging it on her shoulder.

'Tea will be ready soon,' said Mrs Wilson.

Upstairs Janet had sorted out her old slacks and jumpers and her slip-on shoes. 'I'll show John. I bet he is dating another girl', said Janet to herself.

'Janet'

'Coming Mum', replied Janet.

After Janet had sat down and had her tea, she let down her long hair from a bun. It was a shiny black and looked so soft.

'Janet...'

But before Mrs Wilson could get an answer Janet had gone out.

Outside Janet went strolling along till she came to a gang of boys and three girls all wearing bright coloured sweaters and tight black jeans. One of the boys who was sitting on a motorbike underneath a street light came up to Janet.

'Hello there!' said the boy, whose name was Geoffrey. 'Have you come to join our gang?'

'I don't go about with Teddyboys,' replied Janet.

'You'll soon change your mind once you know me,' said Geoffrey. 'I'm good looking. Got a job. Haven't much money—but I'm still your type.'

'Don't rub it in Geff. She doesn't look interested,' piped up one the the girls.

'Come on baby! How about it? I'll take you for a spin on my motor bike.'

'Alright, I'll come', answered Janet. 'I'll do it for spite,' she said to herself.

'I told you, gang,—my charms work!'

'How long for?' answered one of the girls.

The next thing Janet knew she was rushed off to hospital with a broken arm and leg after being trapped under the motor bike for a quarter of a mile. After being carried to the hospital from the ambulance, Janet was made very comfortable. The next day Janet's mother came to see her.

'Where's John?' said Janet.

'Well! Do you suppose a bank manager would want to visit you after you go about with Beatniks?' said Mrs Wilson.

'You can tell him from me if he's scared to get his name in the paper... well, I don't want him as a husband.' snapped Janet.

'Have you see the paper?' asked Mrs Wilson.

'No, I don't want to, either,' said Janet.

Mrs Wilson took a daily newspaper from her basket and gave it to Janet. She read it—'Girl Mixed up with Beatniks'.

'But Mum—who gave this to the papers?' said Janet

'"The Gang Round The Corner", as they call themselves,' replied Mrs Wilson.

'Wait till I get out of this hospital!'

Janet had to stay in hospital for three months, which seemed a long time to her. But the time did pass quickly. She had many visitors. Some were her school chums, and some were old workmates and friends who had seen her name on the front page of the paper.

But there was no John!

The day came when Janet was to come home. Her leg and arm had completely healed. But there was no John to see her off.

Instead, she went home on the 'bus with her mother. When she was sitting on the 'bus with her Mother, Janet piped up—

'Mum, where is John? I want to say Sorry to him for being so horrible.'

'He has gone away to think things over,' replied Mrs. Wilson.

'When is he coming back?'

'I don't know,' replied her Mother.

Three days later Janet had started work again. She heard John was coming home.

She flew home to tell her mother the good news.

'Mum! I know someone special is going to ring the doorbell at half past seven. So I will get ready for a party.'

'Don't count your chickens before they hatch,' answered her Mother, who was frying chips for her husband's tea.

'I know its going to happen,' said Janet.

Janet was so excited that she had no tea.

At half past seven Janet had her best dress on and her new shoes.

The doorbell rang—Janet ran to answer it. 'John Darling! said Janet with her arms outstretched.

'Geoffrey darling, not John!' said Geoffrey. He was not in his slacks and jumper, but in a grey suit and black polished shoes.

'You horrible brute,' said Janet, slapping him across the face.

'But I've come to see if you could come out to a dance. I'm sorry it is rather late to ask you. But you look ready for a dance' said Geoffrey.

'I'll never go with you again,' replied Janet.

'Who is it dear?' said Mrs Wilson.

'Oh, this is Geoffrey', replied Janet

'Oh do come in—I am pleased to meet you,' said Mrs Wilson.

Geoffrey and Janet sat on the sofa and said nothing until the doorbell rang again. Janet rushed at the door and opened it. There stood John. He looked about forty. He had an old blue suit on. He looked pale and Ill. Janet bent to kiss him.

'No don't kiss me. I'm sorry I could not come to see you in hospital. But I have got to have a good talk to you', said John.

'What about?' said Janet.

Now John and Janet settled down on the settee. Geoffrey had disappeared into the kitchen.

'Janet...I've got to break off our engagement,' said John.

'Why?' asked Janet.

'Well, my wife won't give me a divorce.'

'Your wife! You never told me you had a wife.'

'That's why I could not get to see you. You see...it would have got in the paper,' said John.

'Oh, I see,' said Janet.

John got up and left the room. He said goodbye to Mrs Wilson.

'I'm sorry I've been such a nuisance. But she will find a boy friend...'

Janet was left and she sat and cried on the settee.

Geoffrey came in.

'I will be going now,' said Geoffrey, 'Goodbye!'

'Geoffrey...don't go please.'

Three months have passed. Janet is getting married on Saturday, to Geoffrey. John is best man, and his wife is a guest at the wedding.

(Averil Wright, aged 13)

EXERCISE 77

What qualities in a passage such as the following would you commend to Averil's attention?

He sat a long time with his eyes fixed unchanging upon the open gateway, where a little light seemed to fall from the stars or from the horizon, who knows. He was sitting on a log in a dark corner with the gun across his knees. The pine-trees snapped. Once a chicken fell off its perch in the barn with a loud crawk and a cackle and commotion that startled him, and he stood up, watching with all his eyes, thinking it might be a rat. But he felt it was nothing. So he sat down again with the gun on his knees and his hands tucked in to keep them warm, and his eyes fixed unblinking on the pale reach of the open gateway. He felt he could smell the hot, sickly, rich smell of live chickens on the cold air.

And then—a shadow. A sliding shadow in the gateway. He gathered all his vision into a concentrated spark, and saw the shadow of a fox, the fox creeping on his belly through the gate. There he went, on his belly like a snake. The boy smiled to himself and brought the gun to his shoulder. He knew quite well what would happen. He knew the fox would go to where the fowl-door was boarded up, and sniff there. He knew he would lie there for a minute, sniffing the fowls within. And then he would start again prowling under the edge of the old barn, waiting to get in.

The fowl-door was at the top of a slight incline. Soft, soft as a shadow the fox slid up this incline, and crouched with his nose to the boards. And at the same moment there was the awful crash of a gun reverberating between the old buildings, as if all the night had gone smash. But the boy watched keenly. He saw even the white belly of the fox as the beast beat his paws in death. So he went forward.

There was a commotion everywhere. The fowls were scuffling and crawking, the ducks were quark-quarking, the pony had stamped wildly to his feet. But the fox was on his side, struggling in his last tremors. The boy bent over him and smelt his foxy smell.

There was a sound of a window opening upstairs, then March's voice calling:

'Who is it?'

'It's me,' said Henry; 'I've shot the fox.'

'Oh, goodness! You nearly frightened us to death.'

'Did I? I'm awfully sorry.'

'Whatever made you get up?'

'I heard him about.'

'And have you shot him?'

'Yes, he's here,' and the boy stood in the yard holding up the warm dead brute. 'You can't see, can you? Wait a minute.' And he took his flashlight from his pocket, and flashed it on to the dead animal. He was holding it by the brush. March saw, in the middle of the darkness, just the reddish fleece and the white belly and the white underneath of the pointed chin, and the queer, dangling paws. She did not know what to say.

'He's a beauty,' he said. 'He will make you a lovely fur.'

'You don't catch me wearing a fox fur,' she replied.

(D. H. Lawrence, *The Fox*)

8 *Drama and Discussion Work*

The only way to learn how to promote good and imaginative oral work is by live practice. However, discussions need starting points and end up by written exercises; and dramatic work requires synopses, draft dialogue—and can end up as a written play. Here are some examples at secondary modern school level, for discussion of some of the problems that arise.

EXERCISE 78

Here are some comments by children in a class discussion on marriage and the Marriage Service:

'Some men go out with so many other girls they even forget their wife's anniversary.'

'Yes, and some women go out with other men'.

'My cousin...she left 'er 'usband about four weeks ago.'

'Ah, but she've come back.'

'Let me tell it. She's my cousin.'

'Yeah, but I live next door so I know what goes on. She still keeps going with this other bloke, though 'er 'usband kicked 'er out. She ha' got four children.'

'She's havin' another one, mate!'

'Yet she seizes every opportunity to go out with another man.'

'That don't mean because one woman go with another man that every woman does do it?'

'I've never heard my Dad say to my Mum, "Go and get a packet of fags from the pub. She'd say "take this!"'

Here are some of the things they wrote afterwards.

God made Adam first, and Eve after who was made as a companion to Adam...God made the rule as so it should be kept. (Girl, 2A)

Yes because the husband goes out to work and earns all the money, most wives do the washing on Monday and the man comes home to dinner she still hanging out the washing and there's no dinner waiting for him and he's got to fry himself some bacon and eggs for dinner and no man likes that and he gives her half of his wages and hardly ever gets a square meal once a week. On Tuesday most wives go to Cambridge to buy a new hat or a skirt while he comes home he finds a note saying back by 20-2 gone Cambridge buy new hat dinner in the oven custard under grill. They only do housework and they have all the afternoon off because they have finished by dinner time. (Boy, 2A)

I think that a wife should obey her husband because the men are supposed to be the bosses of the house and the women are always jabbering like old Gas Bags and talking over the fence to another old Gas Bag, always always talking, because he is always giving her money to buy clothes, and paint her face. Women should cut out the gaff and get on with some work.

(Boy, 2A)

Firstly iff a wife is willing to be a good wife she should be willing to do anything to help their marriage. Secondly I don't think she would have to obey him because he may say to her go and get the coal in, put the new sparking plugs in the car, or go and chop the wood. The wife would get into a mess with the coal, she'd probably chop her fingers off chopping wood, and more than likely ruin the car for life...Anyway the women usually obeys her husband in some things, because even when he says 'Go and make a cup of tea, dear,' unless he says please I still think its a command.

(Girl, 2A)

If she was to take orders from him he might say come and kiss me when the potatoes were boiling over...

I think men are rather bigheaded and think they can order there wife around if they like. Men don't realise whyle they are at work their wife is slaving away...

If a man wanted to have children he would look funny by himself...

It is not always the man that gets drunk the woman gets drunk as well...

(Girls, 2A)

Explain how you would take part in the discussion yourself and what you would say to them about marriage.

Give details of some sources in literature from which you would read them imaginative material about love and marriage.

EXERCISE 79

Discuss your approach next English period to this synopsis for a piece of 'spontaneous drama' with 4B. How do you make the free drama a genuine family situation?

SYNOPSIS 30/6/61

Michial + Diana are deeply in love, but, Diana's parents do not approve of Michial, On the other hand michials father does approve of Diana. Michial has no mother but he has a sister Susan who goes out with Roger (thats me). Jimmy the sex maniac attacks Diana's mum and michial arrives just in time to save her from injury (and embarrisment) This solves every thing of course and in due course they get married.

Characters

Boy. Michiel Titchmarch } sweethearts.
Girl Diana Noales }

Diana's mother. Joshephine Willmott
" father. David Lester.
Michiel's Father Brian Hardwick
" . Sister Susan Leonard } sweethearts
Roger Woodcock } more or less
Sesc Maniac Jimmy Blows
Scene 1 Diana + Michial snogging on the settee in the living room, Diana's parents come

EXERCISE 80

Here is some dialogue in the exercise book of a girl in the bottom stream of a secondary modern school. Is there anything worth praising here?

John dont worry I dont want to go there;
Jean all right good by,

and she slamed the door in his face

John wait at minet
but it was to late she had all read gone.
John now what am I going to do I she have to try and see her tomorrow, well no good hanging around here may as well go. home and think it over,
The next day.

John hello Jean cant we talk it ~~of~~ over and come to some disson
Jean Talk ~~about~~ about what for instead,

John Well make it up,
Jean I am sorry John. theres nothing to make up.
John What do you mean; There on one eles is there
Jean Well what if there is its got nothing to do with you;
John look I am only trining to be nice,
Jean Well, don't
John all right them I won't be nice, it looks like I got to be rought with you
Jean if you lay a hand on me I will sclem,
John do you think that escard me
Jean Well I wornd you didnt I.
John I don't ~~e~~ care what you esard you Just whant to ~~hat~~ hert me.
Jean no I don't you think you can hert me I Well you rong

John I don't want to think of it
Jean Well perhaps you Better not see me eney more
John dont be silly I want to see you to night
Jean I dont no about that
John I see you at 8. o,clock.
Jean Well all right then
John your a doll.
Jean. I dont no about that
John Well I do
Jean goodby see you to night
it come round 8 oclock.
Jean Iam terribly nerveas
Mum you will get of it.
Jean goodby mum.
Mum goodby my dear
John hello Jean like a drink
Jean yes please
John good what will you have
Jean I have a coco

EXERCISE 81

Evaluate the success of this project in the composition of drama. It was the work of form 4C in a mixed secondary modern school.

THE WAY TO GO HOME

A Radio Play

SCENE I. *In the coffee bar*

Noises off: Coffee cups being rattled, people ordering cups of coffee and Horlicks, motor-bike engine and traffic outside. Door opens.

RAYMOND. Hello, Jonny.

JONNY. Uh!

RAYMOND. Oh, he's moody today.

JONNY. Where's Penny?

MERVYN. She's up the corner, sulking.

BILLY. Two cups of coffee, please.

DIANE. One and six, please.

(*Noise of coffee machine*)

JONNY. Why did you run away?

PENNY. I wanted to; my father always picks on me.

JONNY. Why does he pick on you?

PENNY. I sometimes have a day off work and he moans.

JONNY. It's no good having days off work.

PENNY. I'm leaving home anyway. I'm getting lodgings.

JONNY. You aren't—not while I'm here, you aren't.

PENNY. I am.

JONNY. We'll talk about it over a cup of coffee...Two coffees.

DIANE. One and six please.

JONNY. Have you got any sugar over there, mate?

PENNY. Thank you.

JONNY. What's the good of leaving home anyway?

PENNY. At least I'll get away from my father, and I have got the money.

JONNY. What happened, then?

PENNY. I had two or three days off work last week, and my money wasn't very good and I couldn't give my mother much. My mother didn't mind but my dad did.

JONNY. Why did you run away from home, then?

PENNY. I got in a temper and I went upstairs and I went in my father's drawer. There was five pounds in there I thought 'Should I take it or shouldn't I?' I just lost my senses and I took it.

JONNY. Have you spent it?
PENNY. No, I've still got it here.
JONNY. I think the best thing to do is to take it back and explain to your father.
PENNY. No! I'm not going back to him.
JONNY. Well, you'll have to, Penny.
PENNY. No, you take the money back; I'm still leaving home.
JONNY. No, I can't do that. You'll have to tell him about it yourself.
PENNY. I'm not going back.
JONNY. Well, it's no good of me taking it back.
PENNY. Why should I take it back? He'll only pick on me again.
JONNY. Why? I think you should take it back and tell him how sorry you are.
PENNY. All right. I'll take it back, but not just yet.
JONNY. He won't pick on you. He'll think well of you for taking it back.
PENNY. I'll wait a couple of days before I go back.
JONNY. Well, you'll have to come round my house to sleep.
PENNY. No, I'll go round Margaret's. She said I could go round there.
JONNY. Are you sure? I could easily put up a bed for you.
PENNY. No, I'd better go round Margaret's.
JONNY. Are you sure you'll be all right?
PENNY. Yeah.
JONNY. Don't do anything foolish. I'd better be going or I'll miss my train for work. I shall see you, then.
PENNY. Cheerio. See you here tomorrow then.

SCENE 2. *In the factory*

Noises of clocking-in bell, hum of machinery and talk of girls coming to work.

JANET G. It's going to be another dreary week.
SHEILA. Oh, Monday! I hate it.
DOREEN. Hello, has anyone seen Penny?
PAULINE. Who wants to see her?
JANET G. Don't be horrible.
JANET H. She wasn't at the dance at the Royal last night.
JANET G. You get on my wick, Pauline.
SHEILA. You're always picking girl. You can always find some fault in somebody, can't you.
DOREEN. You always blame something on someone.
PAULINE. What about you, then? I know something about you, too. I know all about you and that boy from down Notley Road—*and* the other one that you were going out with at the same time.
SHEILA. I know something about your friends too, Pauline.

PAULINE. You shut up. You're only jealous because the boys don't go out with you...you're too much of a flirt.
JOHN. You're always saying rotten things about Penny.
ALL GIRLS. You shut up, Sambo. (*giggles*) We saw you out with her last night.
JOHN. Ha! Ha! Very funny! I was out with Pauline last night.
BRIAN. Stop nattering! You're not paid for nothing ... What are you talking about anyhow?
ALL GIRLS. You shut up and mind your own business. Anyhow, you don't do all that much work yourself.

(GIRLS *begin to move off*)

DOREEN. Well, wherever she is, I hope she's all right.

SCENE 3. *Penny's home.*

Sound effects: car-door opening and slamming, footsteps and sound of radio inside house.

LARRY. Mum, here comes a police car. Mum, I wonder if it's about Penny.
MUM (MARGARET). (*in a panic*) I hope she's all right. Go and open the door, Larry.
LARRY. Can't! I'm in the bath.
MUM. Go and answer the door, Fred.
FRED. I'm reading the paper. You go and answer it, love.

(*Knocking on door*)

Oh, I suppose I'll have to go.
POLICEMAN Mrs. Smith?
MUM. Yes...Has anything happened to our Penny?
POLICEMAN. Well, apart from what we've heard from this boy here, we've got no further information.
MUM. Please come in. You know what the neighbours are like...and mind your head on the door.

(*Knocking on door*)

MUM. Please excuse me.
POLICEMAN. Certainly.
SHEILA. Please could you lend me a quarter of tea?
(*neighbour*)
MUM. Not now, please, because I am very busy.
SHEILA. Please...my husband is home asking for his tea.
MUM. Come in then.

(MUM *walks out of room to kitchen*)

SHEILA. Who are you? Got any news about Penny?

FRED. Hurry up with that quarter of tea, Mum. She's got to hurry back to her husband.

SHEILA. Oh, it doesn't matter. Take your time. Well...where is Penny?

FRED. Look, we'll tell you about Penny to-morrow, if you really want to know.

MUM. Here's the tea, Sheila.

SHEILA. Oh, thank you. I'll see you to-morrow about Penny.

(*Door closes*)

FRED. Thank God that nosey parker's gone.

POLICEMAN. This lad says he has seen Penny at the CRESTA coffee bar. He saw her there last Saturday.

ROY. With some mods down there. I saw her with one boy I knew and so I spoke to him...I saw her then all right, but I don't know where she is now.

MARGARET. I wish I knew where she is.

ROY. I'm sorry, I'm afraid I can't tell you any more.

MARGARET. So that's all you can tell us. Is there anything else we can do?

POLICEMAN. Well, we could ask her pals about her and see if they know anything about her. But apart from that boy's statement, we haven't had any information about her.

ROY. Well, I'll certainly ask my pals tonight about her.

FRED. Would you inform us as soon as you find out anything?

ROY. All right. I'll see what I can do for you.

POLICEMAN. Thank you, Roy, for all your help so far. Come and see me tomorrow and tell me what you find out between now and tomorrow night.

ROY. What time shall I come round? I don't leave work till six o'clock.

POLICEMAN. Make it about half an hour after you leave work, then.

ROY. All right. I'll go round the cafe to see my friends about her. Goodbye, Mrs. Durrant. I'll be going now.

MARGARET. Oh, Fred...(*sobs*)...I bet it's gone all round the streets by now.

FRED. Don't you take any notice of the neighbours. They're all a lot of old cows...They get on my nerves...

(*Fade out.* NEIGHBOURS' *voices fade in*)

SCENE 4. *Neighbours gossiping*

JENNIFER. The police car has gone now...and there goes one of them there rockers...I reckon he had got something to do with it...

ROSAMUND. I wonder what has happened to Penny, though. I reckon she has eloped with that boy Jonny...I never did like him very much.

JENNIFER. Nor did I. He looks the sort, you know.

ROSAMUND. Oh...yes...yes...I know what you mean. I wonder if she's...

JENNIFER. I bet you she is.

ROSAMUND. Mm... It's a thought, isn't it?

RAYMOND (*husband*). Are you still nattering? I come home at six and expect some nice tea and all you can do is natter, natter, natter.

JENNIFER. Shut up, you... This is much more important.

SCENE 5. PENNY *writes to her parents*

PENNY.

Dear Mum and Dad,

I'm very sorry about the trouble I have caused but I just can't come back home yet. Don't try to find me as I am staying with one of my friends and I am in good hands.

Please tell Dad that I am very sorry about the money I took from his drawer but I promise to pay it back as soon as possible.

I wish I had not argued with Dad, but I could not stand it any longer. I've tried to come back, but I just can't face it. When I come in ten minutes late at night, he always gets on to me. I am sixteen now and I can look after myself and think for myself.

So please Mum and Dad, for my sake only, don't bother about me.

Your daughter,
Penny

SCENE 6. JONNY *writes to Penny*

Dear Penny,

I am writing this letter to try to make you see reason. You know you love your Mum and Dad, so why not make it up with them now. It will only make it worse if you keep away from them. I hope you still have the five-pound note that you took from your Dad.

If you have not got it, come to the same cafe where we last met and I will lend you the money. I know it will be hard to take it back, but will you take it back for my sake?

Anyway, meet me at the cafe tomorrow night at seven and we will talk things over.

I'll be going to London soon because I have been offered a good job there. I hope you are pleased. See you at seven tomorrow.

Love,
Jonny

SCENE 7. *In the coffee bar*

(*Noise of cars, motor-cycles outside.* GIRLS *enter. Wolf-whistle from* BOYS.

BOYS. Hello girls.

BRIAN H.: Shut the door, girls; there's a draught.

DOREEN. Shut it yourself!

BRIAN H.: Don't be stubborn, dear.

JOHN. Who's for a cup of coffee, you lot?
SHEILA. All right, if it's coming out of your pocket.
JOHN. Right... Six cups of coffee, please, Diane.

(*Noise of coffee machine*)

DIANA. Three shillings, please.
JOHN. Here y'are, then.
DIANE. Thank you.
JOHN. Here's your coffee.
ALL GIRLS Thank you... Ta... Thanks.
ROY. Where's your boy-friend?
JENNIFER. Pardon?
ROY. You know, that one we saw you in the back stalls with?
JENNIFER. You come any more of that and I'll slap your face.
ROY. Come on, then.
JENNIFER. If you weren't so big, I would.
SHEILA. Look. There's Penny sitting over there by herself.
DOREEN. I wonder what's up?
SHEILA. Why hasn't she been to work, I wonder.
JENNIFER. It's not all of us who can afford to stop off work.
DOREEN. I reckon she's not well.
SHEILA. She looks all right to me.
DOREEN. I think I'll go over and talk to her.
JENNIFER. See if you can find out anything.

(*Door opens*)

MERVYN. Cor! Who's opened that door again. Oh, it's Jonny.
ALL. Hello, Jonny... Hi, Jonny.
JONNY. Have you seen Penny?
JENNIFER. She is over there.
JONNY. Thank you. Hello then. Do you want a cup of coffee?
PENNY. Yes, please.
JONNY. Two coffees, please, Diane.

(*Sound of coffee machine*)

DIANE. One shilling please.
JONNY. Thank you. (*To* PENNY) The police are out after you.
PENNY. Yes I know.
JONNY. Your mother told me that the police are looking for you. I went to see her last night.
PENNY. You haven't been round, have you?
JONNY. Your parents are worried about you.
PENNY. Jonny, I have got something important to tell you.

JONNY. What is it, then?

PENNY I can't tell you...(*sobs*)...Oh, dear... I don't know how to put it to you.

JONNY. Come on, Penny. You know you can tell me...Come on, get it over with.

PENNY. Oh...Jonny...I'm pregnant.

JONNY. What?...Why didn't you tell me before?

PENNY. I couldn't.

JONNY. Why not?

PENNY. I didn't know myself until yesterday when I went to see the doctor.

JONNY. Good Lord!...What've we let ourselves in for?

PENNY. Don't blame yourself Jonny. It's just as much my fault as yours.

JONNY. We'll have to tell your parents.

PENNY. I can't. No! They'd kill me.

JONNY. They're the ones who'll stand by you.

PENNY. But I just can't tell them.

JONNY. I'll keep with you all of the time, and I'll come round with you.

PENNY. No.

JONNY. Come on, now; don't be silly.

PENNY. You stay with me then.

JONNY. Of course I'll stay with you. You know I'll stay with you.

PENNY. You will stay with me, won't you?

JONNY. Of course I will.

DIANE. Look (*whispers*) there goes Penny and Jonny. She's crying...I wonder why.

(*Door opens. Sound of cars, etc.*)

SCENE 8. *At* PENNY'S *house*

T.V. ANNOUNCER. ...was sprawling in a plain deal chair, which was tilted back against the wall at a dangerous angle. His arms dangled limply, his legs were spread out, and his magnificent moustache, orange and white with nicotine and age, lifted and trembled with his snores...

DAD (FRED). Oh turn that thing off. I'm trying to concentrate on my pools.

ANNOUNCER. ...like some strange seaweed that is raised and lowered by a...

LARRY. Mum, do you know where my clean shirt is?

MUM. Upstairs in the airing cupboard.

DAD. Oh, my pencil's broken. Now I can't get on with my pools.

MUM. Well, sharpen it then. You won't get nowhere sitting there.

(*Knock at the door*)

MUM. There's someone at the door.

DAD. You go.

MUM. Oh God! I think I do everything in this house.

LARRY. My shirt's not here.

MUM. Oh, be quiet boy. I can't do two things at once. There's somebody at the door. (*Door opens*) Penny! It's Penny! Oh, Penny, where have you been? Come in, my dear. Father, look! It's Penny.

DAD. So you've finally decided to come home, then?

MUM. Have you been looking after yourself? Oh, Penny, have you been having your proper meals?

PENNY. Don't fuss, please Mum.

MUM. Oh, you know we've been worried sick about you.

DAD. I suppose she's been eating and drinking nothing but coffee and sandwiches all this time.

MUM. Oh, be quiet! Aren't you glad to see your own daughter.

LARRY. I ain't.

MUM. You be quiet, Larry, and leave this room at once.

DAD. You look pale, Penny. What's wrong?

PENNY. Are you going to tell them, Jonny, or shall I?

JONNY. Well, I think it's your place to tell them. They're your parents.

DAD. What have you got to say?...Come on, out with it.

MUM. Penny, what's wrong?

PENNY. I'm pregnant, Mum.

DAD. You're what?

MUM. Oh, God! Oh, Penny, don't you know what you've done?

DAD. I suppose it was your fault, you...you...

MUM. Be quiet, can't you? Can't you see...Oh, what's happened? Look at the situation you're in now.

DAD. Never did like the look of him I didn't.

MUM. Oh, Penny! What have you done? I thought you were my nice little girl. Look what you've done, to repay us for everything.

DAD. All you do is go around with girls and never leave them alone.

PENNY. No one is thinking of me.

MUM. Oh, this is some carry-on, I must say. You don't even know what to do next.

JONNY. What I do is no concern of yours.

MUM. Isn't it, my boy?

DAD. Yes, you want to marry her don't you?

JONNY. I daresay I do.

DAD. Well, for a start, you're not marrying my daughter.

PENNY. What's going to happen if he doesn't marry me?

DAD. I won't have you taking *his* name.

JONNY. Oh no? You think of the name you'll get! When you go to work it'll be slung at you...but—er—you don't go to work, do you?

Exercise 81

MUM. Who put our name in the black book and who blackened our front door?

PENNY. Don't blame him for everything.

JONNY. Nobody is going to blacken your paths because you've never made any paths. *You've* never made anything. All you ever do is sit in that chair with square eyes watching that television set.

DAD. What if I do?

JONNY. And you're never doing nothing but supping tea out of the pot. All you seem to do is watch television and sup tea, night after night.

MUM. Jonny! Do you mind!...Look, let's think this out. Here you are acting like two little children...I can't understand you...I can't understand anything any more...my poor little daughter...(*cries*)...Oh, Penny...

JONNY. Excuse me. I'll leave the room.

DAD. (*coarsely*) It's round the back.

MUM. What's going to happen to us? Since you are being so bright with Jonny, I'm sure you can bring up some bright ideas about Penny.

PENNY. Let him marry me, please, Dad...please.

MUM. She wants to know whether you are going to marry her.

JONNY. Well, of course I will. I'll work all the overtime I can get and we'll have a good home, Penny and me will.

DAD. That's what you say.

JONNY. Yes, I *do* say. And I'll say something else too—*You* won't even try to work part time, let alone over-time.

DAD. Well, the jobs just aren't there for people of my age.

JONNY. How old do you think you are? Ninety?

MUM. Look! Will you stop dragging each other down?

DAD. Well, that's nice of you. Very nice.

JONNY. I've got no care for you at all. I've got to think of the future and Penny and me and Penny's baby, so I can't sit here and argue with you all night.

DAD. Well, I don't want him to marry my daughter.

JONNY. Have you ever thought back to the old times when you got married?

DAD. What do you mean?

JONNY. What I mean is have you ever thought about when your Larry was born?

MUM. You didn't have to bring that up. You didn't have to throw that in his face.

JONNY. Oh no? He's got to face it the same as I have.

(*Silence*)

MUM. Yes, we've got to face it.

DAD. I'd rather have the baby put in a home.

MUM. No! We can't allow that. We just can't do that to a little baby. It would be on my mind. Oh, Father you'll have to let them marry.

DAD. But he's got no money! He can't support a family, can he?

MUM. Did you have any money when you married me? We lived in a dreary old flat, just looking at each other and not knowing what to do.

DAD. That's right, we did. And we haven't got any money now. We can't provide them with anything, can we?

MUM. We've got a home haven't we? And we've got a spare room, haven't we?

JONNY. I'll start doing overtime again and I'll get myself a house.

PENNY. We'll manage, Dad.

DAD. We'll have to think about you moving in, won't we?

MUM. Yes. Well, they can use the spare room, can't they?

JONNY. It's good of you.

MUM. Oh, things will work out.

JONNY. Of course they will.

PENNY. Yes, they will.

JONNY. Well, we can't sit here with long faces all night, can we?

DAD. No, we can't. How about a cup of tea, Mother?

JONNY. Tea? Tea? All we're going to think about now is tea. (*Laughs and laughs and laughs.*)

Notes

EXERCISE 1

D represents an adequate response to the request to associate freely about 'apples'. The child begins to break the bounds of cliché at once ('dotted apples') and to think of new words for freshly observed aspects of objects. So the emotional aura of 'apple' is explored—'You can have rotten apples...' meaning 'I must consider the nasty side of experience symbolically'. Then 'throwing apples' is associated with 'orchards places of delight' (a lovely phrase!), while the 'bad' side of the apple as symbol is also kept in view ('Apples evil?...Apple shrivelled up...Bare apple trees'). So the child is moving out towards the patterns of natural life, as associated with human feelings and moods: he is linking the subjective and objective.

E takes up the invitation in a different way—more extrovert, and more concerned to give an account of an actual experience. She conveys the tactile, aural and visual excitements: 'we twist them gently', 'the wasps often sing to us', 'not many usually missed our eyes'. She would understand Keats's *Ode to Autumn*.

C is rather more conventional, following a more stereotyped pattern of progress through the seasons—and it breaks down at the end when inspiration runs out. Yet there are some exciting phrases: 'the air smells of maturing fruit', 'small green and hard but still an apple', 'And many a mouth tries an apple to see if it is time'. Significantly, these exciting lines are ending lines: the child indulges in a conventional 'picture of the season', and then, by building up a realisation, moves beyond the conventional and gives something fresh. (Obviously therefore it is most important not to object to her conventionality—it is not conventionality to her, but fresh—and out of it she makes something fresher.) The last verse is lame, but she has perhaps exhausted herself: the solution for the teacher is to praise the exceptional lines such as those quoted above.

In **A** and **B** the simple processes of humanisation, of symbolic identification can be seen. The apple becomes a symbol of the identity, and of human life in time: for it can seem whole, beautiful and sound (young and good) or rotten from within (old or bad) and liable to disappear, as the dead do.

Here the underlying symbolism is very complex. Perhaps the apple is a symbol of the first 'object' of our relationship, which is the mother's breast. The 'apple of our eye' always has an aspect of being 'forbidden fruit'—because we have once feared, in our earliest infant rages, that we shall eat the breast all up, and so consume the mother-object, and with her, ourselves. Thus the desire for an apple always contains a modicum of guilt:

as a symbol the apple is very complex, and focuses many dealings with one's inner world.

So, stolen apples are like gratuitous invasions of the mother's fecund body (see the boy on scrumping above, pp. 91 ff.). The joy of apples is always accompanied by the threat of wasps ('Apples evil?'), or rotten apples: the story of Man's first disobedience symbolises these fears of the consequences of 'eating the object'. With children, too, sex is confused with eating, and the history of thought shows how men have always found investigation, the thirst for knowledge, and the acquiring of sexual knowledge, to be dangerous and forbidden. The Fall of Adam is thus linked, unconsciously and mythologically, to the Fall of Icarus.

To children, thus, the word 'bad' has a complex ambiguity. A 'bad' apple wrinkles, rots and turns to dust: could this happen (their phantasy-logic asks) to a 'bad' child? Old people wrinkle and die anyway: is this because they are bad? Is joy, like eating apples, bad—so that it always brings the threat of being bruised, caught, beaten, stung by wasps—and, eventually, going rotten?

So, in their simple way, these pieces of 'free writing' begin to touch on deep themes. 'No-one has touched it, they've been told not to': here is the prohibition of Eden. Yet (childish logic suggests) what does it matter if one seizes joy or not? In the end everything goes rotten. Young apples are 'the best you can buy': bad apples are 'best thrown away'.

The possibilities for 'follow-up' are rich: Keats is an obvious indication. There is much in Clare of a relish for natural richness. Why not lines from *Paradise Lost*, Book IV, e.g. 216 ('Out of the fertil ground...) to 246 ('noon-tide Bowrs'); 256 ('Flours of all hue'...) to 268 (th 'Eternal Spring'); and the sensuous description of Eve, 304 ('She as a vail') to 311 ('sweet reluctant amorous delay'). Or Wordsworth *The Prelude*, Book I, 288,

> Oh! Many a time have I, a five years child...

Or Marvell's *Garden*,

> What wondrous life is this I lead!
> Ripe apples drop about my head...

There are also some good passages on the satisfactions of working with crops and fruit in Adrian Bell's novels *Corduroy*, *Folly Field* and *The Budding Morrow* (e.g. *The Budding Morrow*, pp. 56–7, 'A Gift of Apples'). See also passages in *The Open Air*, Bell's anthology (such as 15, pp. 40 ff., on mowing and drinking cider).

On the way natural things can evoke intense unconscious feelings see Edward Thomas's *Old Man or Lad's Love*; also the last thirteen lines of Coleridge's *Frost at Midnight*.

Look up apples in *The Lore and Language of Schoolchildren*.

EXERCISE 2

A simply doesn't get involved: this is what failure looks like in a creative exercise! Of course, there's nothing to say to the child: she is just jingling, and getting the job done, without involvement (though 'betrayed one's sight' shows she *could* have tried). Appropriate unspoken comment: 'And can I have my piece of cake now please Aunty?' It sounds like a breathless recitation, gabbled to please teacher.

B has tried (as the touching remark at the end conveys). The first verse is the best: she is prepared to explore some of the frightening aspects of fire ('a weeping thing'). She also links it symbolically with infant fears, and the disturbing ubiquity of destructiveness ('he was everywhere').

But **C**, from the same lesson, is comparatively a stupendous achievement. Its prose should be recognised at once as Biblical, with a Biblical kind of symbolism, and antiphonal rhythm (see Exercise 3). See my discussion in *The Exploring Word*, pp. 162 ff. This prose poem is not merely about fire—'out there'. From the beginning it is about aspects of human nature symbolised by fire, which is humanised ('*he* is reckless and ruthless'). The antiphonal rhythm (as with that of the Book of Job) springs from the child's intuitive awareness of the ambivalence of experience itself of the conflict between love and hate ('naked tongues of flame reaching high into the sky as if searching for food'; 'he is a giver of heat but he doesn't want you to take it'), and of those manifestations in the outside world of parallel destructiveness within. The antiphonal rhythm goes with these antithetical concepts. As we tame fire in the outside world, he asks, can I tame the fire in myself? Fire seems to enjoy destruction: that's the problem; he purrs, destroying. My problem is that I take joy in hate: how can I resolve this? His magnificent prose poem is an attempt at resolution, and its beauty is wrung from the fear that the fire within threatens his identity.

D is by a spastic child who seems equally to fear that the fire within, of aggressiveness and hate ('ragingly') threatens his identity: or, to put it another way, he perhaps feels that the badness of hate in him has somehow caused his condition ('uncontrollable'), so that he is guilty about being spastic. The threat of annihilation seems worse than death ('I fear not death alone').

I find both these poems deeply moving, and the best examples I know of children unknowingly speaking in symbolic terms of the most profound human fears. In so far as they made something beautiful of their fears they are helping themselves to come to terms with them. All a teacher has to do is 'receive' and applaud.

Follow up: there are some marvellous descriptions of a fire at sea in Joseph Conrad's *Youth.*

EXERCISE 3

The Book of Job is a poetic drama, and its essential theme is the acceptance of the nature of the world, and man's situation in it. So, the full nature of reality must be accepted, and man's inability to wish it away. In accepting the nature of things he is accepting his own weakness, but coming too at a new strength of inner resources: a matching of the subjective and objective worlds.

The rhythm of Job enacts this: the metaphors are felt in the senses, so that each discomforting truth is experienced, in terms of 'felt life'. Yet the terrible aspects of creation, the sealed scales, the joined flakes, the millstone heart of the natural creature which is indifferent to man (i.e. belongs to a different biological system) are beautiful, and fill one with awe. In the awe and beauty are the germs of that acceptance which goes with an acceptance of one's place in the scheme of things (cf. the end of T. S. Eliot's *Four Quartets* and Mahler's *Das Lied von der Erde*).

But this is exactly what the boy author of 2 **C** does: he begins with the phrase 'Fire is not understanding'—which says the same as 'who can open the doors of his face'. And the poetic–philosophical truths are explored in the same kind of direct, simple English metaphors (as in Bunyan and George Herbert).

Students who find difficulty in believing that a child can utter such gnomic wisdom, using his own language for metaphorical purposes, should study the deeper meaning of nursery rhyme and game rhymes (which children naturally enjoy). They should also make sure they can respond to this kind of metaphorical expression: it is, of course, less familiar in our time than it was when common speech followed figurative and metaphorical habits commonly and naturally. That children *can* use such modes shows that common speech could be enriched again were it not that modern mass media and some standardised methods of education (e.g. textbooks and the O-level language paper) artificially depress language habits.

*

Read the following two passages and answer the questions on them:

What is my strength, that I should hope? and what is mine end, that I should prolong my life?

Is my strength the strength of stones? or is my flesh of brass?

Is not my help in me? and is wisdom quite driven from me?

To him that is afflicted pity should be shewed from his friend; but he forsaketh the fear of the Almighty.

My brethren have dealt deceitfully as a brook, and as the stream of brooks they pass away;

Which are blackish by reason of the ice, and wherein the snow is hid.

What time they wax warm, they vanish: when it is hot they are consumed out of their place.

The paths of their way are turned aside: they go to nothing, they perish. (Job, vi)

(1) What is the point of 'is my strength the strength of stones?'

(2) Explain the extended analogy between the way the brethren have behaved, and the changes in the brook. What is the point of the analogy?

(3) Give the point of the whole passage in your own words.

*

Remember now thy Creator in the days of thy youth, while the evil days come not, nor the years draw nigh, when thou shalt say, I have no pleasure in them;

While the sun, or the light, or the moon or the stars, be not darkened, nor the cloud return after the rain:

In the days when the keepers of the house shall tremble, and the strong men shall bow themselves, and the grinders cease because they are few, and those that look out of the windows be darkened.

And the doors shall be shut in the streets, when the sound of grinding is low, and he shall rise up at the voice of the bird, and all the daughters of music shall be brought low.

Also when they shall be afraid of that which is high, and fears shall be in the way, and the almond tree shall flourish, and the grasshopper shall be a burden, and desire shall fail: because man goeth to his long home, and the mourners go about the streets:

Or ever the silver cord be loosed, or the golden bowl be broken, or the pitcher be broken at the fountain, or the wheel broken at the cistern.

Then shall the dust return to the earth as it was: and the spirit shall return unto God who gave it. (Ecclesiastes, xii)

(1) What are 'the keepers of the house'?

(2) What are 'the strong men'?

(3) 'those that look out of the house' and 'the grinders' are references to what?

(4) If your answers to 1, 2 and 3 indicate that these are parts of the body, what then is the symbolism of 'the daughters of music', 'the almond tree' and 'the grasshopper'? (There is no 'right answer'!)

(5) Explain the sixth verse in your own terms.

(6) Say what the passage is about, in one or two sentences.

EXERCISE 4

This is a much more self-conscious piece, full of artifice: even so, the writer has been able to 'speak better than he knows'. He couldn't say what the fire 'meant', but he has been able to record a feeling about fire as a whole experience. Again, the firelight is associated with hate and fear: 'The boy had often heard the sound and had hated it...now he felt warmed and contented'—which links the 'warmth' of the fire with the previous 'hate' of the sound of the clicking mouth. Also, 'The boy jumped and stared at the rows of yellow, uneven pointed teeth and felt himself shudder'.

Here there is ambivalence again, between the comforting domestic scene and the threat underlying it ('cracked and spat') associated with the mouth and teeth. The light of the fire seems like experience, which illuminates a previous innocence: it is as though the boy writing is recording a point at which an infant realises that the toothy hate he fears in his father is not in himself. He wakes from a dream—to see that the hunger in the fire is in the fire, and the unpleasantness of the man's mouth is in the man: he is apart, pushing his own car through a phantasy jungle, in 'an unending cycle of changing lights'.

To get such genuinely poetical writing from a self-conscious writer in the fourth year of a grammar school is a remarkable achievement (teacher, Peter Watson, at Sheffield).

Follow up: several domestic scenes in Lawrence's *Sons and Lovers*, with fires; Blake's *Tyger*; Eliot's The Fire Sermon, from *The Waste Land.*

EXERCISE 5

See *The Lilac Tree* discussed in *The Secret Places*, and in *The Exploring Word* (where there is also an account of a student seminar on this poem). The essential question is: does Florence identify with the lilac tree?

Blake's *Mirtle Shade* is enigmatic, but explores a similar theme of self-realisation—or rather, the danger of destructive and frustrating limits on self-realisation by excessive identification. The protagonist so submits in love to the myrtle that he has prostrated himself, to no avail, only to the forfeiture of life's possibilities. Even the father, who should have helped the protagonist out of the crippling innocence of the bondage of over-dependence, lets him down by only laughing; for this he is sacrificed to the myrtle, but all to no avail. There is no point in mere rejection of the father or in mere Oedipal satisfaction: love has to learn to be free and independent, in its own right.

Using the same kind of symbolism Florence is making her way towards this very independence, of self-realisation: 'Soon, my little lilac tree, we'll be out!'

C, from another girl, shows how easily a child identifies with a tree or other natural symbol, and uses such a symbol to explore her own feelings—here the guilt of pride in her new womanly self: she feels that some retribution might strip her blossoming identity. So, she needs to go on to build her personality on the 'bare boughs': yet the most striking line remains 'And more and more her splendour grows'—which is true about little girls of twelve.

She would at once understand Blake's point (in D) that 'fury' is necessary for fruit and 'truth'. That is, hate must be 'included': without the 'rough winds' that 'shake the darling buds of May' the natural world would remain as 'fruitless and false' as undisillusioned innocence. So would we, if we pretended we were *only* blossom.

Follow up: some of *Songs of Innocence and Experience*; Lawrence's poems *Baby Running Barefoot, A White Blossom, Scent of Irises* (some verses), *The Enkindled Spring, Roses on the Breakfast Table.*

EXERCISE 6

The problem symbolised is that of contact: of finding another in relationship. The protagonist is isolated in black darkness: the bird breaks through. It will not be independent and fly away (it is scared of the light). So, it suffers that annihilation which (the writer fears) is the price of love.

Love is dangerous: this schizoid fear is explored by Blake, Dostoevsky, Sartre, Kafka (all of whom could be given to this obviously very intelligent grammar-school boy). For other work by this boy see p. 45.

But in class he should be commended here for the precision and clarity with which he establishes the atmosphere and symbolism of isolation: 'lean and intense', 'barren shapes...which drifted close to his tower'. And the psychological precision: 'he shut the window on an impulse', 'He and it were beings apart', 'something in its audacious perkiness fascinated him'. 'Delicately strangled' conveys the horror without excess: compare the account of Prince Daniyal crushing a cat's head in *The Near and The Far* by L. H. Myers, or the moments of horror in *Mr. Tasker's Gods* (see above, p. 119)

EXERCISE 7

For discussions of Raymond's work see pp. 11 ff., 29–35, and also pp. 103 ff. in *The Secret Places*.

Fear seems a direct and sincere rendering of the experience of a nameless fear that threatens identity—so that one clings to the solid ground in front.

Follow up: compare the poems on Fear in *Let the Children Write* by Margaret Langdon and invite children to pursue the theme. See also *An*

Outpost of Progress and *Heart of Darkness* by Conrad, in which the nameless fear of evil in the world overcomes the protagonists' subjective world, corrupts them and destroys them.

EXERCISE 8

See the Introduction. Under his 'sexy' exterior Raymond is a baby who has not been able to grow up because he did not have a father. (See the poem in the Introduction, p. 12, which conveys the agony of the illegitimate child.) To him sexual love is what goes on under the 'dark evil trees': because it led to his own life of anguish, for which he seems to be compensating by precocious sexuality. (Note: blet up = belt up; bulter = butler: p. 34.)

See Raymond's short stories in *The Secret Places*, p. 103. Obviously (Exercise 9) he can be helped by putting him in touch with sensitive adult fiction and drama about personal relationships: Lawrence's short stories (*Second Best*, *The Christening*); the opera *Porgy and Bess*; the short stories by Hemingway about Nick and those of Scott Fitzgerald about Basil (in *People and Diamonds*).

EXERCISE 10

'It is still my brook' means 'it is still my identity': as she grows up the girl seeks to preserve a sense of her wholeness and continuity of personality throughout the changes of childhood—towards 'a beautiful...sophisticated' maturity, 'gracefully and gently curving'. Read with an understanding of the symbolism, the poem takes on an additional capacity to touch one's feelings (see *The Secret Places*, pp. 31–2).

Follow up: The Song of Songs, for symbolism of personal richness and value; some of Whitman, for the capacity to identify with aspects of the natural world.

EXERCISE 11

See *Exploring Word*, p. 167. The problems explored here are (*a*) the essential childishness of the personality, and its need to stand up to so much testing and tormenting reality, with such small capacity for achievement and inner resources, (*b*) the way in which outward 'objective correlatives' of hate (the Bomb) make the struggle with one's inner destructiveness more difficult. So, a sense of futility seems to threaten, especially during the 'schizoid episodes' of adolescence.

The language is often borrowed and histrionic ('forgotten thanatoid...'). But the poem is undoubtedly sincere. The only possible comment on the poem is surely to show one has understood it, and has been moved by it—

and this is best done by following up: *The Waste Land*, and *Four Quartets*, surely? And D. H. Lawrence's *Manifesto*:

> To be, or not to be, is still the question.
> This ache for being is the ultimate hunger...

much of *Look! We Have Come Through*; Conrad's *The Shadow-Line*; Koestler's *Darkness at Noon*; Lawrence's *Women in Love*.

My desire would be to give her the work of those who have made the creative effort to 'come through': Conrad, Lawrence, Eliot, and, in music Mahler. That is, those who have expressed the possibility that man can come through his present-day problems by creativity and love. To put her on to many modern works (Amis, Henry Miller, Beckett, Iris Murdoch) would seem to me to betray her to those forces of hate she is seeking to escape and overcome, though of course the more courageous forms of recognition of futility have a place (e.g. Conrad's *Victory*).

EXERCISE 12

The winter of **A** so 'realises' the rat that she begins to imitate its snarl, and so produces the queer mouth-twisting spellings 'gleish evilnesch'!

The symbolism surely works something like this. A child is alarmed by the phantasy projections of its own unconscious—its imagined darts of harm that it shoots at those it hates. It fears that others may have the same power, or that its own aggressive impulses and appetites may recoil upon it. So, Red-Riding-Hood meets the wolf in (grand)mother's clothing (and in mother's bed, where appetite is all mixed up with perceptions of sex and its dangers).

Here the rat is such an emanation from the self, and from others, that threatens. So it is 'undesirable' (and therefore somehow connected with desire) and 'unreliable and wicked', ugly, revolting, unrecognisable, filthy. And yet (like fire in Exercise 2 above) shows an evil pleasure. It sneers, and utters human screams, staring with pleasure.

Poor little author! Here she encounters both human sadism, and the evil in the natural world. Yet her prose remains calm and brave: again, there is no more to say, except to follow up.

Follow up: Lawrence's *Snake, Man and Bat*; Edward Thomas's *Cat*; episodes from Orwell's *Animal Farm*, Henry Williamson's *Tarka the Otter*; Clare's poem about the marten (*Iron Honey Gold,*); poems about fears in *Let the Children Write*.

B is a vivid description of an American kind of frog, more extrovert—though the descriptive words are vivid with recoil: 'milk bubble that bulged', 'low croaking belch'. The writer possibly feels recoil because the frog is like a hostile sibling (milky and belching) which she has hated, and so fears retribution from: so, she runs to her father.

C, D and **E** are pieces of writing about similar fears, in symbolic form. Spiders become the focus for many such unconscious fears of retribution because their behaviour differs so from that of other animals. The infant believes in magic, especially magic of the eye: so, if a retributive emanation were to appear from another's phantasy (as from a sibling who is unconsciously hated and being attacked by mental bolts, as it were) it ought to run away when seen or threatened by a gesture (as a fly does, or a strange cat). Spiders, since they respond to touch and rhythm primarily, have only rudimentary sight, and have survived because they have evolved in self-defence an unappetising appearance (hairy legs, etc. which put birds off eating them), don't respond to normal processes of exorcisement. Hence the terror of them in some children. Children—even grammar-school children—writing about such creatures cannot escape the problem of their unconscious symbolism (nor does Lawrence, of course, escape such a problem in his bat and snake poems).

C describes how she overcame her fear by exploring her sensory feelings about this symbol: she makes a valuable exploration of both objective and subjective experience. We can see how involved she is by her words 'tranced', and her charming abandonment of all 'style' in the aside, 'well it wasn't exactly a walk more of a hop I would have said'... She also enters a new self-confidence, in the escape from fear: 'For once in my life I had owned the confidence of an animal.' Her account is itself a confidence of a very private moment and should be valued as such. Here, certainly, is a piece one shouldn't read to the class without the pupil's permission.

D reveals how the adolescent is still pondering infantile phantasy. She feared that the retributive phantasy-emanation would come and eat her, as she wanted to eat the 'babies inside Mummy'; when eaten she would burst out of him as the babies burst out of Mummy: she wishes to return in their place, horrifying though this is. The analogy with Red-Riding-Hood is obvious. Even as an adolescent girl she is taking no chances: here fathers are useful, and need to allow themselves to be involved in the phantasy. By encouraging such writing a teacher can promote sincerity and directness of expression: it is difficult to be insincere on such compulsive topics.

In **E** the child identifies with the spider, and gives an account of what it might feel like if you were a spider whose identity is threatened by 'ugly fat rude stupid' humans! Despite her poor spelling she creates a somewhat terrifying reversed perspective: the hearthrug 'takes so long to ride through', while a human being is 'a mass of black'. A great triumph, this turning of tables!

Follow up: the spider poems in *Let the Children Write*. For piece (**E**) *A Voyage to Lilliput* perhaps.

F may be compared with *The Lighthouse-keeper* in Exercise 6, and with Lawrence's *Bat*. The description of the actual incident is clearly written, though there are carelessnesses (e.g. 'rustled *through* their rich foliage'?). What is not done so well is the generalisation ('It seemed almost ashamed of its own insignificance and the horror with which its species was connected'). Here is an instance of an exercise where grammatical points can be made to help improve expression: should it be 'horror'?—'connected': this doesn't make sense. There is something faulty about the introduction of the clause by 'with which'. What did the writer mean, 'The horror its species aroused in human beings'?

Why make this point anyway? Isn't it enough to record how the bat behaved (surprisingly calm, apparently)? Similarly at the end, 'free to live its own existence': here a 'correct' and rather mincing way of writing seems to be used to disguise the significance of the bat itself. It is explored as a symbol of *something*, but the writer hasn't quite developed a sense of what. She should either write a realistic account of a creature or make some more subjective use of it (as suggested by the word 'cringing'). Here Lawrence's poem could help: unless she already owes too much to Lawrence, while yet not fully understanding him.

This is an example of a piece of writing which could be consciously improved: 'barged in' jars; 'on detecting my presence' is stilted. 'Soft translucent wings', however, shows that the piece has a tough enough content to bear rewriting. The pupil has possibly been too lazy to get the effect she really sought, and so, here and there, resorts to gesture.

The poem **G** is discussed in *The Secret Places*, p. 22. The poem by Edward Thomas shows a possible follow-up. The boy's poem is genuine, unsentimental and unconventional ('ticks and fleas crawl over him'). To expand this simple vision poems such as Thomas's can suggest deeper feelings about life and death, as symbolised by animals. The author of 'ticks and fleas' would take the irony of 'endless leisure', and the effect of this might well appear in his future work.

H is another charmingly direct and sincere piece. This is by Averil (see pp. 24 and 153–6 and Chapter 3 of *The Secret Places*). Follow up: compare this—

When I was a littel girl
The truth to you I tell
I lived with my dear
Frens a tome they
Keap a littel cow and
I cannot tell you
How I in joyed a ron
To fich her home

Yes I lived with my
Dear frens so kind
Then the cow went
Out to grass and
The time so merrely
Past when I went
In the common
Her to find.

My father whent a way
To hes labour all the day
While my mother all her
Work did do a tome and
The puding was so nies
That was mead with
Milk and rice dount you
Think that I had a good home

It was then a good living
They did get and it was
By the seet of ther
Brow my kind frines
I never can forget
And it was when thy
Keep that littel cow

It was then I lived happy
And free then the
Butter was sent to
Shop and some other
Goods we got the time
Agine I never more
Shall see.

Then some pigs they did
Keep to make ther own
Meat and there gardenes
Well stored with corn
They made ther own
Bred with ther own
Grown were twas befor
My young sister was born.

(Village Woman, quoted by Gertrude Seekell in 'Old West Surrey', in Adrian Bell's anthology, *The Open Air*, no. 37. See also *A Fenland Chronicle*, by Sybil Marshall.)

EXERCISE 13

Children are fascinated (as D. W. Winnicott points out) by fluff, bubbles, rainbows, and so on, because these come and go: their own identities seem as evanescent. So, while this is merely an exercise in describing a piece of paper burning, it takes on a deeper note, because the consumption becomes symbolic of loss of identity. What threatens the identity is hate—the primitive hate that eats: so, to a child death seems like hate eating (see Exercise 22 above, p. 56: the witch has 'about ninety-eight' mouths). These associations are found in myth, too, of course. Here the clue to the deeper note is in the striking phrase, and the 'musical' repetition: 'the colour of death. That black miserable and sorrowful colour...' There is an intensity, too, about the imaginative realisation of the contrast between 'fresh-smelling' (like flesh?) and the 'dirty, fragile' ash that 'crumbles when ever you touch it': the word 'touch' at the end underlies the human analogy, introduced by the word 'killer'. As with fire in the poems in Exercise 2, the worst aspect of the devouring death-hate is its mercilessness.

EXERCISE 14

The coldness in the piece is symbolic of isolation, and a feeling of numbness of identity, and lifelessness: no sensation seems to guarantee vitality. Under the surface is a deeply sad predicament of feeling dissociated and unreal. The headmistress's remark, in this light, seems not only inhuman but cruel. (See *The Exploring Word*, p. 48.)

The piece seems to me extremely good: vivid, moving, frank and open, and deeply moving. Properly received, it could have helped to overcome the 'coldness' of isolation, and to establish a much needed warmth of contact. As is obvious, the girl is really still only a child with a child's interest in simple sensations—and a child's need for companionship.

See above how, ignored by the school, this predicament in alienation can be exploited by commerce (pp. 143 ff.).

EXERCISE 15

The language of this fable seems to me admirable—striking, right in tone, beautifully controlled, while yet pleasantly simple and even childlike ('his prideful heart', 'tipping his head'). A few words are carelessly used (the writer could improve the sentence 'He seemed still, yet rocked slowly, backwards and forwards'; she means 'he kept in one place' perhaps). The third and fourth paragraphs don't seem to me to gain much from not being sentences, as we began with simple fable-like sentences.

But the fable is neatly told, with simple, naive artistry ('laughing and exchanging pleasantries with each other all the time').

Beneath the joke is a deeper one—as hinted at by the reference to the cock's sexual prowess, and the fact that he dies in the barn 'where he made his first conquest', and 'he had seen his father enter here, and never come back.' At the level of unconscious symbolism it is a castration phantasy—in which the 'cock' is punished for his appetite ('idly he wondered whether he would have time for an extra feed before being locked away for the night'). To realise this, of course, only makes the story more charming—the writer being in sublime ignorance. (I was recently amused when an adolescent (single) girl told me a dream in which she had dreamt of giving her husband *coq au vin.* Actually she dislikes *coq au vin*: but she looks forward to the adult pleasures of sexual love, which to her still seems like sophisticated eating—so, *coq au vin.*)

Follow up: Chaucer's *Nun's Priest's Tale*; E. H. White's *Charlotte's Web.*

EXERCISE 16

The author of this piece and of *The Lighthouse-keeper* (Exercise 6) is a very self-conscious practised writer (note 'the sheer abandon of finishing school', 'a shattering defeat for such a sensitive child'). Yet the piece seems completely sincere—and disturbingly so, for the writer seems to identify himself with Philip Ruston.

The symbolism is consciously used, yet superb: 'that soothing green water...water which accepted him—enveloped him'. Being in water is like being in the amniotic fluid, when one is utterly accepted. The problems of reality are like the 'screams' and 'echoes in the baths', because Philip is 'impure' and 'unnatural'.

The words 'impure', 'impassive' establish a precisely realised portrayal of a sensitivity, aware of things beyond the bounds of normal experience. There is nothing excessive about the portrayal of the 'logic' that leads to suicide: it is disturbing in its calm portrayal of the progress of dissociation. The human face is 'the hardness, the sameness': the clouds (senselessly) roll. There is a suggestion of mad hallucination of a paranoid kind ('laughing, suspicious').

The lorry accepts Philip as the reality of life seems not to. That is, the lorry accepts him as he cannot accept reality. Death is 'his soul swallowing himself', which is what suicide is to the suicide, a final act of self-love, self-consumption, in an ultimate attempt to feel real.

Only in the end does the writer dissociate himself from dissociation: he sees (as a suicide cannot) that the consequence is to become nothing; while the 'clouds still roll'.

Exercise 16

The piece seems to me a more-or-less perfect piece of writing, by a child who possibly has severe identity problems, but who also has the penetrating insights of adolescence, and the capacity to use symbols to work on his problems. The teacher's problem here—as English teacher—is to be able and willing to receive disturbing material with probably deeper insights and 'felt philosophy' than his own: and to hold the ring often for a beautiful, but also harrowing, creative quest for identity.

Follow up: Conrad, *Victory*; Howard Sturgis, *Belchamber*; Forster, *The Longest Journey* and *A Room with a View*; Koestler, *Darkness at Noon*; Dickens, *Dombey and Son*; Dostoevsky, *Crime and Punishment*; the poems of Sylvia Plath; *Metamorphosis*, by Franz Kafka.

EXERCISE 17

In the 'lower streams' a teacher gets less by way of conscious artistry: but children can still use styles and modes for their own purposes. Jack, a tough lad from Camden Town, uses a strange mixture of Gothick horror and Shelleyan extravagance to explore his adolescent feelings. His sincerity seems to me indisputable, because of unusual and fresh phrases such as 'my muscles tighten', and the breathless rhythms of 'But no one comes and no one ever will And I'll live in this eternal hell...' and the choric quality of

> Where no man lives
> Where no man loves,
> Where no man lies
> Where no man dies...

These Hamlet-like moments couldn't, I feel, be faked. Nor, surely, could such surreal symbolism?

EXERCISE 18

The impression of Jack's sincerity, even in his adolescent postures, seems to be confirmed by looking at other work of his.

The Whirlpool of Life is like *The Ancient Mariner*—a poem of guilt, and identification with Christ ('his nails pressed deep, he pierced his skin'). 'Moonlit ropes' is a very Coleridgean phrase (as is 'waterfalls of pain', indeed). Death, tiptoeing 'in veils draped black' is like the spectre in *The Ancient Mariner* too.

After 'He grabbed his throat with one last deep gulp' the poem rather flags: but then, *Kubla Khan* stops in mid-career too! An English teacher can surely only applaud such fantastic vision and extravagance, which links this boy's work easily with Coleridge, some of the visions of daemon lovers in folksong (*The Outlandish Knight*) and Greek myth.

B reveals that the capacity for 'grotesque vision' goes with an equal desire for truth to oneself: his poem is closer to Lawrence's insistence on self-fulfilment than to Eliot's caricature of modern apathy.

C is an early poem of Jack's: his teacher was able to encourage him, I feel sure, because he spotted and encouraged, on the 'third ground' of creative writing, the striking quality of his language. To be able to do this requires the teacher's responsiveness to the rendering of physical feelings, in relation to a creative puzzling at the nature of being:

> My hands hang limp all life withdrawn...
>
> Past the place of no return...
>
> On, on where none could come,
> Faster faster to the place where all life was gone...

—which is where 'my sunflower wishes to go'.

To be able to avoid being barred from receiving the poem by fuss about spelling, etc., of course, a teacher needs to be able to accept that a tough boy from the back streets of Megalopolis is likely to write mystical poetry, with a romantic rural topography. Teacher: Jeff Nuttall.

EXERCISE 19

Robert's poem is discussed in *The Secret Places*. An 'infant' poem, it is a tough boy's expression of his unconscious desire to kill the father out of jealousy and take his place with the mother. Of course, a boy fears retribution for such unconscious wishes. So, this poem is beautiful because it marks the creative achievement of an overcoming of Oedipus guilt; it resolves it by a guiltless acknowledgement: 'I killed that man Like he killed me.' Follow up: Blake's *Poison Tree*; the story of Abraham and Issac from the Bible or the medieval play (in *Thieves and Angels*). (see Exercise 73.)

EXERCISE 20

See *The Secret Places*, pp. 15 ff. The story is very charming and engaging, with some striking phrases ('the coloured lights danced up and down her face'). I see it as an 'Electra' story. Clare is Clarissa grown up: Clarissa's father says 'I like her'. The author unconsciously wants to grow up from being Clarissa, to become Clare, who can take her mother's place with the father. She wants to oust the mother ('so she went'). This is how a girl develops her mature personality, by identifying and competing, between her parents—using them as scratching-posts on her way to developing relationships of her own.

Read in this light some of the story is seen to contain an unconscious wisdom that delights one: e.g. 'Oh yes, I think she does, but only because I'm my father's daughter.'

What is striking is that the story is so well sustained—often a sign of the author's involvement in the theme.

Follow-up: the family incidents from Lawrence's *Aaron's Rod* (early chapters); his *Odour of Chrysanthemums*; *Wuthering Heights*; the novels of Adrian Bell; Gorki's *Childhood*; Rex Warner's *Men and Gods*; Jane Austen's *Pride and Prejudice;* Forster's *Where Angels Fear to Tread.*

EXERCISE 21

See *The Secret Places*, p. 35.

This is a good example of a story which is meant to be allegorical-symbolic, but doesn't really get off the ground. It begins like an infant's story-book, moves through T. F. Powys fable style, and collapses into television Western rough-house. The reason is possibly that the little boy is beyond fairy-tale modes, but not yet possessed of any more adolescent modes of phantasy.

The theme of being 'rotten' and 'selfish', and the theme of deceptions, shows that he has a problem of guilt and unworthiness he wants to explore. He can be helped by the right kind of literature: e.g. *Death in the Tree* by Hans Sachs (in *Thieves and Angels*) for instance; fables by T. F. Powys such as *The Golden Gates* or *A Christmas Gift*. Or the Carl Orff opera *Der Mond* would match his macabre myth-world admirably.

The boy's interest in word play ('Jim, Tim, Slim, Bim, Jeff, Cliff, Seff and Jaff') could be encouraged. The teacher could read him the Anna Livia Plurabelle passage from *Finnegan's Wake* ('I feel as old as yonder stone', etc.).

EXERCISE 22

Witches in children's stories are probably often symbols of the badness inside them—the hate they have magically 'thrown' at others returning to attack them. The origin of these hate-emanations are in the impulses to incorporate orally, to 'mouth attack' anyone who thwarts or frustrates the infant. (Actually, as I found after writing these notes, the African tribe from which this story came only gave up cannibalism thirty years ago: and, indeed, it is believed to be still practised for magical purposes).

So, it is appropriate that a witch should have ninety-eight mouths!

Witches seek to 'get inside you' (as by poisoned apples, spells, etc.). As you are trying to export your hate and so be pure and good entirely, you know it is possible to hide bad intentions under a disguise. Just as the wolf (symbol of the oral hate in you) eats grandmother, then dresses in her clothes—so witches turn into beautiful exteriors, to seek to incorporate you.

One way to escape retribution is to make out you were not the same person who uttered the hate: you have changed. This is the same process as

7-2

'splitting' your identity as between the 'pure' you, the jolly you, the hating you and so on. In folklore this 'splitting' is symbolically employed magically, as in weddings, in which two other girls dress up as the bride, and so the evil spirits do not know which girl to enter.

Words are closely linked with such processes of deception by disguise: people still fear to pronounce the Devil's name—they call him 'the Old One', etc., to avoid putting themselves in his power by calling on his name. Similarly, to give one's name may make one vulnerable.

Obviously, it would be fatal to tell anyone, certainly a witch, the word for the bit of the 'split object' into which you have projected yourself for safety. Both the splitting of oneself and the equation of word and thing are schizoid manifestations—that is, in terms of the growth of consciousness they are very primitive, and so are found in primitive lore, nursery rhyme and fairy story. They belong to the very earliest problems of phantasy—even before the capacity to symbolise is fully developed. For this reason they continue to fascinate us, since we all have a backlog of schizoid problems.

In the end the witch shows her savagery, by cutting off the horse's legs: since she is a symbolic projection of our own hate, we fear the way she matches us. So, it is like a terrible dream, that she changes into everything we change into. But we have a secret—which we have not named to her—a secret inner self: and by this evanescent transmigration our identity will escape hate, in order that our identity may continue.

It would be interesting to see what creative writing such a story stimulated. Examples to follow up can be found in Grimm, Hans Andersen, Mary Norton's *The Borrowers*, and nursery rhyme.

EXERCISE 23

Hemingway's use of the lion is symbolic, but rather heavily so. The animal has a 'great head', his 'dark mane' is 'stirring' in the morning breeze, he is looking around' 'majestically and coolly'. The last word suggests that to Hemingway the lion ('bulking like some super-rhino', and with 'his barrel of a body bulking smoothly') is rather like the he-man Hemingway himself. Hemingway's intention (see the full passage in *Visions of Life*) is to use the lion to show up the pettiness of the men ('Get out and take him. He's a marvellous lion'). Yet the contrast is not marked by any deep sense of the waste of the natural world, to serve men's self-aggrandisement and solving inner problems by cheap methods of indulging destructiveness (Hemingway perhaps needed to exert this very destructiveness himself, to make him feel 'great'). If we compare Lawrence's *Mountain Lion* we have something much more sensitive, universal and 'tragic': the capacity to go out in humility, rather than take in and plunder for the sake of one's own identity.

To the child in **A** the lion is noble as a symbol of naive ideals. He is a tragic male creature, but the writing is very direct and uninflated (Hemingway's by contrast *is* inflated). The description of the lion's wound, and its death, despite some conventionalities, is striking and seems more 'real' in places than Hemingway's: Cf. 'little puddles in the dry dust', 'his head laid down in the mud and slime'. The writing is 'controlled' in the right way, without insincere manipulation. It is closer to Lawrence, but without Lawrence's misanthropy.

Follow up: *Tarka the Otter* and *Salar the Salmon*, by Henry Williamson; *Man-eaters of Kumaon* by Jim Corbett; *Out of Africa* by Karen Blixen. *Born Free*, perhaps. *The New Noah*, by Gerald Durrell.

EXERCISE 24

The teacher has to be prepared to unbend to the level of children: this is not always easy for a young adult who has only just managed to put away childish things, and is a little insecure in his new adulthood. The solution to this problem is to meet the fascinating turmoil of family life behind children's writing. Here the little girl is both identifying with the baby bird, but also feeling motherly (as to a baby brother). To be amused, delighted and entertained by such a piece of writing is to find the clue to success, for, once the child sees this, the teacher gets given more!

EXERCISE 25

The essential difference, of course, is that one piece of writing is about the subjective world of emotion, and the other about objective fact. The value of the first is that it exercises sincerity: how genuine the passage is, is shown by such unusual phrases as

> All things that daily give us *confidence*...

and

> ...fear *secretes* itself in us...

The fear of blackness threatens to 'impede': the threat to identity is locked out only by sleep—a form of oblivion. To be awake is to be always seeking 'confidence' against things 'secreted' in us.

These inward problems are much more complex and troubling than outward things. So, a boy who has written about them finds direct factual writing easy enough. There is also the point that to explore one's inner darkness is itself a means to establish a confidence (as I suggested in *English for the Rejected*) whereby one deals more confidently with the real world.

The writer is able to allow that subjective experience is complex, untidy and strange ('every rustle is a spectre'). The imaginative concepts can thus be flexible and ambiguous: but exercising them means that subjective concepts can be distinguished from concepts of concrete entities. So, these categories are not confused: the writer is happy that his objective prose shall be simple and concise: 'The image formed on the retina is inverted and diminished...'

EXERCISE 26

A similar exercise. The record of the 'magnetic sensation' in a fog involves an imaginative making-real: this obviously helps the realisation of the nitrogen cycle, and so helps the writer to write about it in a clear and orderly way. Poor 'factual' writing often marks a lack of imagination—or, rather, a deficiency of training in conjuring up in the mind aspects of the experience being written about.

On fog, see the opening of *Bleak House*.

EXERCISE 27

Classroom exercises may fall down in their appeal to practical extrovert adolescents. And, anywhere, the pondering of outward experience is a valuable faculty to practise. This boy is fortunate in being trained to climb in the Cairngorms in February and to write about it, with the obvious practical purpose of informing others.

That the objectivity of the log does not indicate indifference is shown by the obvious pride behind his (redundant) remark to Mum 'it was the one that the climbers were killed on but we are all right'. Both pieces are real and quite without artificiality or pretence.

Follow up: Scott's *Journal*.

EXERCISE 28

All four poems seem to me perfectly sincere and real, being about painful and disturbing aspects of inward life, with no attempt made to deny these, or to excuse one's worst characteristics.

Hate doesn't literally make one 'swell', nor does it 'devour your whole body up.' But **A** records the feeling of being suffused with rage, and the fear that one's inward hate will consume one's identity. 'Real' too is the observation that hate is relieved, as if it were an abscess, by allowing the poison to be uttered. The internal rhyme here (hole/soul) and the way the poem is arranged in simple lines are indications of the direct art of the less able child. There is an absence of all artifice or literary language, though 'devouring' is consciously used with poetic gravity. And the gravity of the rhythm convinces one of the sincerity.

B is a little more histrionic (compare the poems of Jack, pp. 46 ff.): 'a boiling sea', 'my victim', etc. But the observation of the 'magical' feeling about anger and hate, and the last line seems to show that a genuine problem (one that is with us from infancy) is being really explored.

C is a poem written 'as if written by Isaac': yet the rhythm of the insistent 'I am the loved one' shows that the writer has entered closely into the phantasy, identifying with Isaac. Since he does so, he is writing about real feelings (compare the 'Oedipus' poem, p. 50).

In **D** the 'silvery light' and 'tender loveable lips' are clichés from 'pop', doubtless. But

> Then we will have children of our own
> And when they grow up they will be like us

is from the genuine child, and has the 'real' rhythm of domestic ambition. 'Pop' songs are never as exact about dependence as

> You feel so lost without him...

This is a phrase from the adolescent's genuine (still childish) need to convey to others how much she needs affection, and depends upon relationship.

EXERCISE 29

See *The Secret Places*, p. 7, for the first two stanzas. These are direct sincere child-poetry. Stanzas 3 and 4 are more 'poetical'. Having been praised for stanzas 1 and 2 the writer tries too hard—and overdoes it! Stanza 3 seems an echo from somewhere else: in the last verse inspiration has flown. There's nothing insincere about 'glad that I'am alive': but

> And all the birds twitter for they
> Are happy today

is twee and cosy. However, the increase in literariness marks an advance, and so one can say nothing to the child—only hope that with her new conscious interest she can recapture her naïve first sincerity. This depends now on what she is given: John Clare, or de la Mare, one hopes; Maggie Tulliver episodes from *The Mill on the Floss*; *The Borrowers* or *The Secret Garden* for their mysteriousness, rather than Enid Blyton or even Arthur Ransome, for their mundane securities.

EXERCISE 30

This is an example of a sincerity achieved without a present reality behind it: it is a phantasy explored, in order to be ready to face the reality should it ever be necessary (compare Rose's dealings with actual loss by death, in *English for the Rejected*, pp. 117 ff.). Here death is transmuted as it is in

Ariel's song. The emotional exploration has its own compelling convincing rhythm:

> A face never to forget: so sad.
>
> I knew she was heart broken...
>
> Never did I see such a face.

It thus achieves remarkable universality. Emily Brontë's poem represents the same kind of emotional exploration in an adult poet. For 'reality', by contrast, see Hardy's *Veteris Vestigia Flammae*. And on the distinction see F. R. Leavis, 'Reality and Sincerity: Notes in the Analysis of Poetry', *Scrutiny*, vol. XIX, no. 2, p. 90, winter 1952–3. Leavis says: 'The marks of the imaginative self-projection that is insufficiently informed by experience are there in the poem...in the noble...declamation, and in the accompanying generality, the absence of any convincing concreteness of a presented situation...'

Our child writer *does* give something of this, by contrast. Yet as with Emily Brontë's poem, her poem lays 'a claim to strength that it certainly cannot sustain'. Emily Brontë, Leavis says, 'conceives a situation in order to have the satisfaction of a disciplined imaginative exercise'. A child needs to do this too, for the benefits of anticipating and exercising her maturing recognition of the human situation.

EXERCISE 31

Compare Lear's 'Who is it that can tell me who I am?' **A** is a striking expression of a groping for a *raison d'être* to strengthen the sense of identity: the management of the line-breaks is exact. Clare's poem is perhaps the most profound and poignant exploration of the theme—written after the identity had dissolved. Yet it stops short of self-pity. To read it could help the writer of **A** to realise that there are worse predicaments than his, and that the solution to the question of identity is not in self-pity but in insight.

EXERCISE 32

A by repeating its chorus convinces us of the sincerity of the adolescent mood of feeling unloved. The expression is pathetically unable to convey the feeling: some lines are successful ('The winds blew on', 'He fought against the wind and rain', 'He left no mark', 'his piteous meanings'): other are banal and inept ('he had a lot of pain', 'He felt upright'). A fully consistent record of a mood of depression is given in **B**: a study of **B** should enable an English teacher to see similar rhythms of experience beneath the surface of the adolescent's poem—despite its failure. **B** would certainly make a good follow-up. Note the assonance and the repetition in the first line of **B** and how it conveys a cyclic turmoil in the mind: repetition and short lines in **A** convey something of the same sense of futility.

EXERCISE 33

There are typical adolescent (Hamlet-like) excesses in the pose adopted ('my heart collapsed with utter despair'). But the adolescent does feel like that, and to record such extreme emotional moments can in itself be sincere. Though 'that long trail back' is from 'pop' and 'numbed with truth' is from women's magazine stories, 'The pain must fade and die', and the whole exploration, is the girl's own, and can be built on.

Follow up: some poems from *Look! We Have Come Through!* Perhaps a poem by Wyatt? ('They flee from me...'?) Folksongs (*Died for Love, The Turtle dove, Still I love Him*), *Porgy and Bess,* Lawrence's story *Second Best.*

EXERCISE 34

At first sight these might be exercises in bloodthirsty imaginings. But a few striking phrases should give the clue ('growling with police', 'questioned and questioned', 'vapour of breath in the air'): the incident was a real stabbing, which has frightened the authors.

EXERCISE 35

A is writing as he speaks, so it has to be read aloud to get the nuances of expression—scathing irony, contempt, scorn ('All very funny'). '*The good old days*' at the end has to be read with carefully emphasised derision. It is obviously written by a boy, and so we make allowances for its vernacular, as 'real'. **B** is not: and it is only made to seem as if spoken by a boy. But the purpose is a deep creative one, of portraying the deepest horror of death while attention is focused on the universal, if petty reality, of human life. For an analysis, see *English for Maturity,* Chapter 10.

EXERCISE 36

At Court is real in the same way as 39**A**: there is no artifice ('I said I didn't want to'). The record of experience is good because even painful and humiliating moments are not over-emphasised or left out to save face. 'Don't they both look nice when they are dressed up?' and 'tapped me on the face'—this is parallel to Huck Finn's record of the cruel reality of the Boggs episode, or the vendetta: or, in a less painful way, the scepticism of Aunt Polly. There is a refreshing realism in children's writing because everything is new to them—here the feeling that being charged for such a trivial offence is 'a bit funny', and the observation of how the Bench 'had a little talk'. This realism should be encouraged and can be, by praising this way of writing directly as one talks. (There seems to me however, a great difference between the use of the 'boy's voice' by Mark Twain, and that in *Catcher in the Rye*. Salinger imprisons himself and the reader in a mock-adolescent idiom that limits the concept of human potentialities. Twain uses the mode to see human beings as falling short of a boy's creative sense of moral issues.)

EXERCISE 37

Most students find this passage moves them, by its evident and unself-conscious sincerity. It is undoubtedly real. The child still remembers the details of the reality, which remain part of the life-problem with which he has been left to deal. 'I will never forget the face of the man who was driving the van...The policeman was taking a statement...tears dripped from his eyes and made his face go all red.' This has the realism of children's unflinching exploration of experience; children look around and see the nature of things, and this very realism helps them to survive horror. (Mark Twain uses this capacity, in the extract above, to maintain our attention, with Huck, to the minutiae of the litter of human life, while we take in his father's violent death.)

It is this vivid 'scanning' in the shock of a disaster that yields the 'clear picture' which here so deeply moves us. There is also a background here of rich Irish vernacular, and devotional habit: 'I often wonder if this was a little miracle' belongs to the mother's way of consoling herself. The forty-two car funeral has its place in the community too, in the background. There are obvious connections here to be made with the tragic elements in Joyce (e.g. Dignam's funeral), and maybe in Synge and Yeats (*An Irish Airman Foresees his Death*). See the funeral in *The Aran Islands*, *Emerald Apex*, ed. Price, p. 32.

EXERCISE 38

The realism of this is refreshing and invites the comparison with **B**, and also perhaps Frank O'Connor's *First Confession*, for the common element of the comedy of contrast, between outward devotion—its idealism and its conventions—and inward voices of irony, pettiness, and real conflict within the self. **A** is also touching in the sincerity of its self-revelation: an adolescent often has considerable problems of identification: he identifies with (or she relates to) Christ—but which Christ? Here, the girl wants to confess, but can't find any great sins. She wants to rise to the occasion, and give thanks for joy: but she is troubled by her lapses into banality—'Oops!' and nose-blowing. She is not afraid of solemn feelings nor of genuine sincerity ('For the first time...I pray whole heartedly'): but she's charmingly more complex and full of conscience than the mere religious forms often allow for ('she's a nuisance...sorry God').

B is from the funeral chapter in *Ulysses* in which death as a universal fact in human existence is explored by 'stream of consciousness' realism. Actually of course, it is far from real, since no human being could have such interesting thoughts in such a sustained way. But as a creative mode it creates a great and poignant comedy, of the contrast between the ideal and the petty.

C shows the same 'realism' employed symbolically in great art: the deadly environment, and the register 'gorged with burials' make Mr Dombey's preoccupations futile and destructive of the brief life which is all that is granted us—no more than a 'smoke in the mouth', like that of the young curate.

EXERCISE 39

The piece is bogus: as may be seen by looking in *Songs of Praise*. Helen has taken one verse from No. 699 and another from a few pages on, No. 702. A teacher ought to be able to spot that the concept of addressing the soul, to ask it where its God is, is too 'literary' for Helen, who reveals herself unable to understand the meaning of 'distant realm' ('distance realm' should have betrayed that she was copying: and the stilted 'Men strain'). But if one is to allow that children (*a*) sometimes come out with surprising utterances, and (*b*) often use unconscious plagiarism, then one must expect to be deceived occasionally (as I was!).

Here we have a case of deliberate deception, which needs to be treated as such, in a disciplinary way. Isn't Helen threatening the whole give-and-take teacher–pupil relationship? Of course, it might be that she was unhopeful of ever making any achievement of her own, and could only offer a borrowed one. But she must be brought to see that this way out won't do! 'See me!'

EXERCISE 40

See the account of Rose, the writer of this piece, in *English for the Rejected*, pp. 117 ff.

Rose's mother had died. She turns now to her inward life in symbolic phantasy, now to tackle the outward reality of her predicament. Here she writes a direct account of the death, as a realistic novelist might. But the teacher-reader can tell that it is about her own life, despite the use of the third person—for at the most critical moment Rose gives the game away by relapsing into the first person: 'a lady round they other side of *us*...' So, the realistic detail ('he got up and moved her about...') is seen to be poignantly real. With Rose's work I was often so moved that there could be no pretence at mere objectivity as a 'teacher of English': a sympathetic touch on the shoulder was all that needed to be said. And even to write 'Good' at the bottom seemed impertinence. It is worth noting how many words Rose spells correctly, and how exact the prose is at times.

EXERCISE 41

A is 'competent English' in a sense, but the writer is so utterly in the grip of cliché that he can record little of the real experience of Spring. His figures are such as are pasted on shop windows at Easter—lambs, rabbits with white scuts, cows chewing, ploughmen plodding (their weary way, naturally), foals spindly, butterflies fluttering, etc, etc. As he displays such pasteboard counters, as substitutes for experiences he hasn't really had, so he offers us feelings he hasn't really got; hence his raptures are sickeningly insincere: 'Oh what a wonderful thing to be alive'. If the boy is tough enough, then this surely calls for ridicule? Such denunciation can be salutary. I shall never forget the effect on my own writing of a cataclysmic demolition by my English master (L. S. Harris, Author of *The Nature of English Poetry*, a useful handbook to metre, imagery, and diction in poetry). I had written a sickeningly sentimental piece about Queen Mary opening Norwich City Hall: 'the sun shone appropriately, the queen graciously smiled'—marked 'Tosh! How can you write this insincere drivel?' and more in this vein.

The author of **B** observes actual aspects of the natural world around him ('They could not have been in England long...the conspicuous white rumps of the martins...'). His writing is a bit pedestrian, and his observation is simple: he is just a boy. But he should be praised for his directness (follow-up—Cobbett) and for not pretending to be anything other than he is.

EXERCISE 42

A is a piece of exhibitionism, to display the maximum of 'literary associations', product of a training in the concoction of extraneous 'figures of speech'. Of course, precocious little boys will write like this and one should not discourage verbal pyrotechnics without care.

But in truth **A** tells us hardly anything about the author or his experiences. He inflates his own importance ('I was here, there and everywhere...to offer the sense of security to some younger comrade') and postures ('A broiling sun, obtrusive...' 'As if a tournament of ancient design...').

He is therefore being insincere, though the result is funny enough, and the boy himself would probably enjoy a comic deflation. The piece was written for an exam: and it is just this kind of insincere writing that exams in English generate, though it is not often as amusing.

Exercise 42

Where the criterion of *reality* is concerned, examine the second sentence. Here would be a place to put one's finger, critically speaking to demonstrate to the child that this kind of writing won't do.

'...a *clump* of *tangled* vegetation...' A *clump* is a hard tussocky mass: *tangled* suggests briars, interwoven stems.

'...in the form of reeds and bulrushes...' *bulrushes* are straight, and only a few reeds bend or interweave. It may be possible to have a *clump* of *reeds*: but even so, the image is visual. Reeds stir in the wind, and so are rather lighter in texture than *clump* suggests.

'Waved their tentacles...' Now bulrushes are stiff as pokers, and reeds are like sword-blades. Neither has the least affinity with a tentacle. One could have a tangle of tentacles: but this would be at the other extreme of vegetable texture from reedy growth!

'...like innumerable Excaliburs...' Reeds could look like upheld swords, and bulrushes can look like spears. But even so, 'innumerable', while it would do for grass blades, is excessive for a single *clump* of reeds. As for *Excaliburs*: Excalibur was one sword, which has a symbolic value as jettisoned manhood, seized by the submarine spirit woman. The striking image of it, seized and waved above the water, is distinctly of a *single* blade. To offer an image of 'innumerable excaliburs held aloft by the lady'—is ridiculous: one has a burlesque vision of a perplexed lady grappling with a mass of jettisoned old iron. And in what possible sense could these bundles of old Excaliburs resemble 'tangled clumps of tentacles'? A sword can't be an octopus!

This is the result of training in extraneous figures of speech ('write twenty similes', etc.). Because the figures do not come from any inward need to symbolise aspects of experience, they become grotesque and banal: 'The life-blood of the pan's existence—bacon', etc.

Beneath its belle-lettrist surface the prose is inaccurate and tautologous: 'the wet *reception* which eventually *received* us...relieved us of dust, dirt and other uncomfortable *feelings*' (is *dust* a feeling?).

The attitude to others is unpleasantly patronising and superior ('his familiar but peculiar country burr'...'some younger comrade not quite understanding'). And the deepest fault is that of drawing attention to oneself —to the exhibition of oneself—not to the experience as one to be shared with others. Inwardly one might be annoyed by what seemed the work of a little show-off and prig: speaking to him one would need to exercise the greatest care, in putting before him good models, and the model of sincerity in general. After all, this posturing rubbish is to be blamed ultimately on a teacher who has given him a diet of Lamb and roast pig.

B by contrast is everything that one welcomes. It is unostentatious, and plain. We share not only the experience recorded, but the boy's attitude to it, his secret pleasure in small triumphs. And we end by knowing more about boys, about his character, and that of his master. Such a piece does much for sympathy and insight.

He observes accurately things we might not have seen for ourselves—the curling over ends of the tent-pegs, the 'great wall against the wind', the effect of 'that hairy sort of rope' running through one's hands. We pick up Mr Dow's attempts to urge on his boys, and their mixture of pleasure in being praised, and yet their wry shrugs (consider the tone of 'He said I was just the man for the job', which is somewhere between a pleased blush and a 'Huh!' meaning 'I know what you expect to get out of me by buttering me up').

There are many pleasing incidental asides: he is both fond of Ross, and yet aware of unfairnesses ('I found out later that Ross had got a very sharp axe...we didn't change over till it was too late': obviously Ross, despite all their friendship, had carefully not suggested swapping axes until it was too late). Yet selfishness doesn't spoil the relationship: rather, the author waits until retribution turns up. He is ca' canny, and shows Huck Finn's pragmatic scepticism, 'I just went and watched...they had a time of it...' He doesn't disguise his satisfaction: 'You should have seen Ross's hands.'

The part-cruel, part sympathetic, give-and-take of relationship between boys with all its irony and naïve pleasure, in prowess, one-up-manship, and genuine co-operativeness too are all conveyed without disguise or pretence. It is a very engaging and meaningful piece of prose, because of its reality and sincerity.

Follow up: *Huckleberry Finn* again, *David Copperfield*, Jefferies's *Bevis* perhaps.

EXERCISE 43

A seems embarrassingly insincere: the writer doesn't really care in the least for what he is writing about. Not that he deserves condemnation: his poem is simply superficial and pasteboard.

B, despite its 'grammatical' failures (line 7 isn't a sentence and is not connected meaningfully with anything else), is more successful, with its theme of awakening from hibernating. The last line, even in its inadequacy, is commendably childish: a pleasant contrast to the insincere

O, how I love the radiant Spring!

Follow up: John Clare, Crabbe, Wordsworth, for accuracy in natural observation which is also symbolically charged. Richard Jefferies, Henry Williamson, Adrian Bell and Sturt are also useful antidotes to clichés of the lambs-in-spring kind.

EXERCISE 44

Another fake: the first few lines are from a poem by R. W. Dixon. At least the boy has added a verse of his own. The clue to the deceit is the uncertainty as to whether to leave 'feathers' in the first line, realising this unusual word would give him away. Children are very ashamed of such deceptions usually: a way out might be to ask the boy to paint a picture of the original poem: he could thus 'make it his own', and then perhaps stand on his own feet. It looks as if he reproduced the poem from memory, so the contrivance is not so reprehensible as the one in Exercise 39 above.

EXERCISE 45

I think the poem is sincere, and an expression of the adolescent impulse to 'test the world to destruction', to see if anyone 'cares'. There is a personal problem in the background, as is evident in the 'meant' fall of

> My love I cannot give to anybody
> For I don't get love from them
> But I always get hate...

the way in which the poem is conceived by deliberate artistry, albeit of a simple kind, makes one feel assured that whatever the problem is, it is being wrestled with with some success. A schizoid problem maybe: but not a schizoid poem.

Follow up: The Nick stories of Hemingway; some of the poems of Po chü-I and Li-Po (translated by Arthur Waley). Episodes in Gorki's *Childhood.* Poems by Sylvia Plath.

EXERCISE 46

Because Aloysius can write as he speaks, we have a delightful glimpse into the mind of an African boy: the concern with 'chop' by one who has known famine; the gross obsession with one's inside, its noises and its states of bowel and belly; the preoccupation with petty rights and irritations mixed with grandiose nationalistic ambitions; the combination of disinterested devotion and materialist pragmatism.

And then, from its direct sincerity, the portrayal of the ambitions of the African who looks to the modern world: 'Make we take tings easy. In some years we go become better people. We...ride in luxurious cars...we wak better chop...and marry de earth's beauties.' Could Aloysius come to read and understand Doris Lessing's *Little Tembi* and other stories in *The Old Chief's Country*? And will he see where doubts are expressed about materialist ambitions?

EXERCISE 47

The observation of a child of nine is merciless. It needs to be—we must never underestimate the need a child has to search and search experience for what to us are the most evident and familiar truths (Is fire hot? What does a blind eye look like? What do people smell like?). Here the child makes her own similes from what she knows, and writes what she sees: so, she sees and records things we tend to suppress, because they are disturbing and painful. It seems to us as grotesquely comic as a Beckett play: yet she is only recording direct fact, extrovertly, for the most part. Her comedy is that of the world, looked at anew, from the innocent eye: 'O brave new world!'

EXERCISE 48

See *English for the Rejected* p. 90.

Read the passage aloud (transcript below). This brings out its dogged persistence—as of small boys intending to steal apples. The piece is directly extrovert—the apple is not here a poetic symbol, except as the focus for 'winning'. What is so pleasing is the childish wisdom—the realistic summing up of the situation (enemy: the owner; own troops: small boys). And the calculation of the odds: is it worth it? Note the careful examination of the elements of risks: but yet—'still it is worth getting some Gascoyne's scarlet apples'—this is like a resigned conclusion to a piece of music in which the middle section has explored all the woes that beset striving man.

Follow up: Melville's *Moby Dick*; Twain's *Tom Sawyer* and *Roughing It*; *The Golden Grindstone, Robinson Crusoe, Treasure Island, Tschiffley's Ride.*

Transcript

It comes off of a tree when you pick it is rosy red and before you eat it (it) makes your mouth water it even makes your mouth water when you hear the name Gascoyne's scarlet. When you go scrumping and when you get caught it is worth taking the chance of getting some Gascoyne's scarlet apples. When you go scrumping you have got to be carefull you don't get caught, if you do get caught the man will be waiting for you next time you go to get some more Gascoyne scarlet apples. When I go scrumping all I go after is apples and plums, pear's. When you go pinching apple you do not want to take to many people or you will not get away so quick when there are a lot of people with you a spescally little boys they make to much noise. If you pick apples off of the ground you have to be carfull of the wasps of else they will sting you and the sting comes up to a big bump where ever it stings you.

When you are by yourself and some one comes and you have to climb over the barb wire and get caugh[t] the man will probally catch you but if someone else is with you the can unhook you. Some people when they catch you they might hit you and said he will hit you harder next time he catches you. But some people say they will hit you next time but warn you not to come in the orchard again. But the children could not resist getting some more apples to eat.

It is best getting apples from an orchard where there are no houses. When I go scrumping I do not take bikes because the man who owns the orchard might come along and take the bikes and if you want your bike you have to go and ask for it and that is how the owner of the orchard knows that you were in the orchard. I never take a dark jacket or a red one. Because you will be reconnised very easy because red shows up very easy. But still it is worth getting some Gascoyne scarlet apples

EXERCISE 49

Carp (transcript below) is adequate, direct, extrovert writing: the turns of phrase are confidently literate: 'Carp are the most suspicious fish'; 'I saw a disturbance round my float'; 'He had almost the same tactics'; 'it turned my scales at 12¼ lbs—a nice carp.' As far as practical writing is concerned, we have nothing to worry about with this pupil, where he is interested in what he is doing. (*Carp* would be a good piece to show to the geography or biology teacher, as an example of the kind of English they should expect at best.)

The writer would enjoy Hemingway's *The Great Two-hearted River*, and perhaps Gilbert White's *The Natural History of Selborne* and Henry Williamson's *Salar the Salmon.*

His interest in fish expresses a feeling he has for relationship with the outer world. From this symbolic interest he could be brought to an interest in poetry and to extend his imaginative life, as by being read Ted Hughes's poem *Pike*. This is a rather journalistic poem ('submarine delicacy and horror' is surely the language of the newspaper?). But it conveys with directness something of the malevolence of the natural world: in their world pike are

> a hundred feet long:

and they swallow one another. Such impulses to incorporate threaten us, in dream—and in reality. The eat-and-kill element in fishing certainly emerges in such a poem, in a way a child would be stirred by it. The rather over-simple moralising ('A life subdued to its instrument') and the touch of *hwyl* ('as deep as England') do not obtrude unduly here.

Transcript

The time was 5 a.m. in the morning it promised to be a good day. I dressed and had some sandwiches for breakfast. Today I was going to

Hilton mere pond to catch (if I could) some carp. The bait I had made the night before was ready to be packed. I checked to see if all my tackle was in the bag it was so off on my Bicycle I went.

At halfpast five I reached Hilton Mere pond. I tackled up 10 yds from the Bank I decided to use paste and put a piece the size of a shilling on the hook. I made a cast some fifteen yards near some weeds, then I sat down and waited for a bite. Carp are the most suspisous fish and half an hour later I saw a good one come up to my paste which was floating on the surface. It looked at it and then swam round it suddenly it was gone only to appear a few yards down the pond to look again at the bait. Then he slowly swam up to it and opened his mouth and to[ok] it. He was off in a flash and going like a train for some weeds I picked up my rod and with a firm strike the fish was on, the fish was almost on the weeds I tried sidestrain this turned his head and came towards me, now I was reeling in the slack line like mad then he turned from the bank and the line which had been slack tightened. then it parted with a twang. Line and float went straight into a tree.

I put on another hook, this time for bait I had on a piece of bread-crust. I cast out in the same place as last time and then sat down and waited. This time an hour elapsed before I saw a disturbance round my float. Then slowly it slipped away. I struck and felt the fish which was rather heavy. He had almost the same tactics. The fish went into the middle of the pond and then came back at me at a terrific pace. I was ready for this and by the time he was about to turn I had the line tight he turned and headed for the weeds he got into them so I decided to try hand lining I pulled gently and he came out very slowly his golden side came up to the surface. I had had the fish on for 10 minutes and it was very tired now. I lowered the landing net into the water brought the fish into it. I took it 10 yds up the bank and the hook I took out. I weighed it and it turned my scales at 12¼ lbs a nice carp. I returned the fish to the water and he slowly went out of sight. I packed up my tackle and went home.

EXERCISE 50

If the teacher can overcome his despair at the sight of the scrawled page, he will often find something exciting—as here:

Race Commentary

'Come in, Lamont.' 'Over!' 'Now we are at Lamont.' 'The Ferraris are in the lead...Phil Hill is leading them...Brabham and Moss are fourth and fifth...Moss is fourth and Brabham is fifth...If you listen now you will hear Brabham going through. *Eeeeeergghbroomghrrrr*...Going very well now. Brabham is fifteen seconds faster than the last lap. Oh! What's happened to Moss? Now I can hear a car misfiring...It is Moss in his Cooper...He's going into the pits...Phil Hill is going round Gatwick corner...That is a right and left hand corner...Phil Hill has changed down to third gear... The car is skidding—*eeeeeeckgggggggghcrump*! *Shshshsh*! Hey! I'm still here...The race is still on...Now over to Gatwick corner: to meet you there is Richard Bullard...'

'This is Richard speaking...There is quite a mess here....Phil Hill is quite all right but the racing driver behind him is killed and three spectators ...Two fire engines and one ambulance have come...The Ferraris were still in the lead but there was only one in the race...'

The piece was continued:

'...Brabham is catching up...He is just going round Gatwick. He has to slow down to second gear...Brabham's mate in the BRM is close behind... Three more laps to go...Von Trips is just coming through the 'Z' bend and up to the straight...He is just going to start his second lap...What's happened? His car is slowing down...He was skidding all over the track... It must be the steering...And Brabham overtakes! His team-mate skids near Von Trips' car, so he is out out of the race...It's all over...Brabham goes into win! Back to the studio now...'

Read fast into a tape recorder this is a remarkable and effective pastiche of a radio race-commentary. The pupils can make appropriate sound effects: the author's satisfaction will be enormous!

Now look back at the original: would you believe it! See *English for the Rejected*, pp. 180 ff.

EXERCISE 51

The author shows himself as sensitive and sympathetic: 'I could not intrude on her privacy...' He is also naïve, in a rather childish way—not too far from the children he is describing, in a valuable sense. The price of this is a degree of sentimentality: 'Boadicea revivified, flame-haired, majestic'; and sometimes a lapse into pulp-book language: 'her full body—'; 'snotty-nosed little bastards—'.

But the account is full of well-meaning inquiry into the complexities of teacher-child relationship. Compare the passages about Ursula Brangwen in *The Rainbow* and *Women in Love*: though Lawrence's perception is deeper, we can see how the more relaxed atmosphere of three decades later makes a more human and civilised approach possible—so that instead of suppressing or denying their feelings, child and man grow through them, towards greater self-sufficiency.

Follow up: write a subjective account of a similar experience on teaching practice—of a child who excessively loved or hated you.

EXERCISE 52

To hit an adult so hard that he is knocked out is much harder in fact than in fiction, and a knockout blow might well cause serious injury if not death. A child is unlikely to be able to hit so hard.

So, Jill is almost certainly exaggerating—writing in phantasy what she would *like* to have been able to do—control her uncle's aggression.

Yet the rest has an air of authenticity, even to the knife, and the uncle's remark 'or I will have no ear on'. So, her yarn is a way to overcome her real fear.'

Various other remarks ring true, by their rhythm and idiom: 'I just stood there shaking'; 'Tell him to get off me'; 'No, uncle, honest'. So does the throwing of clothes into the street, the bouncing bottle, and the remark 'Well at least your niece sticks up for you'.

The last remark shows how detachedly the child stands away from it all, and sees it as a human comedy. Her father, she records, has made a decision to protect her. The teacher has no further obligation, I think, except to be aware of what the child *may* be facing, and to hold himself ready to help if need be. In any case, it makes a good story: but whether or not to put it in a magazine is a delicate problem.

Follow up: Huck and his father in *Huckleberry Finn*; Twain's *The Prince and the Pauper*; *Oliver Twist*; Lawrence's *Samson and Delilah*, *Sons and Lovers*; 'An Irish Christmas', a short story from Joyce's *Portrait of the Artist as a young Man* in *People and Diamonds, IV*.

EXERCISE 53

See *The Secret Places*, p. 25

Such remarkable expression from a 'low stream' boy indicates a sudden flow of communication directly from the unconscious. 'Who' for 'how' indicates how uncontrived the expression is. The substitution of 'confused' to rhyme with 'used' confirms that the piece is original, and that the creative achievement was rapid and consuming. (I *may* of course be wrong: it may be an echo: yet even so, why this particular echo?)

Sick, sick, sick in the mind...

has its own insistence, in the rhythm.

If there were a good psychiatrist in the education department I would get in touch with him. If there weren't, I would see what I could do, to offer the author all the sympathetic understanding I could, and to foster his creative effort on his inward problems.

EXERCISE 54

This is by Averil Wright whose work I discuss in chapter 3 of *The Secret Places*. On pages 153 and 158 above may be found two very interesting stories by the same child, written while in 2A of a secondary modern school. An experienced teacher could detect the personal reasons why this story fails. Averil has as yet a child's attitude to sex. She wants to be 'daring'. She embarks on a story of two mixed couples going camping. She strictly indicates 'The two boys sleeping in one tent and the two girls in another': cf. *A Midsummer Night's Dream* II, 2, 40:

> HERMIA. But, gentle friend, for love and courtesy,
> Lie further off; in human modesty,
> Such separation as may well be said
> Becomes a virtuous bachelor and a maid,
> So far be distant...

Even her failure here goes with an important stage in her development, to which a teacher must be alert. As elsewhere in Averil's work, however, even the mere exploration in imagination of the time when she will go off on adventurous expeditions with boys brings fear—and retribution. There is real fear in Averil's words to describe her heroine's hysterical reaction to the storm: 'Jill was very scared. She kept crying and screaming until she was gasping for breath where she was so exhausted': 'where' gives us a chance to take up a matter of making the meaning clear: but we must recognise that the mistake arises because of Averil's troubled feelings. 'Torn to thread' is also a mistake for 'torn to shreds': but it is also a Joycean portmanteau phrase, because Averil is thinking of the threads. At a deep level the tearing is a symbol of dire consequence for being so naughty as to go off with boys alone: for this reason the 'excited' holiday turns into the 'unhappy' one. Averil is not yet ready for such adventures: she still needs her parents to back her, so that she is not 'frightened'. 'I am a girl but I will not prove it' might be a remark you make with Mummy or Daddy as a very little girl: she is on the way to leaving such childish things behind, but on the way to the scared knowingness of adolescence. In her reading she is ready to move from Arthur Ransome to the Nick stories of Hemingway, and then on to D. H. Lawrence's tales of courtship and such writing.

EXERCISE 55

Janice, the author, was married two years later, and I met her with a baby on her arm. I asked her whether she married anyone from the school. 'No,' she said. 'Anyway, we're separated.'

'That's sad,' I said.

'No!' she cried. 'He was a *swine*!'

Shall we, two years before such life-problems have been suffered, reject such explorations of love and sex in English work? Surely only by letting a child down badly?

Janice was illegitimate herself: so like Raymond (see above, pp. 29 ff.), she is obsessed with sex (the phrase crossed out is 'feel my breast')—because it is dangerous and threatening: as indeed it proved to be. (Yet Janice at least now has her baby to love.)

To reject this simple story would have been to add to the misery of it all. 'Accepting' such work may help the child to put in order the emotions it fears ('so she said all right it is all right...'—compare. 'All manner of thing shall be well and...').

For a whole year after she left Janice would stop me and say she was 'writing a book'. In this she obviously found an adult contact which helped her. Here the 'academic' achievement (which is pitiful) seems less important than lending support in a difficult life.

EXERCISE 56

Here is a transcript:

The Kidney man

one day a man kill a wamon. and cut Her Kidney out and eat them. next day. He kill a another woman. and cut Her Kidney out and eat them. and made a awful mess. He was called the vampire. He hab to horrible teeth 91 Thursday januory 9161 a wamom was kill. and a kidney was missing. it was getting serious. nexe thay Find the Body was on marsh ladn and Food-prints in to swamp

THE EDND

See *English for the Rejected*, p. 137

From this writing, with his drawings (reproduced in *English for the Rejected*) and his behaviour (masturbating in class, and so on), it seems likely that Kenneth was mentally very ill—possibly psychotic. A piece like this may not be just a joke, or take-off of a horror film: it may be a dissociated phantasy. Again, good psychiatric diagnosis is called for, and the problem can never be a mere English teaching one.

EXERCISE 57

Harmless exploration of a fascinating theme, followed by a guilty expiation. As Melanie Klein points out, cycling can be a symbol of coition, and sexual prowess: so, as he first emerges towards puberty, a boy may feel sex is so dangerous that one has only to go with it, and one will be destroyed by this strange power. To realise the presence of this fear is more important than to be shocked and angry about the brassière-undoing bit. Of course, this can't be read out. And it might be possible to imply one thinks the 'lovely breasts...good figure' kind of writing is corny. 'She was very sexy' is borrowed, too. Mind you, it is more appropriate to write like this at thirteen than in middle-age!

The piece shows, however, how the pulp/television idiom lends a borrowed sophistication that disguises the true need to explore. What the boy needs is for his interest in love to be accepted, but in such a way as to encourage him to see it in whole terms of relationship.

So, we need to give him the stories of courtship in *People and Diamonds*, passages from *Sons and Lovers*, Beverley Cleary's *Fifteen* perhaps, and even Forster's *Where Angels Fear to Tread*.

EXERCISE 58

If his teacher has been moved by the same boy's Oedipus poem (which means being able to respond to the haunting rhythm of the piece) he will be able, intuitively, to respond to this second poem, which, with its strange bawdy refrain, is so queer and disturbing. Of course, such a poem is difficult to deal with in the classroom, and can't be read out. A teacher might be so irritated by it, and frightened by it, that he would reject it in hostility and shame. But if one is to be able to deal with such disturbed 'low stream' children at all one has to be able to 'take' such things. It is very important *not* to reject the child for this poem, for in it he has exposed some of his deepest fears. To accept it, while making it plain that one couldn't (obviously) read it out, might help Robert a great deal, in his need to overcome the fears that prompt it. Yet the ability to 'take' it really depends on how good one's literary training was—how much one understands 'the poetic function'.

See the strange poem about the dread of masturbation discussed in *The Keen Edge* by Jack Beckett:

> Today a menace romes our earth
> It lay in the deep, the mist of evil
> No one can master this menace today
> But this menace can master you.
> The evil binds and strikes to kill
> Letting you make your death
> You cannot control yourself again
> But you are left helpless to evil
> Once you are struck by this killing evil
> It clings to burn and kill

And gradually crushes innocence
And sinks in until your death.

Beckett says, 'the lad had been terrified by old wives' tales and saw no way out. The poem offered an opportunity to share his desperation and the sharing helped. (Perhaps this instance highlights a danger involved in reading "good" poems to the class).' Such poems perhaps link the guilt of masturbation to a fear of annihilation.

Young teachers might find such poems embarrassing and slight. If when students they are asked to discuss alongside it the songs of the fool in *Lear*, or Blake's epigrams, or poems of Emily Dickinson, they may be brought to be more tolerant of the gnomic expression of the dull, disturbed and rather odd child one finds in 'bottom' streams. To understand such poems and know how to deal with them requires a creative training, which establishes sympathy and understanding. We may compare the value of this with the value in such a situation of mere 'external' psychological knowhow. It would be very difficult to work out the meaning explicitly: an intuitive response enables us to sense at least what kind of poem is here. The fool's songs in *King Lear* are as bawdy, and are associated with the same themes of annihilation and survival. Not only does a reading of *Lear* help understanding—a student who sees the link could then more easily deal with the kind of hostility to such poetic exploration that is often found among colleagues and headmasters.

EXERCISE 59

There seems to be something of a crisis at the end of the first year in the secondary school: children who were happy at writing about dolls suddenly want to write about sex. Here we see in a startling form the italic handwriting of the primary school, about 'little Noddy', on the same page as wildly scrawled pulp-book stuff about the whipping and torturing of girls.

The teacher may see in this a need to heal the dissociation, so that the real inward interests of puberty can be explored in imagination. And this may be done neither by Enid Blyton nor by Raymond Chandler nor Ian Fleming, etc. It requires the best kind of stimulation from sensitive art. But the scrawlier handwriting must be accepted as the handwriting of adolescence—and of that bulk writing from which something may emerge. Of course, the writing doesn't have to be as bad as this. But to force it back to 'italic' may be to force the imagination back to Toy Town, which is not what one wants.

T. F. Powys's fables (*Captain Patch*) might be a way of bridging the gap, since they are 'naïve', but also starkly realistic about love and hate in human nature.

EXERCISE 60

Notes on decoding:

(1) Vowels are likely to be left out ('frm' = farmer), or letters are liable to be transposed, sometimes at quite a distance from one another: thus 'lod' = old.

(2) Other spellings are vaguely phonetic: frmh, vethn, not (for 'knocked').

(3) The origin of the rhythm comes from the pupils' realisation that by repeating one particular string of short words (which he knows how to spell!) he can fill up a 'side'.

(4) The following are important words to decipher: fanit, belhism, sechrus, ruth humit.

(5) Before you finally decide on the value of the piece as writing *read it aloud*.

(6) Now turn to the typeset version.

The Sick Sow

won day The sow was sick and the old frm went four the vethn and the old sow whd't not hethy an fanit and the old frm sidn to vethn the old sow is on hethy so the vethn sidn to the frmh I will cumh and see the lod sick sow sidn the vethn and the frmh went to see the lod sick sow and the vethn and the frmh see lod fat sick sow sidn the frmh and sent at the frmh and not thefrmh ount the big fat sick sow went and ladh down the frmh went two with the big fat sick cow and saw belhism and the frmh went in the house and he sat down and he bav he and sick sow two ladh down and the vethn went and the vent see wat is ron wis and the sick sow went to seph and the vethn went to the frmh house and sick sow the vethn to the framh and the vethn sidn two the old big fat sick sow is a seph and the sick sow not the vetn and frmh run and run up sechrus and the sick sow went to the pigs house and ladh down and sent seph and the frmh not vetn and went bakn to (Melton) and frmh weth to see sick sow and he ruth humit and sick old sow wok up and old sow is beth and ANd.

If you are still flummoxed, here is a tidy version:

The Sick Sow

One day the sow was sick, and the old farmer went for the vet. The old sow wasn't healthy and fainted. The old farmer said to the vet. 'The old sow is unhealthy.' So the vet said to the farmer, 'I'll come and see the old sick sow'.

The farmer went to see to the old sick sow, and the vet came to the farm. 'See the old fat sick sow', said the farmer. But she went for the farmer and knocked him out. Then the big fat sick sow went and lay down.

The farmer went with the big fat sick sow and then he saw he was bleeding.

He went into the house, sat down, and bathed himself. And the sick sow lay down.

The vet went to the sow to see what was wrong with her. The sick sow went to sleep.

The vet went to the farmhouse and the sick sow got up and followed him. The vet said, 'The old big fat sick sow is asleep'. But the sick sow knocked the vet over, and the farmer ran and ran upstairs. Then the sick sow went back to the pigs' house and lay down and went to sleep.

The farmer took the vet back to (Melton). Then when he got back he went to see the sick sow and threw something. And the sick old sow woke up—and the old sow is better.

The end.

Is my polite version too polite?

You could arrange the piece for Choral speaking with drums.

EXERCISE 61

A Ton

They say doing a ton
Is fun
And a thrill,

But when you spill
When doing a ton
You get sent back
To dear old Mum.

You may be dead,
You may be living—
But if you are
It's no thanks from
Doing a ton.

Set out as above the extraordinary scrawled offering takes on a rhythm and shape. And it could even be arranged for choral speaking, or tape-recording. Motto: never say die!

EXERCISE 62

Other children in class pronounced this a poor copy of something on television.

The only phrase I find engaging here is 'she tossed and she tossed in her bed'. I would try to build on this, for example by using the passage from *Sweeney Agonistes*:

when you're alone in the middle of the night and you wake in a sweat and a hell of a fright...

KNOCK KNOCK KNOCK
KNOCK KNOCK KNOCK
KNOCK
KNOCK
KNOCK.

That might awaken something in this rather tedious little boy. So might *L'Enfant et les Sortilèges* (Ravel) or *Der Mond* (Orff).

EXERCISE 63

I have always had a soft spot for this, especially since a Chief Education Officer tried to stop me quoting it in *The Guardian*.

'Tender eyes'/'idolise' is a good rhyme. I would suggest to the author that 'And' is wrong to begin the last line.

Perhaps a music class could invent a tune? The result might turn out better than many 'pop' numbers—which could be examined in comparison. Many are thinner than this: and others merely lean lamely on suggestiveness:

Well I'm a king bee
Buzzin' aroun' your hive;
Well I'm a king bee baby
Buzzin' aroun' your hive
Yeah I can make honey baby
Let me come inside... (The Rolling Stones)

EXERCISE 64

By contrast with pop and imitations of pop, this is agreeably childish in a boy of fourteen: not to need to appear sophisticated is a mark of strength. 'Then that good night kiss: it was an evening well spent' is as plangent as a Chinese poem. (Compare Po chü-I's poem about going to the hills at the age of sixty with a dancing girl of 15.)

EXERCISE 65

Despite its girls' magazine quality this story has a good deal of its own to offer: see *The Secret Places*, pp. 12 ff. Its childishness is revealed by the slip into the first person, and by the moment of fear, at committing herself:

She ran away far into the forest...

An amusing piece of day-dream wish-fulfilment, it contains an underlying sincere preoccupation with relationship and genuineness of affection ('contented with what she had got'!). The humour is not all unconscious: she *intended* to amuse her reader ('before she would say any more he kissed *her*!')

EXERCISE 66

What is remarkable about this story is the way the girl manages to sustain a pastiche of the style of a detective story week after week. While some of the imitations are comical to us: 'Giving a sigh and a moan I got up and strolled up to her, knowing I would be at her mercy as soon as I looked at her', the desire to be 'sophisticated' is touching rather than disturbing. There is also a real underlying fear, of the creature who is 'a bit mad' and is 'put away': and of 'him and his delight in hurting people' The story has its own weird atmosphere, and the author uses pulp modes for her own purposes. It is a great stimulus to others, to have such a substantial story from one of a class.

EXERCISE 67

The story is a magazine story. But how competently it is done—with what a flair! Take the confident opening: 'Jackey was like any other girl with her good points, her faults, and her hopes and dreams...' Compare the opening: 'Lou Witt had had her own way so long that by the age of twenty-five she didn't know where she was...' (*St Mawr*, D. H. Lawrence).

Of course, it would be easy to expose the unreality: the impossibility of such long conversations in the water when one character is drowning! Such faults appear when the story is read aloud to the class: so will the weakness of the 'magical' ending. But within its own genre it is competently done, however superficial. The weakness of it could be usefully exposed by making it an exercise for the class in punctuation: the story wouldn't stand up to such close attention.

The only way of improving such a girl's work is to read her good stories of courtship and adventure. The trouble may well be that her facility is more satisfying than that of writing with more depth. But here the class itself makes a useful fund of criticism: such stories quickly bore them, because though slick they are superficial. Yet the content is relevant.

EXERCISE 68

An earlier draft had a line deleted: l. 3,

> I don't know how he could dress like that.

She has begun to dream of 'the boy she'd like to meet': suddenly he seems a real person, so not at all a mere dream-boat:

> The coat he wore
> Was shabby and grey...

The poem actually is closer (in its touching adolescent sincerity) to Chinese poetry than 'pop': see *Plucking the Rushes, Hot Cake.*

EXERCISE 69

Again, a competent pastiche of the magazine style. If children find they can do it so easily they are unlikely to be taken in by romantic clichés. Besides, behind this day-dream ('about time too'...'I only went out with her because I never seemed to see you...') there are touches of real home, and the desire for real relationship.

This inherent sincerity in children's work may always be found, and awareness of this may help expose 'pop'.

B reveals how pop stories tend subtly to deprave children, by inculcating the values of the jungle. Here every form of aggression is commended, by insinuation: 'Made him want to pull her down a peg or two...'; 'one of those nice, ordinary types'; 'he wasn't particularly nice when he came to it'; 'he'd...fight for everything he'd got'; 'He felt aggressive'; 'He felt his usual sense of power...'; 'He knew how much power he DID have with girls'; 'He was staring insolently at her legs'; 'He was enjoying this'; 'The girl was beginning to look better all the time. Suddenly she WAS worth fighting for'; "Her finger traced the scar"; 'I hate you', she said quietly'; 'Already she belonged to him'; 'He fell...pulling her down'; 'as if it was his kingdom'; 'She didn't resist...she couldn't'; 'He was aggressive...he had the push'.

Everything that is commended here (despite the gesture to 'something' that was 'lacking') suggests false solutions to problems of identity, by being 'tough' and 'aggressive'. This is the phantasy of a decadent commercial cynicism, whose effect is to undermine the adolescent and urge him towards destructive behaviour, as a solution of his anguished puzzlement. Such a cheap attack on youth for money is deplorable: only genuine creativity can help prepare children to resist such subtle inculcation of the urge to 'make it' by being 'big'.

EXERCISE 70

A seems a genuine story, which contrasts strikingly with **B**: the 'pay off' line, 'you needn't bother', conveys to us that 'personal relationships are everything': to Melanie it is cataclysmic. He was pretending to her! So, we see, 'the ultimate goal of the object is relationship': or, to put it more simply, a child knows that what she wants is a good relationship, sincere and genuine love.

The hack who writes phantasies to exploit the teenage market will try, against all the better judgement of his audience, to persuade them into modes of behaviour utterly at odds with their best good sense: a girl has to drive a boy to kiss her. Love depends upon being a trollop according to teenage strip-cartoons. To be a 'cold fish' is a 'failure': how much damage has this kind of play on fear caused by fostering precocious sex at the expense of relational needs?

EXERCISE 71

Comment seems unnecessary.

EXERCISE 72

Again, an efficient parody of the mode: but here not enough parody, and too much satisfaction with this kind of phantasy. Follow-up: *The Killers*, by Hemingway, where the situation is less black-and-white, while sympathies are deeper. Or episodes from Fitzgerald's *The Great Gatsby*, where the rich criminal is exposed as pitiful, and yet found fascinating, or *The Secret Agent*.

EXERCISE 73

A useful starting-point for the discussion of the morality of art. The boy is obviously indulging unconscious Oedipus wishes. As a story, can Eddy be allowed to get away with it? In unconscious terms this means, can we get away without guilt? The answer being No, then it is unreal not to face it. So, this isn't a satisfactory ending.

From such a beginning it could be possible to expose the unreal infantilism of Bond stories ('licence to kill'). Boys can become very heated over discussions of this story, and it makes a useful stimulus for a consideration of what creative works are 'for'.

Follow up: the medieval play *Abraham and Isaac*; Stevenson's *The Beach at Falesa.*

EXERCISE 74

A is a very efficient pastiche of the American pulp war-book mode; at least it shows that a child can do it—indeed such stories are less explorations of the true horror of war than indulgences in violent phantasies of destruction. These have their origins in the destructive phantasies of infancy, and so are associated with fears of disruption of identity.

So, to give children cheap sensational writers would be to stir up fears which a great deal of inward effort is already devoted to dealing with (see M. Pickard. *I Could a Tale Unfold* on horror comics).

But because this story is so well-done, it is itself a 'placing' of violence, since the manner implies a conscious artifice: 'But wait. A fresh burst of screaming...' There is a strange energy of indulgence in horror.

At first genuine writing about war (Graves's *Goodbye to All That*; passages from Hemingway's *A Farewell to Arms*; Barbusse's *Le Feu*; Faulkner's *Crevasse*) will seem less satisfying, because it is about reality rather than neurotic phantasies. But by persistence it should establish a richer appeal.

In **B** the fascination is obviously with the technical details rather than violence. What is amazing is the detail the boy already knows from comics and war books (Dakotas, DC 7's, Horsa gliders, the code name, a red light ...near dropping area, etc.).

This can all be very boring, and boys can fill whole books with it: the boringness seems to be something we have to accept. (Melanie Klein observes that small boys seem to have periods of being extremely boring about details of their obsessions, round which they are building their sense of prowess—and identity).

The author's redeeming quality is his wry wit, which shows here in his 'commercials' between part one and part two! This clownish tendency in him could perhaps be brought out in an organised way.

EXERCISE 75

See *Secret Places*, p. 58, for an extended analysis. A very competent story for a girl of thirteen, on the symbolic theme of running away from home and the anxieties her exploration of independence brings.

EXERCISE 76

Another story by the same girl, in which she begins to explore her preference for a boy (Geoffrey) who isn't Daddy (John = Daddy). The latter 'looked about forty...' and is suddenly seen as too old for her.

The theme of the unconscious symbolism complements that of Ex. 20. For the adolescent girl, as well as taking her mother's place in unconscious phantasy and in growing by identifying, now has to replace the father with whom she hankers to relate sexually, with a partner of her own. This is alarming (because a boy offers less security than Daddy) but also exciting. The motorcycling boy is less respectable than the bank manager daddy: he is a 'horrible brute' (because he wants her sexually). But she goes off with him 'for spite'—out of the recklessness of young life making its own way towards continuity.

EXERCISE 77

Despite their efficiency in telling stories, what children's work lacks most is the capacity to evoke the feel, the look, the smell, the actual sensations of an imaginatively recreated moment. Here Lawrence does just this. The fox is of course symbolic: but it is also a 'real' fox: we are 'with' Henry in the intense moment.

The violence suggests sexual violence: the shooting and death suggest a difference between the mere brute and the civilised human. Man subdues the fox, and makes a fur of him. But the violence of it, and Henry's prowess, are too much for March. Yet she keeps her end up: this is all summed up by her refusal, 'You don't catch me wearing a fox fur...'

Children who write as well as Averil would intuitively understand how effective and grippingly *right* Lawrence's art is—and learn from it, in writing stories.

See also the episode of Mrs Sparsit in the thunderstorm from *Hard Times*, for tense 'atmosphere'; and the Christening of Paul Dombey.

EXERCISE 78

See *The Secret Places*, Chapter 7.

Some possible ways of following up: the novels of Adrian Bell; excerpts from *Sons and Lovers* and *Aaron's Rod* (the early 'family' chapters); *Wuthering Heights*; excerpts from *Middlemarch*; excerpts from *World Without End* by Helen Thomas: excerpts from *War and Peace*; Forster's *Where Angels Fear to Tread*; George Douglas Brown's *The House with the Green Shutters*.

EXERCISE 79

The synopsis in part genuine, part wish-fulfilment phantasy (Superman impresses Mum), part bravado from television 'sex' plays. (They asked me at the beginning, 'Can we do *Street of Shame*, Sir?') The problem is to wean pupils towards what one knows will 'go' with them, and what they can really do: that is, the situation 'inside' the family. How harmless this apparently 'X' certificate stuff is, is shown by the splendid parenthesis: 'injury (and embarrisment)'!

EXERCISE 80

Try reading the dialogue aloud. Then see *English for the Rejected*, pp. 54 ff. Despite Joan's myopic and plain exterior, there is a great deal of life in her dialogue. She catches the underlying cruelty between lovers having a quarrel.

Compare her dialogue with that of a modern play:

[A] GEOFFREY *shifts the sofa. There is old rubbish and dirt under it.*

G. Oh, Jo!

J. I wondered where that had got to.

G. Now you know. It's disgusting, it really is.

J. Oh Geof, the bulbs I brought with me!

G. Haven't you shifted the sofa since then?
J. They never grew.
G. No, I'm not surprised.
J. They're dead. It makes you think, doesn't it?
G. What does?
J. You know, some people like to take out an insurance policy, don't they?
G. I'm a bit young for you to take one out on me.
J. No. You know, they like to pray to the Almighty just in case he turns out to exist when they snuff it.
G. (*brushing under the sofa*) Well, I never think about it. You come, you go. It's simple.
J. It's not, it's chaotic—a bit of love, a bit of lust and there you are. We don't ask for life, we have it thrust upon us.
G. What's frightened you? Have you been reading the papers?
J. No, I never do. Hold my hand, Geof.
G. Do you mind? Halfway through this?
J. Hold my hand.

He does.

G. Hey, Jo. Come on, silly thing, it's all right. Come on there.
J. You've got nice hands, hard. You know I used to try and hold my mother's hands, but she always used to pull them away from me. So silly really. She had so much love for everyone else but none for me.
G. If you don't watch it, you'll turn out exactly like her.
J. I'm not like her at all.
G. In some ways you are already, you know.

[B]

J. Hello Jean. Can't we talk it over and come to some decision?
J. Talk about what for instance?
J. Well, make it up.
J. I'm sorry John—there's nothing to make up.
J. What do you mean? There's no-one else, is there?
J. Well, if there is, it's got nothing to do with you.
J. Look—I'm only trying to be...nice.
J. Well, don't.
J. All right, then, I won't be nice. It looks as if I've got to be rough with you.
J. If you lay a hand on me I'll scream.
J. Do you think that scares me?
J. Well, I warned you, didn't I?
J. I don't care what you said. You must want to hurt me.
J. No I don't. You think you can hurt me. Well, you're wrong.
J. I don't want to think of it.

J. Well, perhaps you'd better not see me any more.
J. ...Don't be silly...I want to see you tonight.
J....I don't know about that.
J. I'll see you at six o'clock.
J. Well...all right then...
J. You're a doll!
J. I don't know about that.
J. Well I do.
J. Goodbye. See you...tonight.

Joan Stall's realism makes passage **A** look sentimental and posturing ('we don't ask for life...(*sob*)...we have it thrust upon us...')

EXERCISE 81

The play is much influenced by television drama, but it has more sincerity, and more *concern* for people. It plunges *in medias res*—of pregnancy, which seems to obsess secondary modern school children. But the main interest is in the parents' rejecting reaction, and the way this may be overcome. Of course, the family dialogue falls short of effective realism: but it is more sincere than **A** in the notes to 80 (p. 224).

It lends itself to possible improvement by example. Here Conrad's or Lawrence's dialogue would be more valuable than that of most 'realistic' modern drama, such as *Billy Liar* (which I find unreal and false).

Relevant are the comments below by children taking part:

'I have really enjoyed my English lessons because we can think for ourselfs and that is one thing I always wanted to do and now I can.'

'Personally I have learnt more in the last three weeks than I have ever learnt before...The work we have been doing has helped me to think, and I think that it very difficult to do so at short notice unless you think about it.

I have also learnt how to handle very difficult problems and have confidence with other people.

I particularly liked helping to bring the rough copy of the script to sense and type it out. In the play I am the Director, and I find its a very responsible job to do.'

'These lessons have helped us to think for ourselves and helped us with our speech as well as using our imagination, it has been great fun and I enjoyed doing it. I liked the acting quite a lot as it has helped me to speak more outright as I am inclined to hold my feelings back.'

'I find that doing this play and playing someone else is interesting very interesting it is active, sometimes it was very hard to find words like the last part of the play, but we managed.'

Exercise 81

'We have learnt more of life this term than in the past three years. We have learnt how to think, how to speak and good manners...'

'...We've been learning about life a bit more. Also we are learning it in our heads and not in books and we have learnt how to say things more easily to other people.

The teacher didn't have to shout at us to be quiet because we knew when to pay attention to him. The boys didn't play about at all and have been taught to understand the risk the girls have to take in life.'

Write a report to a Governing Body which objected to the play.

ADDITIONAL NOTE (See Introduction, p. 17)

Hear is Lawrences's poem in full:

Song of a Man who is not Loved

The space of the world is immense, before me and around me;
If I turn quickly, I am terrified, feeling space surround me;
Like a man in a boat on a very clear, deep water, space frightens
and confounds me.

I see myself isolated in the universe, and wonder
What effect I can have. My hands wave under
The heavens like specks of dust that are floating asunder.

I hold myself up, and feel a big wind blowing
Me like a gadfly into the dusk, without my knowing
Whither or why or even how I am going.

So much there is outside me, so infinitely
Small am I, what matter if minutely
I beat my way, to be lost immediately?

How shall I flatter myself that I can do
Anything in such immensity? I am too
Little to count in the wind that drifts me through.

This may be compared with the boy's poem *Black Skeleton* in detail.

Both poems are fascinating as examples of the symbolism of 'hostile objects', that is, of threats from the 'bad objects' in one's inner world. (The word 'objects' here means 'an entity with which one is in relationship'.) As W. R. D. Fairbairn, the Scottish psychoanalytical theorist writes, when someone we need and love ceases to love us [this may be experienced by a very young infant as] persecution or attack.

Then the lost (or hostile) object, now become a bad object, is mentally internalised in a much more vital and fundamental sense than memory. An inner psychic world has been set up duplicating the original situation.

This 'internal world' in which we struggle with 'bad objects' is one in which we always feel frustrated, hungry, angry, guilty and profoundly anxious. So, we need continually to 'work' on this inner unrest, by dreams and symbolism. We try to 'compel them (the bad objects) to change into good objects': to keep our inner world whole and integrated is the impulse of cultural activity.

Both Lawrence and the boy author of *Black Skeleton* fear that they may be annihilated as by outward symbols of internalised bad objects. The boy turns the tables by tearing the thundercloud apart before it can 'come too far down' and touch him: by 'thinning it' into white, he seeks symbolically to turn it into a good object. Lawrence, by accepting his predicament, escapes the cosmic wind that threatens him. The withdrawal of love evokes fears in him, such as he knew, as all of us do, in infancy: when love seems withdrawn, then we fear we shall be annihilated. By looking with profound sincerity at this fear Lawrence discovers an invulnerability. Note the common reference to evanescence of identity, which is a feeling all children have, and which poets seem to have more than their fair share of:

> The wind blew through him...
> ...I am too
> Little to count in the wind that drifts me through.

This acceptance of one's mortal situation seems to bring a psychic invulnerability rather than the reverse: which is what we mean by 'coming to terms' with the truth of experience. As T. S. Eliot said, 'Humility is endless'. The same openness to inward experience is to be found in Lawrence's poems, especially *Manifesto*, about the inward consequences of his discovery of his wife as a separate person.

BIBLIOGRAPHY

Beckett, Jack, *The Keen Edge* (Blackie)
Clegg, A. B. (ed.), *The Excitement of Writing* (Chatto and Windus)
Ford, Boris (ed.), *Young Writers, Young Readers* (Hutchinson)*
Hourd, Marjorie, *Coming Into Their Own* (Heinemann)*
Hourd, Marjorie, *The Education of the Poetic Spirit* (Heinemann)
Hourd, Marjorie, *Some Emotional Problems of Learning* (Heinemann)
Langdon, Margaret, *Let the Children Write* (Longmans)
Marshall, Sybil, *An Experiment in Education* (Cambridge)
Thompson, Denys, and Jackson, Brian (eds.), *English in Education* (Chatto and Windus)*
Walsh, J. H., *Teaching English* (Heinemann)
Whitehead, Frank, *The Disappearing Dais* (Chatto and Windus)*

Notes on Symbol Formation, referred to in the Introduction, is a paper by Dr Hannah Segal in the *International Journal of Psychoanalysis*, vol. xxxviii, p. 391.

For further lists of books on teaching creative writing, on English and on child growth and development see the present author's other books on teaching English and also the bibliographies in those above marked*.

INDEX OF TITLES, FIRST LINES AND SUBJECTS OF EXAMPLES

Index

INDEX OF PASSAGES AND POEMS QUOTED FROM PUBLISHED SOURCES